Mathu of Kenya

Mathu of Kenya

A Political Study

Jack R. Roelker

HOOVER COLONIAL STUDIES
Edited by
Peter Duignan and Lewis Gann

HOOVER INSTITUTION PRESS
Stanford University, Stanford, California 94305

The Hoover Institution on War, Revolution and Peace, founded at Stanford University in 1919 by the late President Herbert Hoover, is a center for advanced study and research on public and international affairs in the twentieth century. The views expressed in its publications are entirely those of the authors and do not necessarily reflect the views of the staff, officers, or Board of Overseers of the Hoover Institution.

Hoover Institution Publications 157

International Standard Book Number: 0-8179-6571-8
Library of Congress Catalog Card Number: 76-20294
Printed in the United States of America

To Jim

CONTENTS

PREFACE   ix

ACKNOWLEDGMENTS   xi

INTRODUCTION xiii

I.   BEGINNINGS—1910-1929   1

II.   TEACHER AND SCHOLAR I—1929-1934 . . 29

III. TEACHER AND SCHOLAR II—1934-1944 . . 44

IV.   LEGISLATIVE COUNCIL REPRESENTATION I—
      1944-1951 70

V.   LEGISLATIVE COUNCIL REPRESENTATION II—
      1952-1957 107

VI.   ELECTORAL DEFEAT—1957-1958 134

      CONCLUSION 149

      NOTES 154

      A NOTE ON SOURCES 179

      SUMMARY OF SOURCES 181

      INDEX 195

PREFACE

Hoover Colonial Studies Series

The last three decades or so have seen a revolution in the historiography of modern Africa. Historians once devoted their attention largely to the conquerors and builders of empire; their colonial subjects went mainly unrecorded. Then the pendulum
started to swing the other way. Imperial history began to fall from academic favor. Scholars attempted
to write the annals of modern Africa in African terms,
with the colonial period no more than a cruel but
short-lived interlude. Some academicians went even
further. The historians of Africa were to assume a
political mission: they were to assist in nation-
building and to lend their skills to bring about the
triumph of a particular ideology or a particular
class. The term "Eurocentric" became a word of
abuse beloved by reviewers anxious to denigrate those
authors whose political philosophy they happened to
dislike.

Yet the history of the Europeans in Africa cannot be separated from the history of Africa at large.
No reputable historian of Eastern Europe, for instance, would deny historical legitimacy, say, to a
study of the Ottoman conquerors of Albania or the
Austrian invaders of Bosnia. Similarly, the policies
of a British governor in what is now Tanzania or the
exploits of a Belgian military leader in what is now
Zaire belong to the history of Africa just as much as
they belong to the annals of Great Britain or of
Belgium, respectively.

Students concerned with the history of the Europeans in Africa, moreover, enjoy advantages today
that were not available to their predecessors half a
century ago. A mass of new archival material has recently become accessible in depositories both of the
former metropolitan powers and of the independent
African states. In addition, colonial historians can
now draw on a great body of sociological and anthro-
pological material largely unavailable in the early
days of European colonization.

To take advantage of this new material and to
reanalyze the colonial period as a phase of Euro-
African history, the Hoover Institution has launched
a new program of scholarly inquiries organized around
the theme of African colonial studies.

One major series, directed by Peter Duignan and
Lewis H. Gann, will deal with the men who modernized
Africa -- <u>Agents of Empire</u>. This project, interdis-
ciplinary in approach, will cover all colonial powers
in sub-Saharan Africa. It will be concerned with the
transference to Africa of Western institutions and
modes of production, techniques and skills, ideas and
ideals -- in short, with the total Western impact on
Africans. The project will seek to answer the following questions: What were the situations faced by
the agents of colonialism both in their efforts to
govern Africans and in their idealogical justifica-
tions for doing so? How did African societies react
and respond to foreign rule? What effects did Europeans have on African societies? What were the se-
quences of adjustment and change?

Complementing this project will be a series of
edited versions of primary sources (diaries, letters,
and journals and reports). We have also planned a
volume of contributed essays on notable colonial
governors as well as one on Belgian governors of the
Congo.

Professor Harry Gailey's study of Sir Donald
Cameron was the first in the "Hoover Colonial Studies
Series." We are now pleased to introduce the politi-
cal biography of Eliud Wambu Mathu, the first African
representative to sit in the Legislative Council of
Kenya, by Dr. Jack R. Roelker.

We trust that this and subsequent studies will
help to elucidate and reinterpret the colonial past
of Africa.

                                     Peter Duignan

                                     Lewis H. Gann

ACKNOWLEDGMENTS

This study would not have been possible without the encouragement and assistance of countless people. The extensive travel and exploration of a multitude of libraries and archival collections which the research required was greatly facilitated by the cooperation of numerous librarians, archivists, academic colleagues and friends. To all of these I owe an irrepayable debt.

Special acknowledgment can only be made to those who have been of most specific assistance. My primary appreciation must go to Eliud Mathu for the numerous hours he spent with me in interviews. I also received exceptional cooperation from Mr. B. A. Ohanga in the interviews he granted me. For constant academic encouragement and inspiration, I am forever indebted to Dr. Robert Gregory. I am also genuinely grateful to Dr. Roderick J. Macdonald for his support and generous assistance. In addition, I would like to thank Oliver Bickford, William Gitobu, Robin Kamau, Edward Stralinsky, David Wilkin and Fred Morton for their help during my stay in Kenya. I am also particularly appreciative of the translating assistance given by Leonard Muthoga, and of the typing and proofreading of Mrs. Gloria Gross.

I would also like to thank Mr. Nathan Fedha, Kenya Government Archivist for his constant cooperation. Similarly, the officials of the Presbyterian Church of East Africa Archives, of the Christian Council of Kenya, of Edinburgh House and the Church Missionary Society Archives were all unfailingly helpful.

Finally, I am most grateful for the generous Fulbright-Hayes Research Fellowship. Only with this financial aid was the essential research possible.

Jack R. Roelker

INTRODUCTION

Eliud Wambu Mathu was a leading African political spokesman during a critical period of Kenya's
colonial history. On October 5, 1944, he was appointed by Governor Henry Moore as an unofficial
Member for African interests and the first African
representative to sit in the colonial Legislative
Council. He continued in this role without interruption until May 1957. These were turbulent years in
modern Kenya's history - years of tension and bitter
struggle. Racism and violence were intense but so
too were demands for human equality and political
freedom. The stability of the colonial administration and the privileged status of the European settlers, both of which seemed so secure at the start
of this period, were being fundamentally challenged
before its end. The social and political change in
this period was rapid and dynamic, even revolutionary. Eliud Mathu had a role in producing this
change, and the object of this study is to examine
that role and to evaluate its contribution to the
development of the Kenya nation.

An eclectic approach to a study of this kind
seems most effective. The focus is a description of
Mathu's political career in the Legislative Council
with the purpose of determining its place in the
broader spectrum of African protest in colonial
Kenya. Thus the emphasis is largely political, and
there has been no attempt to achieve a full scale
and multifaceted biography. Nevertheless, especially in the earlier chapters, the biographical
method has been employed as the most facile means of
describing the origins and development of Mathu's
character, his social outlook and political philosophy. After these influences have been traced,the
core of the book concentrates on a detailed account
of Mathu's political career, the essence of which is
the analysis of the policies he pursued in the Council. Along with his parliamentary representation,
Mathu's relationship with "Mau Mau" and his position
in the popular elections of 1957 and 1958 are studied
and evaluated. Besides this political description
and analysis and biography, a third approach of com-

parison is used in a section devoted to a broader
study of the social and intellectual attitudes prevalent among the African elite in the years of
Mathu's political prominence. The position of
various members of Kenya's black intelligentsia of
the 1940s and 1950s on questions such as race, western culture, and political independence is examined
and compared to Mathu's views in these same years
with the purpose of providing some perspective. This
multiple approach, while somewhat unwieldy, seems the
most thorough way of examining Mathu's parliamentary
career and placing it in the context of Kenya's political development.

Because the concern of this study is with
Mathu's political significance, only a cursory description has been given of his life since 1958.
With the election of that year his political career
ceased, and a new era in Kenya's political development was firmly launched. Mathu remains active even
today, but his significance as a political spokesman
ended with the introduction of popular elections in
1957-58. He has never returned to politics since
that time, and indications are that his historical
relevance will rest with his contribution as a member
of the colonial Legislative Council.

Three particular characteristics of this study
have made it peculiarly difficult to arrive at a
sound assessment of Mathu. The first of these relates to the traditional problems of historical perspective and its special significance in the study of
modern Africa. The primary advantage of historical
writing is that by its nature of dealing with events
of times past it allows the scholar a more objective
view. One is removed in time from his subject and
can see it in a broader scope and with a cooler head.
It can be argued with some justification that the
events since World War II are too recent to allow
this detachment full play. Certainly emotional involvement with the events of the period has been a
big factor in the evaluation of Mathu obtained in
oral research from a number of Kenyans. Young leftist scholars, such as Grant Kamenju and Benson Kanti,
see Mathu as nothing more than an opportunist, a
lackey of the colonial regime. Older men, such as
James Jeremiah and B. A. Ohanga, who shared Mathu's
experience as nominated Legislative Council members,
offer a far less critical evaluation of his career.
Given this situation, one might argue that this entire

study would best be put aside until more time has
passed. But for the historian interested in African
politics there is no real alternative to taking this
disadvantage in stride. Mathu was among the very
first of Kenya's Africans with any substantial western education, and, as noted, he was the first
African granted a formal voice in the government
machinery at colony level. He was connected in some
way almost from the very first with the organized
political activities of his people. The unusual
rapidity of the chronology of modern Africa's political history necessitates a greater focus on relatively recent events than would occur more generally
in historical writing.

The second difficulty encountered in this study
involves the use of the interview as a major re-
source. In providing information for this study,
despite his limited leisure, Mathu agreed to frequent
meetings and to a series of taped interviews in which
he provided an oral autobiographical account of his
career. These meetings have been a rich source of
new information. Nevertheless, because they were the
product of historical reflection, the image that was
projected rarely escaped fitting an intellectualized
mental conception which was Mathu's self view. This
seems an unavoidable weakness whenever oral research
is employed. It can be overcome only by balancing
the data from such interviews against other sources.

A final problem confronted in this study involves the temptation, especially real to an American
writing about African political resistance, to view
this resistance as directly analogous with the black
struggle against white supremacy in the United
States. This has been particularly difficult in
assessing the significance of Mathu's political
career. In his own reflections, Mathu stressed the
influence of Booker T. Washington on shaping his
philosophy. Given this self-interpretation, there
was a clear temptation to follow this thesis through
as the central focus of this study - to make Mathu
the Booker T. of Kenya, or perhaps a representative
of a school of reformers throughout colonial Africa
for whom Washington was the archtype. Such an interpretation might have dramatic impact. It would certainly be welcome as a clarifying contribution to the
study of colonial Africa. But to employ this theme
the writer must not ignore certain discordant historical facts which significantly weaken the efficacy

of the analogy.

Perhaps the most obvious of these is the fundamentally different racial composition of colonial
Kenya and the antebellum United States. Although
both were dominated by white political establish-
ments, the European community of Kenya was never more
than 10% of the total population whereas Washington's
America always had a white majority of at least 80%.
The strength of Kenya's Whites came from the support
of the British Crown. But this support was always
ambivalent and grew increasingly so as the intensity
of African nationalism increased. This basic demo-
graphic dissimilarity essentially alters the validity
of tracing a parallel between the careers of Mathu
and Washington. The necessity for compromise in
Washington's circumstances was much more real than in
Mathu's. Indeed one need only note the effectiveness
of the more revolutionary tactic of passive resistance as employed by Gandhi in India and Martin
Luther King in the United States to make a similar
point in reverse. While Mathu certainly was influenced by Washington's concepts, the circumstances in
which they were employed were notably different, and
the need for such a cautious approach can be more
genuinely questioned.

A second contrasting factor in the careers of
Mathu and Washington is evident in the divergent
character of the entire spectrum of Black American
and Kenyan African protest. The most distinct aspect
of this contrast is chronological. Washington lived
and died in an era when accommodation to the terms of
white supremacy remained prevalent among America's
Blacks. W.E.B. Du Bois formidably challenged this
approach but his Niagara Movement was soon absorbed
into the dedicated but elitist and white-dominated
N.A.A.C.P., and Washington's compromise attitude remained entrenched. Mathu was still a relatively
young man when "Mau Mau" erupted, and shortly thereafter his "half a loaf" tactics were rejected for the
more militant demand of "Freedom Now!". While this
difference should not alter a scholarly assessment of
Mathu, and while he did "move with the changing
times" to a considerable degree, it is nevertheless
a notable discrepancy in any effort to demonstrate a
real correlation between his career and that of
Washington.

Finally the feasibility of classifying Mathu as

representative of any specific school of African
spokesmen is basically contrived. Certain similarities might be seen between Mathu and earlier West
African personalities, such as J.E.K. Aggrey or
Casely Hayford, or with the more contemporary Henry
Chipembere of Nyasaland. But equally as many differences between these men can be shown. It is natural
for the historian to seek for a broad thesis. But
the factual basis for this thesis must be genuine.
Mathu's career is an essential part of Kenya's political history. To portray it as patently illustra-
tive of some broader African school of protest would
be dishonest.

To reject the idea of Mathu and Booker T. Washington having parallel careers is not to deny the influence of Washington on Mathu's thought. Indeed,
all of Kenya's politically active Africans who were
part of Mathu's era seem to have had a remarkable and
early awareness of black American spokesmen. Knowledge of Garvey, Du Bois, The Crisis magazine, and
especially Washington from World War I onward was
universal with these men. This political activism in
the United States was clearly a stimulant to them.
Mathu undoubtedly studied Washington's work and used
it as a foundation for many of his own beliefs. This
association between the two men is real, and the circumstances that produced it will be traced as one
element of this book.

As a final introductory note some justification
of this study might be warranted against the frequent
cries of irrelevance met in the research. The tendency of political historians today, both in Africa
and in the West, is to emphasize the radical phases
of their subject. In Kenya, for example, numerous
studies of "Mau Mau" have been made almost to the ex-
clusion of all other aspects of modern political activity. Mathu was involved in the militant politics
of his country. But if one were to define his political philosophy and the position he held most consistently in his career, it would be that of a liberal or moderate. He was never detained, and his support during the Emergency was ambivalent. Yet even
if his stand had been reactionary, a study of his representation would be worthwhile. For a nation's
political history to be recorded truly requires examination of the full spectrum of its operating elements. To isolate and expand upon only one faction
is both naive and prejudicial. Only a distorted

picture can result. This account of Mathu's career
in the Legislative Council is intended as a contribution to a better understanding of one area of African
political development and coincidentally of the attitudes and tactics of the British administration during this colonial era. If it succeeds in this it has
value, and its relevance is justified.

Eliud Wambu Mathu

CHAPTER ONE

BEGINNINGS--1910-1929

Undoubtedly the yeast of civilization is
stirring the Kikuyu strongly.

Kiambu District Commissioner,
1918[1]

In Kenya's Central Province the circumstances of
Britain's penetration were such that virtually all
the essential elements to emerge in the relationship
between the colonial presence and the Kikuyu population were evident as early as the 1920s. The equi-
vocation of the administration's objectives is evidenced by their active postwar recruitment of settlers and simultaneous expressions of African paramountcy. The influence of the Christian missions and
their paternalistic kind of cultural penetration was
also entrenched. The settler community was politically organized, and its authority had grown steadily
since the days of Sir Charles Eliot early in the century. All these phenomena have been extensively recorded and need no evaluation.[2] There is no historical revelation in the statement that the fundamental
factors of Britain's occupation of Kikuyuland were
plainly present in the years following World War I.
Nevertheless, the point is important for an appreciation of the atmosphere of the area at that time.

What has not been sufficiently recorded and is
not fully appreciated as yet by historians is the
quality of political awareness present within a core
of the Kikuyu community in post World War I. Scholars concerned with the subject uniformly agree that
the Kikuyu were the vanguard of Kenya's politically
conscious Africans. They might agree also that among
the Kikuyu could be found advanced political ideas as
early as the 1920s. But the emphasis in their accounts most often presents a different impression.
Descriptions of African politics in Kenya consistently stress the evolving nature of political consciousness.[3] The travel abroad of African soldiers during
World War II is given as the major broadening factor

which produced the heightened political activity of
the 1950s. This kind of analysis is valid and useful. But at the same time it should be emphasized
that this evolution, this growth of political awareness, was primarily a quantitative process, an expanse in the numbers of men involved. It was not an
evolution of political philosophy. A reading of
Kikuyu political statements of the 1920s would show
that virtually all of the political concepts and demands of a much latter period were expressed then.
Race consciousness, the self-help doctrine, and the
numerous specific grievances ranging from land reform
to compulsory education are some of the most important of these. It was in this decade following the
first Great War that the real political awakening of
Kenya's African community occurred.

Clearly, this period was a critical one in modern Kikuyu development. The establishment of colonial control had produced a profound upheaval. By
1920 the primary effects of this phenomenon were being experienced. The character of the colonial relationship was taking form. The political consciousness of the indigenous population was awakened. It
was in this atmosphere that Eliud Mathu grew to manhood.

Mathu's birthplace had been witness to change
even before the impact of colonialism became emphatic. His village was Riruta, in the Dagoretti Sub-
District of Kiambu District, Central Province. The
original inhabitants were Dorobo, a hunting people.
The predominantly agrarian Kikuyu first settled
there in a small community early in the nineteenth
century. They moved down from Mount Kenya and were
granted a section of land by Dorobo for the payment
of 200 sheep and goats.[4] Only two _ithaka_ (land
titles) were established at this time, and official
expansion was not effected until the turn of the century.[5] During the nineteenth century the pastoral
Masai had become dominant in the area. During the
century the Kikuyu community also had grown. In the
1890's internal rivalry splintered the Masai, and the
Kikuyu paramount Chief Kinyanjui wa Githerimu, with
British support, used this situation to expand Kikuyu
control. He allied with one Masai faction and, for
this assistance, was given extensive territory to the
south of the original Kikuyu _ithaka_.[6] Thus settlement is recent to much of Kiambu, and the region was
the scene of considerable change in the nineteenth

century.

Change remained the rule in this area in successive years. But, more and more, it was due to the
European presence and was more profound. Dagoretti
was among the first sections of Kikuyuland to be developed. Lord Lugard, as agent for the Imperial
British East Africa Company, established the first
Kikuyu station there in 1890. Although Kikuyu reaction caused this effort to fail, construction of the
Uganda Railway through this region in 1900 was the
beginning of intensive colonization. The military
superiority of the British made their advances virtually inevitable, but circumstances contributed to
their success. A wave of famine and disease was
weakening the Kikuyu, and in this situation much of
the land which they might have used remained unculti-
vated. It was land sublimely suited to western occu-
pancy. In the years immediately following the railway's penetration, development began in earnest. Administrators, missionaries and settlers moved in, and
the colonial process, with all its reverberations,
was launched.

By 1910, which Mathu estimates as the year of
his birth,[7] the colonial government had established
an administrative framework in Kiambu. Dagoretti,
Mathu's home area, was administered as a large sub-
district which included both African reserve and settler farm land.[8] The reserve area was divided into
six locations, each under the control of a gazetted
chief. Mathu lived in Location 13, that of Paramount
Chief Kinyanjui to whom he was remotely related. A
modified system of indirect rule was applied in these
locations, and each Monday the chiefs and elders of
the sub-district met to form a Native Council with
authority which was primarily judicial.[9] Direct administrative responsibility, however, belonged to the
District Officer, then entitled Assistant District
Commissioner, resident in the government headquarters
at Dagoretti town. Apparently the primary duties of
these early administrators were the supervision of
poll and hut tax collection and of labor recruitment
for settler plantations.[10] Toward these ends the
chiefs were used as intermediaries, a policy which
significantly augmented their position, and disturbed
the traditional balance of authority.[11] Nevertheless,
the system was effective. Partly as a result of
these alterations, the political and economic nature
of Kikuyu society was swiftly and fundamentally al-

tered in these years.

　　The severe hardships which the Kikuyu had been
experiencing were terminating by the time Mathu was
born. Farming was again productive, and 1912-13 was
described in the Annual Report as "a record year for
crops." Maize and beans flourished, and the harvest
of newly introduced white potatoes was "magnificent".
Livestock prices rose, so that the selling price of a
sheep increased from rupees 7/- to rupees 10/-. Pro-
fit was such that hut taxes were paid "ungrudgingly".[12]
Much of this tax money, however, came from the wages
of those who had migrated to Nairobi or to settler
farms to find employment.[13] Despite this out-flow,
Kinyanjui's location had a thriving population. The
epidemic of diseases which had devitalized the region
earlier had subsided. Census figures for 1912-13
estimate that a total of 7,789 people lived on the
17,700 acres here.[14] Most men had two wives, and each
woman averaged three children. According to administration accounts, land was ample in this location
for the peasant farming which these women performed.
A typical plot was five acres of which three were
farmed and two left fallow, and the avilable land was
reported to be more than sufficient to provide this
acreage.[15] This farming went on peacefully. The colonial administration had quelled the traditional
warfare resultant from Masai raids. While the establishment of British control caused serious disorient-
ation among the Kikuyu, from the standpoint of simple
economic output, this period was one of increased
productivity which was partly the result of this
same control.

　　Economic growth was clearly not sufficient balm,
however, to ease the suffering the Kikuyu experienced
as a result of British takeover, and dissatisfaction
with their new rulers was unmistakably prevalent at
the time of Mathu's birth. An important evidence of
this is found in the record of an interview with
M.W.H. Beech, a Dagoretti Assistant District Commissioner, held with the oldest male resident of the
sub-district on December 12, 1912.[16] This man was
"Chief" Gatonye, the last survivor of the Njeroge
circumcision age group. His point of view was largely traditionalist, opposed to western penetration,
and in stating it he presented some of the specific
grievances which were to remain part of the protest
movement until independence. Much of his criticism
was directed against the settlers. "We want more

land," he stated. "The Europeans have taken too
much: they have taken what we bought ourselves . . .
if our foot touches their land, they fine us ten
goats . . . Europeans give us allotments on forest
and uncleaned land on their estates. After cleaning
it and planting we are often summarily turned off."[17]
Despite administration statements that the Kikuyu had
abundant land, this issue of land reform, which would
be first on the list of grievances throughout the
years of protest, was already being presented by
Gatonye in these early years. But his protest extended to other areas as well. He expressed a willingness to pay hut tax which he considered essential to provide funds for maintaining peace and protection against the Masai. There was a second reason
for his support of this tax. It was calculated on a
village basis, i.e., a man was responsible for the
huts of his family unit, and it therefore conformed
to the Kikuyu communal style of life. The poll tax,
on the other hand, he strongly opposed.[18] This was a
tax on the individual, and it worked against the communal feeling. Each man was responsible solely for
his own tax so that an independent attitude and com-
parative spirit were encouraged. Gatonye opposed
such change, and as an extension of this, he opposed
migration of his people to towns or settler farms.
"They are different men," he stated on those who migrated. "They disobey the orders of the elders and
think only of themselves."[19] Similarly he opposed
western education. Those who attended schools were
"mission boys", and they too were afflicted with the
individualism Gatonye saw as a destructive force.[20]
His testimony taken as a whole is unique personal
evidence of the tension created among the Kikuyu as
a result of colonization. A broad reading of archival sources for the period indicates that Gatonye's
position is typical of his people in these years.

Although proportionately a definite minority,
as Gatonye's criticism implies, there were those
within the Kikuyu community who were actively accommodating themselves to the changing times. It is a
truism of Kenya history that the Kikuyu adapted to
western culture in greater numbers and with less resistance than other Africans in the country. But
this adaptation was never unqualified. The records
of early district officers in Kikuyu areas stress the
conservatism of their charges.[21] The accommodation
which did occur was gradual. Mission schools were
established in Dagoretti. The Church of Scotland

Mission (CSM) was the first of these and began educational instruction in Kinyanjui's location in
1908.[22] The African Inland Mission (AIM), The Church
Mission Society (CMS), and the Roman Catholics (RC)
followed.[23] These schools which, besides religious
instruction, emphasized technical training, e.g.,
agriculture, carpentry, masonry, were the only formal
source of western education offered. An indication
of the effectiveness of these missions in acquiring
converts is available in the formation of the Kikuyu
Mission Volunteers, a Carriers Corps during World War
I which mustered some 1,800 men from mission stations
throughout Kikuyuland.[24] In addition to these mission
adherents, other Kikuyu were absorbing western culture in the towns, on settler farms, and in other
units of the Carrier Corps. In 1917 an estimated 500
Africans were employed in Nairobi offices and
homes.[25] As has been noted, labor recruitment for
farms was an active undertaking of government officials, and the appointed chiefs were expected to
cooperate in the process. Taxes created a new need
for money which also quickened the labor flow. The
fact that white settlement first flourished in Kikuyu
areas made a degree of accommodation essential, but
beyond this it is clear that increasing numbers were
actively seeking knowledge of the ways of the West.
Predictably European innovations also appeared in the
villages. A district officer describes this development in 1918 and gives some indication of the gradual
rate at which it occurred:

> Yearly the Kikuyu became more sophisti-
> cated . . . shop keeping on a small scale
> is becoming very popular, mainly native res-
> taurants but cloth is also sold: This is
> symptomatic of advance. Estimation in
> rupees rather than in goats is gaining
> ground: a few ploughs have been bought, two
> flour mills erected [.] European clothes
> have been adopted by many headmen one or two
> of whom have bought mules for riding. Or-
> dinary younger natives also are adopting
> clothes to a greater extent.[26]

Clearly, then adaption was a growing phenomenon. It
was slowly winning converts and was affecting the
character of life within the reserves.

An important personal consequence resulted from
this adaption. For the first time each individual in

Kikuyu society was faced with a choice of life style.
The fact that most of them, well into the 1920s
were continuing their traditional existence made any
decision to do otherwise especially difficult. The
reality of this difficulty becomes clear when applied
to the specific situation of Eliud Mathu.

Mathu's origins were humble and wholly traditionalist. They are best described in his own words:

> My parents were not educated; they were
> typical Kikuyu parents. Call them raw if
> you like, but they did not know anything
> about anything else besides Kikuyu tradi-
> tion and Kikuyu ways. . . . Now my father
> and mother never went to school. They were
> very elderly. . . . My mother was never a
> Christian. My father was never a Christian.
> They hated everything modern. They did not
> want to see the Europeans nor to have any-
> thing to do with them. They knew nothing
> about them, and they did not care to know
> them. They were typical Kikuyu who loved
> to live as Kikuyu.[27]

Mathu's father, Mathu wa Kamwengi, had three
wives, and the first of these, Wambui, was Mathu's
mother. The family was poor but held some prominence
because Mathu Kamwengi was the village medicine man.
He led the community ceremonies and sacrifices. He
also had been an important warrior in battles against
the Masai. He was a member of the eminent Acera
clan, the same clan to which Kinyanjui belonged.
Mathu's mother is described by her son as having been
"very self-reliant" and "respected because of her industry and intelligence."[28] She bore six children of
whom Mathu was the youngest. It was a family of
minor distinction, with no real resources and with an
active resistance to western innovation.

As his origins prescribed, Mathu's early youth
was spent in the traditional way, and in his situation, as later, his unusual abilities were manifest.
He wrote:

> During my boyhood, I did not pass any day
> in idleness. I had to look after my father's
> sheep and goats, eagerly and willingly, so
> much so that the animals caused damage to a
> man's garden only once, when I had interested

myself in working with clay with the other
boys. 'He never takes part in unreasonable
games or useless disputes,' said my parents.
During the boys' dance sessions, I was, undoubtedly, in the first place as leader of
local dances. 'He was the smallest of the
boys, but because of his knowledge and
intelligence he was able to lead and guide
ngucu, mumburo and even nguru which is the
dance of the young men,' said my eldest
brother.[29]

Mathu was very young when he lived this way. He
was probably no more than ten when his life began to
change. But in these years he was high-spirited and
absorbed in his surroundings. He reflects on his
childhood as a happy time and on his traditional
origins with pride and respect.

The important influence which began to alter
the routine of Mathu's days was his contact with the
missions. The decision to attend school was wholly
his own. It sprang from a yearning for self-improve-
ment which, Mathu later felt, had within it an element of guilt stemming from a particular incident of
his boyhood. He related this episode and its effects
as follows:

I remember quite well on one occasion when
I was very unkind and cruel, my mother and
brothers were ill and because of the way my
brothers used to beat me, I took that opportunity of revenge when they were ill. This
I did by stoning them and giving them no
food as a punishment for their previous unkind actions to me. When they got better,
they did not seek revenge. I felt my wrong
deeds after a time, I felt as if I should
be a better lad if I knew how to read and
write, and more than that if I knew who
Jesus was of whom I was hearing quite often.[30]

The CSM ran a free elementary school at Riruta,
very near Mathu's home, and he began attendance here,
without his family's knowledge, in 1919. His sheep
and goats were kept for him by a friend, and each day
he set off with them and returned as if he had spent
his day in the fields. As circumstances would prove,
he rightly judged that his parents would oppose his
attendance. But his contact with the school and his

instruction in Christianity stimulated his ambition
and changed his outlook so that he determined to
abandon certain traditional customs and continue his
connection with the mission.

The schooling at Riruta was directed to produce
this response from its pupils. Officially its stated
objectives were given as follows:

> The Elementary School enables boys and
> girls to learn the elements of Reading,
> Writing and Arithmetic, to enable them to
> read the Gospels, and to lay a foundation
> for work of a more practical nature. Stress
> is laid on the foundation of Christian
> character and of habits of industry and
> cleanliness.[31]

The Reverend John W. Arthur, who directed the CSM
schools in Kikuyuland, was a medical doctor from
Glasgow. He was strong willed and autocratic in his
approach which had as its goal the "mental and
spiritual advancement" of his pupils.[32] By this was
meant the rejection of traditional institutions such
as polygamy, "immoral native dances", and the "vile
rite" of female circumcision and the adoption of
Christianity and European customs in their place.[33]
He expected obedience from his African subordinates
and considered African political activity "Bolshevic
Ante-Order" and "Communistic."[34] This attitude was
not unique. It is the familiar paternalism upon
which most mission activity was based. It brought
literacy, skills, and erudition but, at the same
time, it devastated the confidence of many in their
traditional heritage and left them with no real cultural roots. Mathu was affected in this way, and
though he retained a respect for his origins, he
gradually became almost wholly absorbed into the
European culture. This development was largely the
result of his mission education.

His education continued steadily from 1919 but
not without difficulty. His deception of his parents
was not successful for long and with its discovery
came condemnation and a beating. He submitted to
their order to end his studies but not without a
qualification which reveals the missions' success:

> I gave up my schooling with the hope that
> I would once more be a reader and a Christian.

> By this time I made it strictly known to my
> people that even if they strictly forbade
> me to go to school, I would never from this
> time, take part in family sacrifices and
> ceremonies of any description. 'As a token
> of my obedience, I am ready to do everything
> else as to the tending of sheep and cultiva-
> tion of the garden, but I will never join you
> in things concerning ngoma (departed spirits)
> or any other thing disagreeing with the Chris-
> tian religion,' said I to my people.[35]

Shortly thereafter, Mathu's father agreed that his
son's education should continue. This was undoubtedly a difficult decision, especially given his position as medicine man for the village. But Chief
Kinyanjui came to Mathu's aid and recommended to
Mathu Kamwengi that he allow his son to study.[36] It
was evident in discussion with Mathu that this approval by his father meant much to him:

> . . . in 1920 he gave me permission and he
> purchased the required paraphernalia which is
> necessary for a boy to go to school-- a slate,
> a slate pencil and a primer in Kikuyu. So I
> got permission from my father. He refused
> any of his children but he permitted me, and
> I am the only one. Even today none of my
> brothers and sisters have ever gone to school
> because my father is now dead, and it would
> be a curse if they did against the will of my
> father. My father gave me his blessings and,
> I think we say, and the local people say,
> that Mathu has succeeded, even going to
> Oxford and getting a degree because his
> father blessed him to follow this line.[37]

He returned to Riruta in 1920 and attended until the
following year. In addition to his work in school,
he was able to obtain additional materials from the
mission which he would study at night. "I had a
little hand-lamp I used to read with when in bed as
the native huts have no tables or lamps," he writes.[38]
He was then able to attend school regularly, and,
with his evening study, was able to reach intermediate standard by 1921. This entitled him to progress to a higher school.

Mathu was admitted to the CSM Intermediate
School at Ruthimitu near Dagoretti town in 1921 and

with his attendance came some new developments in his
educational career. This school, like the one at
Riruta, was tuition free, but it did require that its
students supply study materials beyond those used at
the lower level. To acquire these Mathu needed money,
and he raised it from the sale of farm produce in the
local market. He began a vegetable garden beside the
Nyongara River. He also assisted his brother with
his hens and was given eggs to sell in return.
Clearly these were busy days, but despite these multiple activities he also found time to begin religious instruction in earnest. Before being baptized
into the Church of Scotland one had to take a
Hearer's and Catechument's Course. Mathu enrolled
for this in 1921 and studied under William Njoroge,
a Kikuyu Evangelist who encouraged him. He continued
to excel at school. His teacher, the Reverend Musa
Gitau, in a reference written for him stated, "Wambu
is the best of my boys and attends school punctually
daily. He is a boy out of the ordinary."[39] His
study at Ruthimitu continued until 1923, and in these
years his decision to continue his education was for-
tified both by his scholastic success and by encouragement from his African teachers who made a similar
decision before him.

In 1923 Mathu began a three year term of study
at the CSM Central School at Kikuyu which Dr. John W.
Arthur supervised directly, and although he completed
his program here successfully, there were some difficulties to overcome at the start. This institution
was a boarding school and admittance to the course
depended on the pupil's passing a Vernacular Certificate examination. Mathu sat for his exam and failed
in 1923. Despite failure he was told that he could
attend classes at the school as a non-boarder and
could repeat the exam at a later date. Kikuyu was a
distance of eight miles from his home, and Mathu com-
muted sixteen miles each day for a year and a half.
Often, as he made this journey, he was given a lift
by a passing cyclist, one of whom was Johnston Kamau
(Jomo Kenyatta) who had studied carpentry at the
Central School and was living at Kikuyu. In 1924
Mathu repeated the required examination and scored
well. He was admitted by Arthur to the boarding section and given a job as dormitory cook because of his
inability to pay the required fees.[40] It is interesting to note that despite his ambition and the difficulty he had had commuting the long distance each day,
Mathu had some qualms about the new boarding situation

and had to be encouraged by Arthur personally before
he agreed to move from his home into the dormitory.
He gives no reason for this reluctance, but it is
understandable as the natural apprehension of a boy
of fourteen who had to decide on his own to leave
his village surroundings and move into a new community. A variety of courses was offered at the
school, most of them for practical vocational skills.
But there was also a Normal School, and it offered a
literary course of which the stated aim was "to train
teachers of a sufficiently broad outlook to provide
not only for the needs of the scholars of their village schools but also to assist in the spiritual and
material advancement of the community to which they
will later be sent."[41] Three months after his enrollment as a boarder, Mathu was admitted into this
course. The staff at Kikuyu felt that he displayed
the leadership potential a teacher required. So in
1924 he began training for the vocation he would consider throughout his career as his natural calling.[42]

Besides being the start of his involvement with
teaching, the year was important for Mathu for a number of other reasons. The Headmaster of the Normal
School was George Andrew Grieve, a man who was to influence Mathu significantly, and this was the beginning of the relationship between them. This was also
the year of Mathu's baptism into the Presbyterian
Church. He had completed the required course of instruction in 1923, but his baptism was delayed because it was felt that he was still too young. It
might be noted that Mathu's parents did nothing to
discourage his religious conversion. Their attitude
is described as follows: "Having given me the right
to go to school, they never curbed any authority of
mine after that point."[43] Despite his conversion,
Mathu continued to abide by the primary traditions of
his people. His absorption in study and his life
away from home prevented him from performing many
activities typical of Kikuyu youth, e.g., hunting,
living with his age set in independent huts, and
early marriage. But in this same year of his formal
initiation into the Christian faith, he also was
initiated into Kikuyu manhood through the prescribed
ceremony of circumcision.[44]

The coincidence of these two initiations in 1924
vividly illustrates one of the fundamental conflicts
in Mathu's development which tragically he never de-
cisively resolved. Caught between the values of

Africa into which he was born and those of Europe
which he was acquiring through his mission education,
he was =constantly confronted by a duality of essentially divergent cultures. It was a dilemma with
which every Kikuyu of his generation had to cope to
some degree. But because of his future political
prominence it is particularly vital to note how Mathu
came to terms with this problem. Kenyatta would do
so, almost cathartically, in his defense of traditional culture in Facing Mount Kenya. Mathu's LegCo
colleague, B. A. Ohanga, also resolved this conflict
by conversely embracing western attitudes and describing those of Africa as "raw" and "pagan."[45] But
no such easily definable commitment is ever evident
with Mathu. By this time in his life he had made
some clear choices. He had decided, wholly on his
own, to go to school. He had become a Christian.
These decisions, as has been noted, led him to reject those customs of his people most criticized by
the missions. Other traditions he by-passed from
practical necessity while away at school. But his
circumcision is indication of a continued identification with his origins, of some desire to maintain
connection with his roots. Similarly, as will be
seen, his interest in and qualified participation in
the activities of African political organization in
these student years suggests some early interest in
freeing Kenya from colonial control. Throughout his
parliamentary career he urged his people to modernize
and at the same time preserve those aspects of their
traditional culture which had positive value. Thus
his position remains vague. He had clearly wrestled
with the problem and perhaps resolved it for himself,
but it was a resolution difficult to define and
therefore politically precarious.

The root of the problem in this conflict was
Mathu's fundamental moderation. He was consistently
pragmatic in his approach, seeking to find a workable
compromise. In this particular case of conflicting
cultures he advocated a blending in which the major
element would be western. This position, while perhaps realistic, was not politically advantageous.
His failure to fully embrace European values annoyed
the colonial administration, and his limited defense
of traditional culture would alienate him from the
African leadership that was eventually to emerge.

Besides his fundamental moderation, however, a
second factor in explaining Mathu's pragmatism is his

concern for his personal survival. There is irony in
this since it often worked against him, but it remains a pertinent element in his behavior. As his
career progesses Mathu's steady commitment to certain
objectives for his people is clear. But the intensity of this commitment is often determined by an
assessment of the political scene and the security of
his particular position within it. While he manifests definite principles, his methods and vigor vary
depending on his personal situation. To a degree
this is attributable to the nature of the time--the
formidable task for a Kikuyu of Mathu's day to digest, adjust to and attempt to positively influence
the colonial establishment. In these circumstances
it became essential in Mathu's eyes to create and
maintain for himself a satisfying personal environment, and the force with which he pursued his principles was to some extent dependent on the degree to
which this threatened his private domain. Thomas
Hodgkin in his Nationalism in Colonial Africa makes
much of urban Africans finding solace in their isolation from their lost communal heritage in welfare
associations and similar groups. Mathu was such a
man. He formed no welfare group but, throughout his
career, created for himself a sense of community in
the situation in which he was at the time. In this
way he could escape the loneliness which might otherwise have caused isolating and incapacitating bitterness. That there were other options is obvious as
seen by Kenyatta or the early career of Harry Thuku.
But Mathu was inclined to compromise and to preserve
his personal stability if it did not require the vio-
lation of his basic beliefs. Alliance High School
was the first community into which Mathu settled in
this way, and it provided him with a creative environment with which his cultural duality could
blend.

The character of Alliance High School, which
was founded in 1926, was determined by a series of
compromises from a more ambitious initial scheme.[46]
The Alliance of Protestant Missions, which ran the
school, was established at a conference at Kikuyu in
1913. It was a joint organization of the CSM, CMS,
African Inland Mission (AIM), and Gospel Mission Protestant Societies. After World War I a surplus of
Ł6,000 was granted by the Trustees of the East
African Red Cross to this organization to be used for
African medical services. Coincidentally at this
time the CSM had assigned to the Alliance 100 acres

of land at Kikuyu for the purpose of establishing an
African college. It was, therefore, agreed that this
college should be initiated as a medical school uti-
lizing the funds from the Red Cross. Buildings were
erected, but a complexity of difficulties involving
staffing problems, in-fighting among individual member missions, and government opposition led to its
abandonment. The result was a compromise agreement
in 1925 that the buildings be used for the purpose of
a high school managed by the Alliance with government
cooperation.[47] Provisions and money were provided
for an enrollment of 50 students, and it was hoped
that Senior School Certificate could be used as the
admittance qualification.[48] This too proved too ambitious a proposal, and initial enrollment was 24
pupils, the highest qualification of whom was the T3
certificate. A final compromise was the selection of
the school's principal. It was hoped that a man of
impressive academic background could be brought in
from a higher educational institution outside the
colony. Several qualified candidates applied but
again difficulties arose in the decision of appointment. While this went on, George Grieve had been
employed as Acting Principal, and it was intended
that he would serve as assistant to the man appointed. But because of disagreement on a final choice
and because Grieve was functioning well, he was asked
to take the Principalship and accepted, on August 5,
1926.[49] Kenya's first secondary school was officially opened by Governor Sir Edward Grigg on October 1,
1926, and despite its inauspicious beginnings became
the center of academic excellence for African education in the colony.

Grieve remained Principal at Alliance for 17
years, and his character was an important influence
on the school and on Mathu personally. Indeed the
relationship that developed between Grieve and Mathu
had a fundamental shaping influence on Mathu's development and to a considerable extent determined the
values in which Mathu would be schooled through most
of his academic career. Grieve first came to Kenya
in 1920 after service in the army had disrupted his
teaching career in Scotland. His university degrees
in the arts and in education were from Edinburgh, and
he taught teacher training at the Kikuyu CSM School,
and at Tumu Tumu after accepting the Alliance appointment.[50] While at Kikuyu he met T. Jesse Jones, there
on behalf of the Phelps-Stokes Commission, and a
friendship developed. As a result of this Grieve
visited the United States and observed the experiment

in black education at Hampton Institute. He was pro-
foundly impressed. His view of African education in
Kenya and of Alliance High School specifically was
influenced by this visit. Hampton's primary goal, as
conceived by its founder General Samuel C. Armstrong,
was the "training [of] selected Negro and Indian
youth for efficient, Christian service."[51] Students
were taught that personal fulfillment came from dedi-
cating themselves to working, virtually as missionaries, among their own people.

> What is commonly called sacrifice is the
> best, happiest use of one's self and one's
> resources--the best investment of time,
> strength, and means. He who makes no such
> sacrifice is most to be pitied. He is a
> heathen, because he knows nothing of God.[52]

This ideal was adopted by Grieve as his own. "To
give consecrated Christian service is the only worthwhile result [of education]", he writes, "all the
rest . . . is subordinate to this end."[53]

In applying this objective, Grieve incorporated
two specific elements of Hampton into the Alliance
curriculum. The first of these was a commitment to
"the building of an African civilization"[54] by
creating a course of study with an African perspective. In a pamphlet on the school published in 1928
he states:

> There is no desire to divorce the
> interests of the student from their own
> native life and customs. No European
> education would be considered complete
> without knowledge of the development of
> the civilization and culture on which it
> is based. So it ought to be with the
> African.[55]

Accordingly, he included a course in Bantu Studies as
a requirement at the school. Secondly, as Armstrong
had done at Hampton, he sought to prepare his students for careers in practical areas which would be
directly beneficial to the community.

> I look upon it [Alliance] as a school in
> which the attempt is to be made to train
> African leaders; and that the attempt to do
> so is to be made through the medium of a

training, cultural in the first instance,
and later to develop into a definite training, here or elsewhere, in some profession,
through which the qualities of leadership
will be enabled to find expression--teach-
ing, medical work, commerce, agriculture,
etc.[56]

Three areas of specialization, in teaching,
clerical and agricultural training, were offered at
the school. This was in the form of a one year
course in addition to and following the general two
year "cultural course" of literature and science subjects.[57]

Despite Grieve's enthusiasm for and adoption of
much of General Armstrong's educational approach,
factors intervened which stopped Alliance from developing into another Hampton Institute. The most influential of these was the development of Makerere
College in Uganda which was established in 1921 "for
the training of artisans" but was rapidly evolving
into a center for higher learning.[58] By 1935 it offered a course of study "recognized throughout the
British Empire as a creditable conclusion to a secondary course."[59] The "cultural course" at Alliance
was the most advanced academic study available to
Kenya Africans. As a result of Makerere's growth,
this "cultural course" became a prerequisite for admission, and Alliance became a kind of preparatory
school with an almost wholly academic emphasis. Upon
completion of the two year course in science and the
arts, after 1935, the brighter Alliance student went
to Makerere rather than enrolling in the practical
training offered at Alliance. A second factor
responsible for the limited influence of Hampton on
Alliance is the, perhaps unconscious, ambivalent behavior of Grieve. Although he frequently expressed
his confidence in Armstrong's ideas, his actions often contradicted them. Bantu Studies and practical
training courses were both adopted by the school, but
neither was really integrated into the core of the
curriculum. As noted, the specialized technical
courses became mere addendum to the academic curriculum, offered only to those who opted to remain at the
school for a third year. Similarly the Bantu Studies
course, while a requirement for all students, remained an isolated subject. All other courses retained
a strong western orientation. As a result, in 1931,
the school was described by a former member of the

Phelps-Stokes Commission as follows:

> The pupils are divorced from home
> interests and home conditions. The
> knowledge is imported through a foreign
> medium. Theory predominates even in
> agriculture. The course on Bantu Studies
> is just another class-lesson.[60]

While Alliance was no Hampton, Grieve's support
for Armstrong's ideals continued throughout his
Principalship and had a notable effect on some of his
students. Unlike Carey Francis, who would succeed
him, Grieve's style was subtle and unassuming. He
established a friendly rapport and visited the homes
of his students, travelling the countryside by motor-
cycle. This approach had appeal and many of his
pupils listened when he encouraged them to pursue
"Christian service." One who was led in this direction was Peter Mbiyu Koinange who left Alliance to
study at Hampton by Grieve's design.

Perhaps most notable is Grieve's influence on
Eliud Mathu. This influence is clearly realized and
appreciated by Mathu whose praise of Grieve is unqualified:

> Mr. Grieve was an aid not only to me,
> but he is the father of higher education
> in East and Central Africa. He helped not
> only me--he helped those who helped them-
> selves. He was a devoted man. A teacher
> in the true sense of the word, and he en-
> couraged those who wanted to go forward.
> He encouraged me, and he helped me tre-
> mendously to get where I did get to.[61]

His help to Mathu was indeed multifarious. As his
master he taught him not only the prescribed schedule
of subjects but also shorthand, and later, Latin and
Greek. He saw an uncommon enthusiasm for academics
in Mathu and encouraged his scholarship. Undoubtedly
he incorporated his personal educational philosophy
into his teaching. Perhaps even more importantly, he
allowed Mathu access to his personal library which
included abundant literature on black education, and
it was here that Mathu first discovered the writings
of Booker T. Washington. Grieve discussed Washington's educational concepts with his student and told
him of his positive impressions of Hampton Institute.

Mathu was clearly affected by these ideas and carried them with him throughout his career. In this way Grieve reinforced Mathu's interest in teaching and aided and helped shape his academic advance. He was also a personal ideal in Mathu's eyes. He ran Alliance quietly, almost democratically. He taught by example and by encouragement. Under his direction Alliance provided a relaxed yet intellectually stimulating atmosphere in which a student with enthusiasm, such as Mathu, could go far.

Mathu was among the first group of 24 boys to qualify for admission to the new school, and this achievement already began to distinguish him as academically advanced among his people. Early in the preliminary planning for the school it was realized that the set admission standard was unreasonably high and that the anticipated enrollment of 50 pupils was extravagant. Qualifying exams were given in February 1926, for which boys who had obtained the English Leaving Certificate were permitted to sit. This is the level which Mathu attained at the CSM Normal School.[62] The competition was colonywide, and because of the involvement of the four major Protestant mission societies, it is likely that most of those qualified sat. Nevertheless, only 14 qualified, and Mathu was one. Another 10 were admitted on probationary terms and with special authority from the Education Department.[63] The average age was 19, and some were as old as 23. According to Kipkorir, most of these pupils came from Christian homes in which parental encouragement was a factor in their son's achievement.[64] Certainly Peter Koinange, the other member of the group whose accomplishments would rival Mathu's, had the considerable benefit of both family wealth and a Christian home.[65] Given these circumstances Mathu's achievement was virtually unique. His advance was entirely his own doing, and he was among the youngest in the group. His reaction to the news of his acceptance has been recorded and is evidence of his enthusiasm for his chosen pursuit:

> One day I met Mr. and Mrs. Grieve near the Kikuyu Church. The very words I said were, 'Sir, have I passed the examination?' A very soothing and precious reply came out of my master's mouth, 'Yes, Eliud, you have passed.' I cannot express in words the feeling that came into my heart when I knew without doubt that I was to be one of the

first Alliance High School students.[66]

With this began a connection with the school which
would continue until 1942. It would provide him opportunity to prove his ability, and to acquire a reputation as an outstanding member of his community.

The school ran smoothly, if perhaps more slowly
than desired in its early years, and Mathu thrived
there. Provision had been made in the budget for
three Europeans and one African on the staff, but it
took some time to fill these places. For the first
year everything was handled by Grieve with volunteer
assistance from his wife and from an occasional community resident. In 1927 James Stephen Smith and
Leonard Beecher arrived and the European staffing was
complete. The African vacancy remained open, however, for want of anyone qualified to fill it. Mathu
continued to excel academically and impressed his
masters. J. Stephen Smith taught agriculture and established a Scout Troop in which Mathu became active.
His recollection of Mathu is worthy of note:

> Mathu was the cleverest we had had
> through our hands. Both Grieve and I
> thought the world of him. He couldn't
> be kept back at all. He was the type
> who decided to learn shorthand and
> within three months had mastered a
> course which normally took a year.[67]

Following the first two years study, Mathu successfully completed the prescribed examination. Surprisingly, in view of his later studies, he scored
best in agriculture, science and math. His score in
English, which would later be among his university
subjects, was his poorest grade.[68] For his final year
he resumed teaching at his specialty, having been reinforced in this decision by Mr. Grieve's example:

> I chose teaching every time! I always
> said it. I must say that Mr. Grieve im-
> pressed most of us - he was a very devoted
> teacher and got quite a number of us to feel
> that we would like to join the same profes-
> sion. He gave us an urge, and so I chose
> to be a teacher. I didn't want to be any-
> thing else.[69]

His enthusiasm is plain. Indeed, these were happy

years for Mathu. He found satisfaction and recognition in his studies. He also was busy in other ways.
School sports, such as tennis and track, became avid
hobbies. He continued his vegetable farming as a
means of raising fees and was permitted a plot of
school ground for this. His private mastering of
shorthand has been seen. He grew to love music and
was much in awe of Reverend Beecher's talents in this
field. As noted, he also read privately from
Grieve's personal library. His favorites were biographies, especially of famous Blacks, and he tells
why:

> These histories about the lives of great
> Africans and American Negroes had a lot to
> do with influencing my character - trying
> to live up to these tenets - and I am still
> interested in biographies because that's
> where one can see how he matches with those
> who have shown greatness.[70]

Besides Grieve's encouragement and recollections
about Hampton Institute, a second circumstance helped
to stir Mathu's interest in Booker T. Washington. As
previously noted, Peter Koinange had left Alliance
without completing his course and had gone to Hampton
Institute. Mathu became curious about this school
and studied Washington's Up From Slavery with special
interest to learn of its origins. This book had considerable impact and would be remembered by him at a
later time when he was developing a rationale for his
career in government. He also read of Abraham
Lincoln, and this too gave him inspiration in future
years. During these secondary school days, Mathu's
curiosity and ambition seemed boundless. He was experiencing the special excitement that comes when a
keen mind born in isolation first discovers a vast
new world.

In addition to his academic pursuits at Alliance,
Mathu also followed with interest the political activity of his people. The historian's difficulty in
tracing this situation is that, beyond oral testimony, no records, such as letters or diaries, exist
which might describe the extent of this interest.
Secondly, except in one small capacity which will be
noted, Mathu had no real connection with any of these
activities but only followed them as a supporting
spectator. Taken in context, this relative political
passivity has its own significance as an indication

of Mathu's priorities at this time. While it is
notable that, as a schoolboy, he did study his country's politics and follow the demands of his people,
it is equally relevant that this interest was accompanied by no public active participation with any
cause. Reference has been made to the broad scope of
ideas existent in Kikuyu politics in the 1920's.
Mathu knew of them and would emphasize many of them
years later in LegCo. But at this time his primary
interest was on his personal academic growth and on
cultivating his relationships at Alliance. Nevertheless, an examination of the most significant of these
political ideas is essential for an understanding of
the shaping influences on Mathu's philosophy as a
foundation for his future parliamentary career.

The emergence of organized political protest
among the Kikuyu was the result of growing discontent
against the policies of the post World War I colonial
administration. As earlier noted, traditional
Kikuyu, such as Chief Gatonye, had expressed dissatisfaction with the British over taxes and loss of land.
But at the same time there was some appreciation of
the improved agricultural situation and the security
against the Masai for which the administration also
was responsible. The World War, and the policies
which followed it, changed this. Some 150,000 men
had been recruited, mostly as porters, to serve in
the German East African Campaign, and many of them
were Kikuyu.[71] They were given only minimal provisions and, perhaps because of this, stricken with in-
fluenza and plague. A total of 46,618 died, almost
all of disease.[72]. The survivors returned believing
that they would be rewarded for their service only to
find new restrictive legislation and higher taxes. A
Fort Hall missionary describes their plight:

> No serious attempt was made to distribute
> a bonus to those natives who had come through
> the campaign, or to secure war widows and
> aged parents from the destitution which the
> loss of their able-bodied relatives entailed:
> Later the hut tax was raised (1920) from
> rupees 5 to 8, wages were cut (a general
> scale being recommended and accepted by the
> majority of the white settlers which reduced
> all wages in the proportion of 3 to 2) and a
> registration ordinance was passed, the annoy-
> ance of which was aggravated by its applica-
> tion on several occasions within the Reserve

itself.[73]

In addition, more highland acreage was alienated to provide for the settling of British war veterans, and an active recruitment campaign sought to double the settler population.[74] Kiambu was described as potentially revolutionary in the late war years when reports of war dead reached the people. "A gloom spread over the native population and in the writer's opinion the Reserve was in a condition where any spark might have caused a dangerous outbreak."[75] Solace was sought in immediate pleasures, and drinking and dancing "became exceedingly rife."[76] This atmosphere developed even before the creation of the new taxes, the wage cuts, and the adoption of registration. Clearly the situation in the 1920s was restless and critical of white rule.

Two Kikuyu organizations emerged in the immediate postwar years, and, while they differed in their tactics and the emphasis of their protest, many of their grievances overlapped and taken together included virtually all of the issues, save political independence, with which African politics in Kenya would be concerned throughout the colonial period. The Kikuyu Association was the first to emerge, probably in 1919.[77] It was an organization of chiefs and headmen, founded by Paramount Chief Kinyanjui with the encouragement of CMS missionary Canon Harry Leakey, and carried the support of the administration. It was committed to presenting petitions to the local officials in the way that was legally prescribed. Later, in 1921, a second association was formed. This was Harry Thuku's Young Kikuyu Association (soon converted to the East African Association), and, because of its more militant approach, it was quickly proscribed by the administration. Thuku distinguished between the colonial government and the government in England and declared his loyalty only to the latter. "The D. C. is nothing to us," he wrote to a friend, "because we know that all men are subjects of King George."[78] His organization's petitions by-passed the local officials and were sent directly to the prime Minister in England. He also worked closely with the Indian community, a policy which, especially in this period, alienated all European elements and their allies in the colony. Thus Thuku was arrested and exiled in 1922, and his career as a militant was over.

The significance of both of these associations
to Mathu's career is not in the details of their
history but in the content of their programs. The
Kikuyu Association, because it was organized by
government appointed chiefs in the reserve, was
essentially moderate and expressed rural demands. Its
main concern was land reform, and its goal was to obtain title deeds which would officially declare reserve land the property of the ithaka holders. It
accepted the alienation of the settler highlands but
sought to insure Kikuyu control of reserve lands allotted to them by the government. Land reform would
remain throughout the colonial period the primary
demand of Kikuyu protest. It was first formally expressed here, albeit temperately, by this association
of chiefs. But the Kikuyu Association had other demands. At a meeting at Dagoretti on June 24, 1921,
a list of grievances was presented to the Chief
Native Commissioner.[79] It included protest against
use of women as plantation laborers, opposition to
native registration (kipande), dissatisfaction with
the increased hut tax and demands for government
schools for African education. A later memorandum,
presented in 1924, repeated these grievances and
added several more, e.g., demand for medical services
and for African representation in the Legislative
Council.[80] Admittedly the expression of these demands was always cautious and beseeching, but it is
noteworthy that the Association did have an extensive
program of grievances not unlike that sought by Kenya
Africans even into the 1950s. The East African
Association also had a series of demands. The roots
of this organization were in Nairobi, among the mission educated men who were employed primarily as
clerks. Thuku was influenced by the similarly
oriented Young Baganda Association and by the Indians,
and the emphasis of his grievances was urban. While
there is evidence in government reports, in secondary
sources, and in Thuku's autobiography that he was
concerned with the land question, it is significant
that primary accounts of EAA meetings, and the correspondence of the Association with London, contain
no mention of this issue.[81] Rather, their meetings
emphasize such things as abolition of kipande,
government education for Africans, and opposition to
wage cuts. The organization also stressed, in
stronger language than the Kikuyu Association, the
need for African representation in the legislature
and called for extension of the franchise "to all
educated British subjects."[82] Here too then, was

another expression of grievances which would have a
long history in the African politics of Kenya. Indeed, Mathu's demands in the Legislative Council in
the 1940s and 50s were to differ only minimally
from the memoranda and resolutions of these two
associations operating in a period some 20 to 30
years before. That this was so does not imply a lack
of awareness or growth on the part of the Kikuyu, for
these grievances were an expression of fundamental
injustices of the colonial situation. This predica-
ment is evidence instead of the rigidity of the administration and of the frustrating circumstances
within which African politics in Kenya had to function.

Thuku's arrest and the banning of his organization did not cause Kikuyu political activity to cease
in the 1920s, and the expression of grievances became more extensive and specific, if not more adamant, as time went on. The Kikuyu Association continued to receive government and mission support and
remained active throughout the decade. It still
stressed land reform, and in its petition of 1928,
prepared for the visiting Hilton Young Commission,
called explicitly for repeal of the 1915 Land Ordinance which provided no guaranteed boundaries to reserves. As in earlier petitions it called for the
granting of individual title deeds "according to our
custom."[83] Also more explicit was the Association's
request for legislative representation. Twelve members for African interests were requested--four
Africans, four missionaries and four government officials. All of these were to be elected by the
Africans themselves because "we are in a position to
know those who really know the interest of the
African."[84] The Association continued to be dominated by chiefs and to work through the local administration. They lost considerable support in 1929 when
they stood behind the CSM condemnation of female circumcision. Thuku's followers also retained a formal
vehicle of protest which continued the policy of pre-
ferring negotiation directly with London to dealings
with local officials.

The tragedy surrounding the events of Thuku's
arrest had the ironic effect of heightening support
for his cause while forcing it to operate less openly. Jomo Kenyatta, who had been a member of Thuku's
organization, described this result: "The idea of
union had taken hold of the people's imagination, and

instead of being killed the Association was driven
underground."[85] James Beauttah, who at this time
worked as a postal employee, claims that the succeed-
ing Kikuyu Central Association (KCA) was formed by
him, together with James Njoroge, at Njoroge's house
in Pangani in 1922,[86] so that very little time
lapsed between Thuku's arrest and the reorganization
of his supporters. But whatever the chronology of
its origins, the KCA flourished later in the decade.
In 1925 its members sent a petition to the newly
arrived Governor, Sir Edward Grigg, which, undoubtedly as a precaution against proscription, emphasized
their commitment to legality and stated their purpose
as "protecting and safeguarding by constitutional
means the interests of the Kikuyu community and their
rights and liberties as citizens of the British
Empire."[87] This document contains an expression of
grievances including the new demands for coffee growing rights in the reserves and for the release of
Thuku and his colleagues as well as the earlier
sought land reform and educational and medical services.[88] Of greater interest than this 1925 petition
is a longer document prepared for the visit in 1929
of Sir Samuel Wilson, Permanent Under Secretary of
State for the Colonies. This memorandum contained
specific numerous demands such as the call for a
Common Electoral Roll, opposition to a settler majority in the legislature, and land reform. Most significant, however, is the attitude expressed in the
document toward race. Request was made for six representatives of African interests in the legisla-
ture--three of whom would be African, two European,
and one Indian. With regard to the African members
it stated:

> The Association is not opposed to imported
> Negroes to represent Native interests in the
> Central Legislature. What we really fervently
> want to see is a black man on the Council.[89]

Here is an expression of real consciousness of race.
Negritude and race consciousness are concepts which
would become part of militant politics much later in
the nationalist movement. But literate Kikuyu were
already knowledgeable about race problems in the
United States and were identifying with black spokesmen there. Beauttah, as a postal worker, was able to
obtain legally banned literature such as the NAACP
newspaper Crisis, and the writings of Washington,
Garvey and DuBois.[90] He also was influenced by the

Gold Coast educator, J.E.K. Aggrey, when he visited
Kenya in 1924 and told the Africans "an eagle cannot
become a fowl" which in Beauttah's words meant "an
African cannot become a white man and should not try
but should be proud of his race."[91] The cultural
confidence manifested by the KCA in the female circumcision crisis in 1929 is but a corollary expression of his growing racial pride. Here too then,
along with the specific grievances, is another evidence of "modern" political concepts traceable to
the earliest decade of organized Kikuyu politics.
It is evident that a literate and aware African
living in these years would be exposed to nearly all
of the ideas essential to Kikuyu politics throughout
the colonial period.

As has been noted, while Mathu was a schoolboy
he followed the activities of these political associations. Harry Thuku had become an anathema to the
missions. He had begun as a "mission boy" with the
CMS but had spoken out harshly against missionaries
in his speeches. For years after his arrest he was
used by mission teachers as an example of misspent
talent and so, ironically, remained prominent in the
students' minds.[92] Mathu refers to Thuku's early
efforts as having been "ahead of their time", and
today he claims that he, and virtually all of his
classmates, looked to Thuku with great awe in these
years.[93] Mathu further followed political developments by reading the local European newspaper, The
Leader, which was available at his boarding school.
Finally, his education brought him a unique opportunity to gain political information. Because of
his advanced English he was sometimes used to help
prepare official correspondence. As he explains,
"Jesse Kariuki and even Mzee (Jomo Kenyatta) used to
come to me to draft memoranda to go to the House of
Commons."[94] Indeed, with his relative Kinyanjui and
the Kikuyu Association this assistance became so frequent that Mathu worked as the chief's private secretary during his holidays from school.[95] Because of
the similarity of the issues of these early years and
later years, Mathu's involvement with his people's
politics in the 1920s has some relevance. It was
largely a passive interest, clearly subordinate to
his studies, as it is evident that he was by nature
more scholar than activist. Yet that experience he
did have would serve as a useful foundation for his
as yet unanticipated political career.

Some broad conclusions can be made concerning Mathu's beginnings. He had come far, largely on his own initiative, from origins that were harsh. The years of his boyhood were a time of rapid change for his people, but he had an exceptionally practical attitude and adapted well. He had found a satisfying niche in the academic community of Alliance and was wholly involved, manifesting broad interests and experimenting widely in the many facets of that world. He had a remarkable mind and a genuine enthusiasm for study. Although not singularly bookish, his clear ambition was for teaching. He was politically aware but only peripherally involved in the activities of the Kikuyu associations. He had no proclaimed intention or seemingly conscious anticipation of becoming politically active. His aspirations were primarily for his own personal development, to continue his studies and achieve a kind of personal self fulfillment.

It must also be said that it was these characteristics that distinguished him in the eyes of his masters. Despite his desire to build "an African civilization," Grieve and his colleagues were colonialists of the paternalistic type, and Mathu's character ideally suited the objectives they had set for their students. His keen mind and seemingly insatiable academic enthusiasm, together with his interest in teaching, made Mathu a prize pupil. That he was impressed with Booker T. Washington's philosophy and might employ this in his teaching was similarly attractive and compatible with the paternalist's conception for Kenya's future. Aggressive African political activism was repugnant to the Alliance staff, and Mathu's scholarly ambitions showed no indication of taking a political bent. It was an almost symbiotic union in which Mathu and the Alliance masters seem to satisfy one another's needs.

CHAPTER TWO

TEACHER AND SCHOLAR I--1929-1934

This lad is one of the most advanced
young Kikuyu Africans, showing not only
his keenness to go forward in education
but above all things to extend the Kingdom
of Christ.

Dr. Arthur, 1932[1]

The period from 1929 to 1934 was a crucial and
solidifying stage in Elius Mathu's development in
which the principles he absorbed as an Alliance
schoolboy were strengthened and adopted as his own.
He spent these years first teaching at Alliance and
later studying at the South African Native College
at Fort Hare. In both of these experiences George
Grieve played an important part. He continued to
guide Mathu's development and influence his character. Thus Mathu's basic environment and outlook
changed little from his student years. Teaching and
study continued as his primary interests. His exposure to and enthusiasm for the concepts of Booker
T. Washington increased and crystallized. In part
as a corollary to this, his faith in Christianity
grew. And similarly politics remained a peripheral
concern. Fundamentally these years were a logical
progression from his secondary school days, spent in
intensive study, exploring in greater depth the intellectual world of western culture and accepting
the values of his missionary mentors. However by
the end of this period the ideas he had acquired had
been fully assimilated and integrated into his philosophy. He acknowledged his commitment to a particular point of view and sought to apply it for the
first time. He was yet to manifest any independent
perspective incompatible with that which he had
learned. But by 1934 he had exchanged his schoolboy
diffidence for a new assurance. He had clearly ma-
tured into a self-possessed adult with conscious
principles.

Because of the restricted educational resources

available to Kenya's Africans in these years, Mathu's
distinguished position in the ranks of Kenya's
African elite is not a difficult fact to trace. The
establishment of Alliance High School is the key development here. Its founding marked much more than
the mere appearance of a new school in the colony--
it was an historical event. Grieve's plan to make
it an African Hampton basically failed. But given
the realities of colonialism, with its intrinsic
European ethnocentrism, it was largely because of
this failure, and the adoption of prep school standards, that it acquired a reputation as the colony's
most prestigious African educational center. It provided the first opportunity for Kenya's Africans to
secure quality formal schooling of a type that would
allow them to proceed to college or university. And
throughout the 1930s it remained the only source for
African secondary education in the colony.[2] This institution, therefore, had the unique responsibility
of educating the great majority of the African intelligentsia that developed in Kenya in the colonial
years.

     This renown associated with Alliance is one fac-
tor in explaining the satisfaction Mathu felt as a
teacher there. The colonial British view of the
African at this time was at best paternalistic and
more commonly blatantly racist. Accordingly the
career alternatives that would be offered to the
gradually emerging westernized Africans would be se-
verely limited.[3] Mathu was the forerunner among
Kenya's formally educated Africans. He was among the
14 students to pass the school's general examination
after the first two years of study were completed.[4]
He was also the only student of the 24 who made up
the first class body to successfully obtain the
Senior Secondary Teacher's Certificate at the end of
his third year.[5] And in 1931, when efforts were being made to find him a place at Fore Hare, he was
still the only African in Kenya to have reached this
level.[6] Because of these pioneering conditions,
Mathu faced the most restricted career opportunities,
and a position as the sole African master on the
staff of the colony's most respected African school
was clearly a prize. It brought him recognition both
among his own people and the British, and this was to
some degree responsible for the pleasure he found in
his work in these years.

     Another aspect of the atmosphere at Alliance

that suited Mathu at this time was its stated purpose of preparing its students for a life of "Christian service." However nominal this motto was becoming, as the competitive academic climate grew, Grieve never abandoned it, and he impressed it upon Mathu. Moreover this goal was reinforced by Mathu's study of Booker T. Washington who saw education as "the sole and only hope of the Negro"[7] and who encouraged his students to endeavor "to build up the Kingdom of Christ on earth."[8] In these years Mathu had a clear life plan. He was Grieve's protege, and Washington offered historical support. Alliance seemed the ideal place for him to fulfill his mission to serve his people through teaching Christian culture.

A final reason for Mathu's happiness while on the Alliance staff was the escape from isolation he found living within a virtually self-contained community with values similar to his own. As previously noted, a major difficulty any African must face if he chooses to pursue western education is that he simultaneously cuts himself off from his traditional society. Core African values are in direct opposition with those of Europe. Any quest for personal recognition and individual self-fulfillment is foreign to the communal perspective of the Kikuyu. Because he was among the first of Kenya's Africans to make this choice, this threat of cultural separation was especially real for Mathu. But at Alliance he was an example for the students who were set on a course similar to his own, and this was reassuring. Too he found greater social acceptance from his European colleagues than he might have in a situation of similar responsibility in the civil service or private business sector. Because Alliance was a boarding school, this sense of community was especially strong,and staff and students lived in close proximity to one another on a common campus. The variety of social, athletic and club activities resulting from these circumstances provided a satisfying environment sufficient unto itself. Consequently Mathu's transition into a largely western existence was much less difficult than it might have been.

While Mathu's scholastic success was certainly a factor in his appointment to the Alliance staff, the compatibility of his character with the ideals of the school were at least of equal import. Principal Grieve's interest in Mathu's early development has been seen. From its inception it was intended

that the school should employ an African master, and
it is probable that while a student Mathu was being
groomed by Grieve for this spot. The fact that
Mathu, despite his scholastic ability, was not immediately sent abroad for higher study as Peter Koinange had been is evidence of this fact. Instead he
was tutored by Grieve and encouraged in his desire
for teaching. The actual appointment was made in
March 1929 by the science master, J. S. Smith, who
was Acting Principal while Grieve was on leave.[9] But
this was mere formality, and the order to make the
appointment came from Grieve.[10] In any case, the two
men were of one mind as to the character of the person selected. Like Grieve, Smith advocated the
Hampton philosophy and described the school's objective as "to send him [the student] out as a converted and consecrated man who will make himself opportunities for Christian service."[11] Writing of the
factors which led to the selection of Mathu, Grieve
gave as a major point that "he was a sound Christian."[12] Clearly this aspect of his character was a
vital factor in the choice of Mathu for the position.

While it is notable that the intensity of
Mathu's Christianity is somewhat more evident in
these Alliance years than it would be later in his
career, it appears to have been nonetheless genuine.
He studied the Bible avidly and was active in raising
funds for building a new CSM chapel at Kikuyu.[13]
He would remain a Christian in later years and serve
consistently as a church elder, but this aspect of
his character is not as omnipresent after his departure from Alliance. It is likely that the ardor of
his religious fervor as a teacher was at least in
part the result of his success and personal fulfillment in the European and mission-centered academic
world. This does not imply that he was consciously
calculating and molding himself into a desirable
image. Rather it was simply an integral aspect of
the community in which he was living, and the greater
his success within that community, the greater his
enthusiasm for its values.

From the start of his teaching career at
Alliance, one of his most effective roles was that
of a bridge between the African students and the
European staff. Grieve was concerned about this cultural barrier and wrote of it in the Kikuyu News:

> However closely the European teacher may

be in touch with his African pupils, a good
African teacher can do a great deal to
smooth over any difficulties that may arise
from time to time and to cement the bond
that already exists between white and black.[14]

The Board of Governors also anticipated this difficulty and felt the solution was to establish firm
control. When the school's structure was being decided in 1926, they recommended that the African
teacher, for whom budgetary allowance was made, be
"a good disciplinarian in the nature of a drill ser-
geant who is good at games."[15] Mathu was not this
sort, but he did ease cultural tension because, in
Grieve's words, "he had . . . the confidence of all
the students."[16] As will be seen, the most dramatic
incident in which this intervention was required
would come later in the decade, after Mathu's return
from Fort Hare, but it was an important aspect of
his teaching in these earlier years as well.

Besides teaching math and science in these
years, Mathu was involved in a number of additional
school activities, two of which were innovative. The
first was the initiation of a school library. No
money was being allotted for this purpose in 1929
when Mathu joined the staff. To remedy this he began to collect books and donations from the community. He also made a request to the school's Board
of Governors which resulted in the regular assign-
ment of a portion of the budget as a library fund.
Mathu became librarian and later, as the collection
grew, organized its cataloging.[17] He also was responsible for the founding of the Alliance High School
Old Boys Club. This occurred in January 1931 at a
Teacher's Refresher Course which was held at the
school.[18] The club's main objectives were:

> 1. to keep the old boys in touch with
> the school and with one another.

> 2. to influence old boys to put into
> practice the motto of the Club and to be
> proud of it.[19]

Mathu chose this motto which was "Concordia in Pace"
(Unity in Peace) and designed the emblem on which it
was placed. This was a shield showing the motto
along with an open Bible and a pair of doves in
flight carrying an olive branch.[20] The Club's con-

situation required that the administration be dominated by the old boys themselves, a fact which would
have later significance. The Principal was Club
Patron and an ex-officio member, but it was stated
that he need not attend meetings, and Grieve did not
take any direct part.[21] The Club flourished throughout the 1930s. Records of meetings indicate a
steady increase in membership and attendance. Besides these two activities, Mathu also was involved
as Smith's assistant in Scouting and with games. It
was clearly a busy and happy time for him. In
Grieve's words, during these first teaching years
Mathu "proved faithful in the work allotted to him,
and willing to shoulder any burden."[22] More than
this, he created responsibilities for himself beyond anything required of his position.

     After three years as an Alliance master, a com-
bination of circumstances resulted in Mathu's departure to South Africa for further study, and, not
surprisingly, George Grieve was again instrumental
in bringing this about. As the academic reputation
of the school grew, Grieve was anxious to build a
professional staff.[23] Moreover, proposals were being discussed to expand the teacher training and
commercial courses at the school into two year programs.[24] Mathu was happy in his work but was also
showing interest in following Peter Koinange's example and continuing his education. He had begun
saving from his ₤75/year salary in the hope that
some opportunity might develop.[25] In 1931, Grieve,
seeing this as a chance to satisfy Mathu's wishes
and at the same time retain him as a teacher and improve his qualifications, came to his aid. It was
another example of the symbiotic circumstances in
which Grieve and Mathu mutually benefitted.

     As with Koinange, the choice of school was
Grieve's, and, while not Hampton, it was an institution much like Alliance that incorporated elements of
the Hampton tradition. Mathu describes how this
choice was made:

          I wanted to pursue higher education. I
     did not know where. Makerere did not exist
     then as a place for higher education, and
     so I took the advice of Mr. Grieve. Fort
     Hare was founded by Scottish missionaries,
     so he knew of it. I didn't know anything
     at all. And he told me that the only place

I can get you to is Fort Hare.[26]

Grieve was a friend of Alexander Kerr, the Principal
of the South African Native College at Fort Hare.
He knew that like him, Kerr had visited Hampton and
that Kerr's philosophy was in many ways like his own.
It was a further step in grooming Mathu for his future as an Alliance master.

If Grieve was paternal in his behavior in this
undertaking, the local administration was almost uniformly negative, and the Alliance Principal had to
maneuver skillfully to escape their censure. The
money Mathu had saved was not sufficient to allow
him to meet all the expenses the study in South
Africa would involve. In October 1931, therefore,
Grieve discussed Mathu's ambitions with Evan Biss,
the Acting Director of Education, and proposed that
the Local Native Council be asked to grant him a
scholarship.[27] Biss was non-committal and suggested
that Grieve see the Chief Native Commissioner, an
F. D. Wade, and discuss the case. This was done, but
Wade was not very encouraging. He expressed the fear
that Mathu's study in South Africa might produce a
steady flow of future students after him, and such a
development, it was felt, would be premature.[28]
Grieve wrote Biss about this meeting and, undoubtedly
as a tactic to aid Mathu, argued that this situation
would not result:

> In Eliud's case, I do not think there is
> much danger of forming a precedent, as he is
> the only student who has yet gained Senior
> Secondary Teachers Certificate. You may
> remember looking through his papers at that
> exam. I believe you considered that he had
> done well. I think it is not likely that
> there will be more than a very few to pass
> this exam within the next ten years. I do
> not know of any other student whom I would
> have recommended for aid to go to Fort Hare.

> His case is a special one, too, in that
> it is very desirable that there should be a
> highly trained African on the staff of this
> school.

> I should be grateful if you would con-
> sider his case favourably when the matter
> is brought to your notice.[29]

Circumstances and some quick maneuvering by Grieve
aided Mathu in these dealings and made his departure
possible. Biss became sympathetic and was influential in easing the plan through the reluctant administration and in supporting Mathu's academic
qualifications against the queries of the educational
officials in Pretoria.[30] On January 27, 1932, H. S.
Scott, the Director of Education for whom Biss had
been acting, returned from leave and wrote Grieve
that he was "a good deal disturbed" about the
arrangement for Mathu.[31] Fortunately, this occurred
after the required scholarship was granted by the
Local Native Council. This body had met on January
18 and awarded Mathu 600/- per year for the duration
of his study.[32] This resolution was proposed by
Chief Josiah and carried unanimously by the Council's
African members.[33] The District Commissioner, who
was in attendance, had disapproved but "in view of
the unanimous opinion" had withdrawn his opposition
"but without enthusiasm."[34] Grieve anticipated
trouble in his meeting with Director Scott, and so,
despite the fact that Mathu lacked the necessary
landing permit required for his admission into South
Africa, he sent him off immediately before Scott
could present an obstacle. Mathu left Nairobi on
January 29th. Grieve saw Scott on the 30th, and the
Director was forced to admit his helplessness. "I
am afraid there is nothing we can do," he wrote.[35]
Thus, because of Grieve's quick action, and despite
the Director's disfavor, Mathu's hopes were realized.
The permit required for admission to the Union was
sent by air and was waiting when the ship arrived at
Durban.[36] His first adventure abroad had begun.

As Grieve had expected, the approach to education followed at Fort Hare was much like that of
Alliance. The school was established as the South
African Native College at Fort Hare in 1915 by
Alexander Kerr.[37] After considerable pressure from
the African community, the South African Government
agreed to its founding and recruited Kerr in London
as its first Principal.[38] He held this position
throughout Mathu's enrollment years. He differed
from Grieve in that he was a layman, but like the
Alliance Principal he was a Scotsman, a Presbyterian,
and had a strong interest in black education in
America. He too had visited Hampton Institute and
applied elements of its approach to Fort Hare.[39] As
at Alliance the course of study began as a broad
"liberal arts" course and then focused on specific

professional training. In its early years, the
school's main function was to advance students merely to matriculation level, and this continued
throughout the 1930s. But in 1925 the school was
incorporated into the University of South Africa and
could carry matriculated students on through the degree programs of that institution.[40] Thus the areas
of specialization were more numerous and more advanced than at Alliance, e.g., the ministry, teaching, medicine, law, civil service, journalism and
agriculture.[41] Kerr's personal objective was to
provide "education that fitted a man (or a woman) to
understand the world in which he lived, the world
that had been shaped by the forces of civilization,
and in which he desired to live."[42] Like Grieve,
Kerr also supported the stress on "Christian Service" practiced at Hampton. His institution's constitution specified that it was to be "a Christian
College and all members of staff were to be profes-
sing Christians.[43] Despite his lay background, Kerr
held that "the Christian tradition and practice
should . . . be fully honoured."[44] Thus Mathu's
first venture outside Kenya in some ways brought him
to an environment not very different from his home--
a black educational center training an elite class in
the cultural traditions of the West.

    Other aspects of South Africa were considerably
different from life in Kenya and required significant
adjustments, one of which was academic. Mathu found
the educational standards far more advanced than
those of Alliance. Perhaps because of this, he was
not permitted to begin studying for a degree as he
had intended but was enrolled in a program leading
to a matriculation certificate, that would then make
higher study possible. Even at this level, however,
Mathu's academic preparation was inadequate. He was
the only student at Fort Hare from outside the Union
and its adjoining Protectorates. The majority of his
peers had formerly attended the nearby Lovedale CSM
School which had been established nearly a century
before and was a highly respected institution. For
the first half-year, Mathu was forced to spend virtually all his time at study in order to advance himself to a comparable level.[45] "I am now up to the
ears for December exams; they are difficult ," he
wrote Dr. Arthur at this time. It is notable that
during these years at Fort Hare Mathu had some temporary problem with his eyesight and wore spectacles
for a time.[46] It may well have been the result of

this intensive study schedule which he was forced to
follow. In any case, he successfully overcame his
educational handicap, and Kerr wrote that the results
of his matriculation examination, taken in 1934, were
"highly creditable."[47]

A second aspect of South Africa which required
some adjustment from Mathu was the reaction to a more
advanced race problem. This had two main aspects,
the first of which was the experiencing of the omnipresent color bar. Kenya society, too, was at this
time highly segregated, but, in Mathu's own words,
"it was never as so clear cut as in South Africa"[48]
Neither was it so conspicuous. Compared to Kenya,
South Africa's white population was immense. From
the standpoint of sheer numbers, the experiencing of
the separate races policy must have had a profound
effect. And seeing this, Mathu could anticipate a
potential fate for Kenya. As a corollary to this,
living in South Africa made Mathu vividly aware of
the white supremacist mentality and was a valuable
lesson for his dealings in subsequent years with factions of Kenya's settler community in the Legislative
Council. A second significant aspect of Mathu's
association with South African racism was that it
made him more aware of the potential of organized
protest activity among Africans. South Africa had
been colonized considerably longer than Kenya, and
because of this, the black population there was more
elaborately organized as a political force. Most
significant in these years were the activities of
Clements Kadalie, leader of the Industrial and Commercial Workers' Union (ICU).[49] In the 1930s
Kadalie lived in East London, which was very near
Fort Hare, and was endeavoring to prevent the disen-
franchisement of the Africans of Cape Province. Representatives of other organizations, such as Marcus
Garvey's Universal Negro Improvement Association and
the Communist Party, were also active there in these
years, and, while Mathu remained apolitical, his exposure to this sharp activist environment certainly
had an effect.

Without a doubt, however, the single most important influence on Mathu in South Africa was his association with Davidson Don Tengo Jabavu. By this time
in his life, Mathu had made most of the primary decisions regarding the general course he hoped his
life would follow, i.e., that of a westernized
Christian educator. While Grieve had encouraged him

in this direction and helped to ease the way, ultimately this decision was Mathu's, and he pursued it
through considerable obstacles. He had enthusiasm
and great ability, and even at this time, he had
gained recognition. But, paradoxically, because of
this success, he felt himself to be something of an
outsider among his own people. Because he was among
the first highly educated Africans in Kenya, he was
isolated by his achievements. As a result, his relationship with Jabavu had special significance. In
Jabavu Mathu found a true mentor--a fellow African,
older than himself, with similar values, who had much
to relate. Jabavu had been on the Fort Hare faculty
from its founding. Unlike Mathu he had the advantage
of encouragement and financial assistance from home.
His father, John Tengo Jabavu, was the founder and
editor of the first Bantu weekly newspaper, Imvo
Zabantusundu.[50] He was also a Christian and a pio-
neer for more advanced education for his people.
Consequently he sent his son to the University of
London where Davidson graduated with honors in
English. Upon completion of this degree he went on
to obtain a Diploma in Education from Birmingham
University. Perhaps of most significance, he also
visited the black schools of the United States, and
was especially impressed in 1913 by Tuskegee where
he met Booker T. Washington two years before the
latter's death.[51] Mathu describes Jabavu's influence on him as "tremendous."[52] A friendship grew up
between them based on a mutual intellectual respect.[53] Mathu had come to Fort Hare with only private tutoring in classical languages, whereas his
classmates had been formally trained in both Latin
and Greek. With Jabavu as his Latin teacher, Mathu
finished first in this area on his matriculation
exam despite his lack of previous formal training.
According to Mathu, this performance "absolutely
stunned" his teacher. "He was always talking about
it, and as a result he became so friendly."[54] At
the same time Mathu was similarly impressed with his
master's mind:

> This man, he had two qualities--he was a
> classical scholar, and he was a first class
> musician. . . . I must say I did share quite
> a lot of his enthusiasm and his exactitude
> in studies.[55]

This friendship was clearly a boon to Mathu's decision to pursue a life of teaching.

Of more historical importance than Jabavu's encouragement of Mathu's academic career, however, is
the influence he had on his student's view of the
world. Until this time there is no evidence of a
public reaction by Mathu to any aspect of Kenya's
colonial regime. Undoubtedly there were policies he
opposed. But he remained silent and passively
focused on his studies and teaching, enjoying the
satisfaction and recognition of being Alliance's
first African master. On his return from South
Africa, however, this situation would gradually
change, and Jabavu's example was instrumental in
bringing this about. As has been noted, Jabavu was
involved in South African politics. He led the Cape
Native Voter's Association and in 1935 served as
President of the All-African Convention at Bloemfon-
tein which was organized to formulate a policy to
combat Prime Minister Hertzog's proposal to abolish
the franchise for Cape Coloureds.[56] While he was a
Christian and an academician, he was also politically
outspoken and an activist against that which he considered unjust. He spoke out against the racist policy of his government which he argued had reduced
his people to "landless, voteless helots; pariahs,
social outcasts in their fatherland with no future
in any path of life.[57] Like Mathu, Jabavu was a pro-
ponent of pragmatic adaptation to western culture for
his people, but he saw this as a selective process
rather than blind acceptance of all things new. In
an address to African teachers in 1920 he stated:

> Today you must not rest satisfied with
> what satisfied your fathers in their days.
> Move with the times and seek to improve
> your houses as well as your persons and
> belongings. Do not stick to a thing just
> because it was the custom of your parents.
> On the other hand, I do not intend that
> you should throw overboard everything
> that belongs to the age of your forefathers;
> for some of their customs were the result
> of long experience.[58]

Thus Jabavu encouraged Mathu to be more outspokenly
critical of certain elements of colonialism--to protest against policies he considered unjust and to
practice selectivity in adopting only those aspects
of western culture that he considered beneficial to
his people. This was Jabavu's most original contribution to Mathu's growth. It was in large part re-

sponsible for Mathu's noticeably more independent
spirit upon his return to Alliance in 1934.

A final way in which Jabavu influenced Mathu was
in supporting and strengthening his interest in
Booker T. Washington. Jabavu refers to Washington
repeatedly in his writings. The following description is typical:

> He [Washington] lives in a world of
> realities, often stern realities, not one
> of dreams, idealisms, or vague impalpable
> abstractions . . . he has a personal and
> direct attitude, not an impersonal and
> detached one, toward men and things--an
> attitude that preserves him from faulty
> generalizations about these. . . . Early
> in life he understood more clearly than
> others that there was a genuine, nay,
> pathetic, desire on the part of his
> countrymen for education, for civilized
> conveniences and machinery. With his
> knowledge of their needs he sought to
> furnish these, and has done so with
> subtle diplomacy. The Negroes have again
> and again, and in multifarious ways shown
> their appreciation of his service and its
> tangible nature. He has taught them what
> it is necessary to know; he has taught
> them the dignity of labour and impor-
> tance of material development. Indeed so
> much stress has he laid on the acquisition
> of chickens and pigs, bank accounts and
> property, that he has lent himself to the
> misinterpretation of being materialistic
> and, if not irreligious, morally in-
> different to the claims of religious pro-
> paganda. No greater mistake was ever
> made. He is as religious as a man can
> be; and his regard for the Bible and its
> meaning to man's life is fully given in
> Up From Slavery; to him it has been a
> real guide.[59]

In keeping with this positive description, Jabavu
saw education as the key to change:

> The cure lies in our being able to
> produce well educated Native leaders
> trained in a favourable atmosphere, who

> will be endowed with common sense, cool
> heads, with a sense of responsibility,
> endurance and correct perspective in
> all things.[60]

And along with education Jabavu too argued for economic growth:

> We are all working for the same end,
> to save Africa from virtual serfdom,
> There will be no divergence of opinion
> as to the need of self-help and a more
> effective mobilization of our economic
> forces for that purpose. We should find
> a solution for an escape out of poverty
> by all practicable means within our
> power. So long as we are an impoverished
> community we shall never rise and scale
> the heights of success to which our
> mental and physical capacity entitles us
> to attain.[61]

Finally, all of this development should have a
Christian base. "In our stage of civilization," he
writes, "the most important person in our village is
by general agreement the minister of the gospel."[62]
Taken together, Jabavu's support for Washington's
philosophy helped strengthen Mathu's confidence in
these same ideals. In this aspect Mathu learned
nothing new but saw Jabavu as an affirmation of
values he had chosen for himself at Alliance.

Mathu's friendship with Jabavu, therefore, had
a vital influence on his development. It confirmed
his belief that intellectual and material development was the key to racial justice and that his role
in this process should be that of a teacher. It also
gave him confidence to criticize and speak out
against injustice. Largely as a result of this relationship, Mathu's South African experience
strengthened his decision to teach and encouraged
him to defend his principles against attack.

When Mathu won his grant from the Kiambu Local
Native Council, both he and Grieve expected that it
would continue until he completed the studies required for a university degree, but this hope was
not realized. Grieve's quick action had succeeded
in preventing the Kenya Education Department from
vetoing the grant before Mathu's departure. But he

could not overcome their pressuring the Kiambu
Council for a later withdrawal of funds. In 1934,
immediately after Mathu had successfully completed
the matriculation exam, his grant was terminated,
and he was forced to sail home. H. S. Scott, who
had balked at the arrangements in 1932, was still
Director of Education, and it is likely that his actions were instrumental.[63] Alexander Kerr lamented
this decision after the fact and praised Mathu's
scholarship as well as "his gentlemanliness and
general courtliness of bearing."[64] Mathu left South
Africa in late January and returned to his position
at Alliance with a £13/annum salary increase.[65] His
study plans had been thwarted, but he had had an en-
riching experience--his values had been strengthened,
and he manifested a more confident leadership upon
his return.

The five years from 1929 to 1934 were vital to
Mathu's growth. This was a time of testing and af-
firming his decision to teach and render "Christian
service". It was also a time of maturation when he
adopted certain principles as his own. By the end
of this period his fundamental character had been
formed. He returned to Alliance in 1934 confident
of the worth of a life dedicated to educating his
people into the modern world.

CHAPTER   THREE

TEACHER AND SCHOLAR II--1934-1944

In a young country like Kenya with its
new influences and diverse problems, it is
people of strong character that we need to
lead their people to higher goals. We look
up to education to help produce strong,wise,
courageous and faithful African leaders who
will inspire others to a sense of duty,
loyalty, trustworthiness, temperance, justice
and other virtues.

Eliud Mathu, 3 January 1938[1]

The ten years from his return from South Africa
until his appointment to the Legislative Council in
1944 were a time when Mathu found greatest fulfillment in teaching, expanded his perspective with further study abroad and finally was forced to re-
evaluate his total life-plan because of changing circumstances at Alliance. There is irony in these
events. Mathu's satisfaction and confidence as an
educator are in full display in these years, but
after his return from graduate study in England, when
his professional training was at its peak, he confronted a crisis which ended his comfortable career
as an Alliance master. The significance of this
period is the view it gives of a Mathu that might
have been--a lifetime educator, much like Jabavu,
whose interest and involvement in politics remained
peripheral and largely academic. Well before any
difficulty at Alliance developed, liberal colonialists anticipated the appointment of African representatives to the Kenya Legislative Council and selected Mathu as a front runner for such a position.
But Mathu gives no evidence of having coveted this
role, and there is some question whether he would
have accepted his appointment in 1944 had his
career at Alliance not been shattered. Until this
turning point he continued to perceive himself as a
scholar and teacher.

Mathu's position in Kenya upon his return from Fort Hare was characterized by a much greater recognition from the colonial community and a more active and effective involvement on his part in both school and community affairs. These were the years, from 1934 to 1938, when he found most success in teaching. Compared with his later political career, this period was tranquil and low keyed, but in its own context it was a rich and satisfying time without the complications and pressures of later years.

Mathu resumed his responsibilities at Alliance without difficulty. He had resigned in 1932 but with the understanding that he would be reappointed upon his return. He recommenced his teaching of math and science and, because of the expansion of the practical training curriculum, also taught agriculture. His style in the classroom was that of the traditional schoolmaster who dominates each lesson and provides more information than most students can grasp. Observation reports of his classes describe his approach:

> This teacher has a pleasant manner, and has some ability in framing questions. He is too inclined, however, to lecture. Some of the material appeared to be beyond the Form I pupils in this group.

> Eliud Mathu was seen during a theoretical lesson on "The Rotting of Organic Matter." He made good use of his materials, specimens of the stages of the decomposition of a mealie cob. He speaks fluent English with an occasional slip in grammar or pronunciation. His lesson was well planned. He is inclined to do too much of the talking himself and should try to let his pupils have a greater share of the mental work of the lesson. In showing his specimens around the class, he sometimes told his pupils what to see--a fatal mistake in science teaching. The lesson provided a good deal of information, though some of it was revision. The teacher's questioning at the end of the lesson was good.[2]

In addition to his teaching, Mathu again supervised the library and continued his involvement with scouting. He was also assigned as housemaster to a dormi-

tory.   He continued his interest in sports and in
1935 represented Kenya as a long distance runner in
an athletic competition in Uganda.   At Alliance he
organized a tennis club for the boys.   With no real
difficulty, he easily settled into the life style he
had followed in his earlier years.

        Beyond this snug academic existence, however,
Mathu now began to employ some of the lessons gleaned
from D. D. T. Jabavu at Fort Hare.   He became more
outspoken and pursuant of positive change in the interest of his people.   The first evidence of this was
the organization in 1934 of the colony's African
teachers into a union, the Kenya African Teacher's
Union (KATU).[3]   The motivation for this action came
directly from Jabavu who had been chairman of the
Cape African Teachers' Association in South Africa.
While Mathu was at Fort Hare, a second Kikuyu, James
Gichuru, joined the Alliance staff.[4] He and Mathu
became close friends and together launched the KATU.
It was their intention that it should be colony-wide,
but, perhaps because of tribal friction, it never
effectively extended beyond the teachers in Central
Province.   All of the officers were Kikuyu, with
Mathu serving as Chairman and Gichuru as General
Secretary.[5] Even within Central Province the recruitment of members and election of officers moved
slowly, and while regular meetings were held on a
local level throughout the mid-1930s, a General Conference met only in 1938.   This conference was well
attended and expectations were high, but the enthusiasm proved abortive.   In that same year, Mathu
again departed for further study abroad, and the
association faded.   Because of the still embryonic
nature of the teaching profession among Kenya
Africans, Mathu's leadership was a vital catalyst
in the success of the KATU.   Had he not left, it is
likely that the Union would have endured and expanded.   Even with its failure, however, the effort has
relevance to an understanding of Mathu's development.
This attempt to create a colony-wide interest group
is evidence of his growing self-confidence and community commitment.

        In an address at the 1938 General Conference in
Nairobi, Mathu demonstrated this new confidence by
criticizing the blind ethnocentrism of European
colonialism.   His argument was predictably pragmatic
and accepted the European presence as an inescapable
reality.   "Western education and civilization gener-

ally have come to stay in Africa", he stated, and
consequently "Africans must reap the benefits of this
education." Nevertheless he emphasized the need to
proceed with caution:

> Since the advent of the white man in
> Africa, African life and culture have
> naturally changed to some extent. White
> civilization is submerging African civili-
> zation and unless the African takes steps
> to preserve what is good, and there is
> much that is good, in his culture, this
> good will eventually and regretfully
> disappear.[6]

This position was a far cry from the diffident student of the pre-South Africa days.

As guidelines for the form that education in
Kenya should take, Mathu suggested four primary aims:

(1)   to develop the physical, intellectual
      and spiritual sides of man.

(2)   to raise the economic, social and
      political standards of the African.

(3)   to produce leaders for progress.

(4)   to break down barriers between races
      and to promote cooperation between
      the Africans themselves and between
      them and other races.[7]

Taken together he argued that these objectives would
make the school a microcosm of the kind of community
towards which Kenya should strive. Training should
be practical as well as intellectual for service to
the community. Christian values should be instilled
because "the African cannot do without God" and
"Christian principles are most fitted" to his traditions. Racial cooperation should be pursued since
"Black and White are all in the same boat" and "must
all sail through together or drown together." Finally,
he stressed the African's responsibility to help himself:

> The Government and Missions can only help
> us on a certain distance along the road of
> progress. We have to do the rest ourselves.[8]

In this address Mathu's indebtedness to the
ideas of Booker T. Washington is again evident. But
it is an interpretation of these ideas that goes considerably beyond Mathu's earlier emphasis on educating leaders in Christian values and practical social
skills. In this address, while incorporating these
concepts, Mathu also stresses Washington's principle
of self help and quest for racial harmony. During
his previous years of study, Mathu had discovered
Washington and found his ideas appealing. In this
speech it is clear that by this time in his life this
appeal was more than merely academic. He had digest-
ed and adopted much of Washington's philosophy. He
had used it to formulate a positive working program
of his own. In 1938 Mathu was in his late twenties
His years of intellectual exploration basically had
passed. His fundamental philosophy was formed, and
the study he would do beyond this was to be under-
taken mainly for the practical purpose of making it
possible for him to obtain a position from which he
could apply the tenets of this philosophy in a more
effective way. He had acquired a maturity and a
commitment to a set of values toward which he sought
to lead his people.

Another example of Mathu's new assertive leadership occurred at Alliance in 1937. The school was
steadily growing during these years. Until 1938 it
remained the sole secondary institution in the
colony.[9] Its enrollment in 1937 was 125, and while
the majority were Kikuyu, there were also a good
number of Luo and Kamba.[10] Ethnic consciousness was
strong, and considerable friction developed among the
Kikuyu and Kamba against the Luo--primarily because
the former practiced circumcision and looked upon the
uncircumcised Luo as unclean. In 1937 an incident
occurred during a soccer match in which a Luo student
kicked a Kamba, an intolerable insult in the view of
the circumcized youth. The incident passed momen-
tarily, but that evening, and again the following
day, fighting broke out in which the Kikuyu allied
with the Kamba against the Luo minority. Because
they were so outnumbered, the Luo became fearful and
left the school for Nairobi. Grieve could not control the situation. He called on the Board of Governors who met in emergency session. But before any
action was taken by them, Mathu went before the students and reprimanded them strongly. He shamed them
for their hostility and was successful at reestab-
lishing order. The Kamba student was expelled, and

the Luo returned.[11]   Without Mathu's intervention
this minor affair might have become serious. His effectiveness indicates a strong rapport with the students. The common ethnic origins between himself and
the rebellious boys was certainly a factor in his
success here. But by this time three other Kikuyu
had also joined the Alliance staff.[12]   Yet it was
Mathu's action that brought results. More and more
he was being viewed as a respected leader by his
people, and especially by those who had been his
students at Alliance.

Examples of Mathu's greater involvement in community activities are also evident in these years.
He sat on the Kiambu Local Native Council and was
ordained an elder of the Presbyterian Church at
Kikuyu. He was a member of the Education Department's Advisory Council on African Education, a dele-
gate to the Makerere Commission which met to raise
Makerere to the status of a college, and a member of
the Christian Council on Race Relations. With one
notable exception these connections were not particularly influential--he had no real impact and under-
took no remarkable policies. Their primary significance is that they illustrate Mathu's growing recognition by and concern for the community.

The one case in which Mathu's presence did have
special effect was his representation on the Christian Council on Race Relations (CCRR). His negative
reaction to the policies of this body was such that
he brought about its collapse. The CCRR had been
created in 1933 by the Kenya Missionary Council (KMC),
and from the start there were problems.[13]   It was
to be composed of local Protestant missionaries of
the KMC who in turn appointed additional lay members
of the community, e.g., members of the Legislative
Council, officers of African political associations,
representatives from the local press, government
officials and other community leaders. Its stated
purpose was to bring about improved race relations
"by consultation between representative members of
these races gathered together in goodwill for the
examination of differences, the elimination of difficulties and with a view to the discovery of a common
basis of discussion and agreement."[14]   To do this
successfully in the circumstances of the 1930s
would have required major compromise on the part of
both Africans and Europeans, and the emotional climate was such that this was not possible. In addi-

tion, the predominant attitude of the CCRR manifested
little tolerance or appreciation of the traditional
African values. It was typically paternal. During
its first year, members of the Kikuyu Central Association attended, but their relations with the missions were already disturbed due to the female circumcision controversy. These initial sessions were
strained affairs, and KCA cooperation was soon withdrawn.[15] In 1935 the European Elected Members of
LegCo similarly withdrew, claiming that the Council
was "distinctively, though obviously sincere, pro-
native, and your actions would appear calculated to
encourage natives to look for grievances."[16] Thus in
1937, when Mathu was appointed as a member, the
Council's position was already precariously weak.

Mathu attended several sessions, found the
policies expressed unacceptable, and finally resigned. The Native Registration Ordinance, established
in 1921, was discussed, and a Committee was appointed to formulate revisions for recommendation to the
government. Mathu opposed any form of registration
and refused to sit on this committee.[17] In the
spring of 1938 a deputation from the Council met with
the new Governor, Sir Robert Brooks-Popham, for the
purpose of discussing the objectives of the CCRR.
Mathu criticized the report of this meeting and argued that the Council seemed to be striving "to
supplant purely African organizations."[18] Then in
July the Council met with Mr. H. R. Montgomery, the
newly appointed Member for Native Interests in
LegCo. He was unpopular with Africans and was asked
by the Council if he could legitimately represent
Africans in the Legislature. Montgomery argued that
"he represented African interests and not Africans
themselves."[19] He stated further that "some Africans
were like children," and that he must use his own
judgment in deciding what their interests should be.[20]
Despite the offensiveness of this position to the
Africans, the Council supported Montgomery. Mathu
resigned, stating that "the Council's tendency was
towards the continued repression of the African."[21]
He was followed by James Jeremiah, an African postal
employee and future LegCo member. The already un-
stable Council did not survive. Its paternal attitude had alienated both settler and African support.
Mathu advocated compromise and the cooperation of the
races, but the approach of the CCRR undermined his
dignity. He would not tolerate its self-righteous-
ness and insensitivity to the traditions of his

people.

Besides his teaching and community activities, Mathu also continued his formal studies during these years. Before his departure from Fort Hare, he was advised by Kerr that he could continue toward an Arts Degree through correspondence.[22] Mathu agreed and began almost immediately upon his return home. Despite his full teaching schedule and other involvements, he progressed rapidly. "I studied night and day and weekends," he relates. "Every night I put water to my feet so that I wouldn't sleep, or poured cold water on my head or applied a towel with cold water to keep awake."[23] He completed the course early in 1937, only slightly longer than it would have taken had he remained a regular student on the Fort Hare campus.[24] He received his B.A. from that institution, and, as a result his salary was increased to ₤120 annually.[25] He became the second Kenya African, after Koinange, to hold a college degree.[26] Every indication is that his main motivation in obtaining this degree was to improve his status as a teacher. Certainly a career in politics did not seem a feasible ambition for an African given the temper of that era's administration. But even with this reality fully considered, Mathu's focus seemed almost totally geared toward education.

The years from 1934 to 1938 at Alliance were significant to Mathu's development. It was the time when he found greatest satisfaction in his teaching. It was also the period when he began to receive recognition from the community. But most important, it was during these years that his philosophy jelled. He was coping with the inevitable conflict resulting from the dual cultures in which he lived. His discovery of Booker T. Washington and subsequent association with D. D. T. Jabavu had given him the foundation. With increasing assurance, he now began actively to apply these principles. He was no longer fundamentally a student. Without abandoning a basic respect for his traditional heritage, he sought, by gradual assimilation and pragmatic adaptation, to direct his people toward adoption of Christianity and the culture of the West. During these years, and for several more to come, the method he applied for extending these objectives was that of teaching.

Although Mathu's basic outlook had been formed by this time, his formal education was resumed for

two years of graduate study in England. This experience, which extended from September 1938 to August
1940 had a broadening effect on him personally and an
enlightening effect on many of those in Britain who
met him during his travels and whose view of Africa
was considerably altered as a result. Mathu's general perspective remained constant in these years, but
his commitment to expanding the rights of his people
was strengthened by his association with London's
"Black Bloomsbury" among whom were many Africans, and
his confidence in his own ability was heightened by
the success of his social and academic performance in
these sophisticated surroundings. The primary significance of this experience was to add polish and
assurance to Mathu's character and to expand his reputation, especially within liberal circles in
Britain.

      To an even greater degree than was true of the
earlier excursion to South Africa, this study in
England was the result of liberal colonialist effort. In the former case the incentive was largely
Mathu's, while the arrangements were manipulated by
Grieve. In the second case neither the initiative
nor the arrangements were Mathu's own. It was Margery Perham (later Dame) whose efforts brought about
a British Council grant. At this time she was teaching colonial history at St. Hughes College, Oxford,
and, in connection with this position, had visited
Kenya in 1937 to gather research. She came to the
Alliance campus and was introduced to Mathu by
Grieve.[27] She spent considerable time with Mathu
and was clearly impressed by his character and intelligence. She met with the Director of Education
and discussed the possibility of alloting funds for
Mathu to study in England. Upon her return home, she
discussed this possibility with Reginald Coupland,
Professor of Colonial History at All Souls College,
Oxford. She also went to Sir Harold Nicolson, a
personal friend and member of Parliament, and sought
his assistance in obtaining a grant.[28] She had virtually immediate success. R. H. Wisdom, Kenya's
Acting Director of Education obtained the approval of
the Alliance Board of Governors to allow Mathu a
leave.[29] He also made Ŀ120 available from the Education Department's General Savings to help finance
living expenses.[30] Shortly thereafter, a full
scholarship plus Ŀ50 was granted for a course in
English at Exeter University by the British Council
for Relations with other Countries.[31] Mathu readily

accepted the opportunity. He sailed for England from
Mombasa harbor in September 1938.

It is worthwhile considering the reasons for the
awarding of this grant, especially when contrasted
with the difficulties met with earlier in obtaining
moneys for South Africa. The explanation lies in
Perham's effective maneuvering and in the receptive-
ness of appropriate administrators to the idea of
developing an African elite. The intention concerning the role of this elite varied among these officials, but uniformly there was a general willingness
to provide Africans with opportunities to do higher
study.[32] Perham's clear intention was to prepare
Mathu for a place in the Legislative Council.[33] "I
think he will find a great position waiting for him
in the leadership of his own people." she wrote early
in 1938.[34] For this reason she was especially eager
that he be schooled in government.[35] She was employed by the Colonial Office to write reports and
through this connection interested its officials in
Mathu's potential. A. J. Dawes, head of its East
African Department, wrote that he was "particularly
interested in him (Mathu)" and that he "ought to be
encouraged to take a lead among his own people."[36]
Colonial Office influence was then employed both on
Administrators in Kenya and on scholarship trustees
in England to aid Mathu's education.[37] Coupland also
gave enthusiastic support. Even before meeting Mathu,
he described him as "a remarkable man" and as "one of
the leading members of the little group of educated
East Africans whose opinion is going to have a certain importance in the future."[38] But Coupland did
not see Mathu's potential as primarily political.
Rather, he expected Mathu to continue as an educator, "especially when the new possibilities of higher
education at Makerere begin to materialize."[39] John
Murray, principal of the University College of the
South West, Exeter, which Mathu first attended upon
his arrival in England, also viewed him as an educational leader. His hope was that Mathu would head
a teacher's training college to "build up in Training
Colleges the teaching force for the African village
schools."[40] Like Coupland, he approved Mathu's grant
and described him as "an outstanding man . . . well
worth making the best possible job of."[41] With the
backing so influential, one can easily understand
why Perham's efforts were successful.

Clearly Mathu's character was as important a

factor as his intelligence in his being chosen for
this grant. The scholars and administrators who encouraged him sought to groom an African elite to
assume leadership roles in the colonies. Generally
speaking they were looking for a certain type of personality in their quest for candidates. There is
some difficulty in giving a detailed description of
this type, however, because there was some variation
of opinion among the selectors as to what these details should be. For some, such as Lord Lothian of
the Rhodes Trust, the emphasis was clearly on an
African of superior intellect but with little aggressive force:

> He must be a person who can stand an
> education at a high class white university
> without becoming spoiled, who can meet
> colour prejudice . . . without becoming
> embittered and who can go back to his own
> country where he will have to take his
> place as part of the subordinate race
> without going "red".[42]

This assuredly is a blatant racist description, and
one which helps to justify the condemnation of those
who argue the hypocrisy of the liberal British colonial cause. Perham and Coupland, on the other hand,
were more genuinely liberal colonialists. They opposed the settler domination of colonial administrations but at the same time held that benevolent European leadership must prevail for many decades until
it had attained a solid modern, i.e., western-
oriented, base. Consequently both Perham and Coupland sought men who were genuine leaders but who were
also gradualists with a penchant for western culture
and a willingness to pursue piecemeal change in the
complex racial and political climate of the colonial
community. They wanted practical men who could remain cool and operative in the settler oriented atmosphere in which they would have to function, and
who would represent a model for their people.
Mathu's pragmatic philosophy, European life-style
and scholastic achievements seemed to suit this design. Perham described him as a man of "strong
character . . . stable" and with "quiet restrained
common sense."[43] Coupland called him "highly intelligent and remarkably open-minded."[44] They saw in
him the potential for the kind of durable moderate
leadership which they believed would be required for
the Africans to make successful inroads against the

domination of the settlers and to gradually evolve
toward self-government in colonial Kenya.

Mathu's personal ambitions did not change with
this grant--his intention was to use the additional
education to improve his status as a teacher. It was
intended that he should take a course in English
leading to the English Proficiency Certificate which
was specifically intended for students who did not
have English as a first language. Mathu had taken
an arts degree at Fort Hare and felt he would have
little to gain from this line of study. He accepted
the grant without objection, but immediately upon his[45]
arrival at Exeter, he arranged to have this changed.
In his own words his objective was "getting myself
better equipped for my work as a teacher."[46] Obtaining the Teacher's Certificate was obviously the most
direct way of accomplishing this end.

During Mathu's first year in England, his most
noteworthy activity other than his studies was a
visit he paid to Scotland. Before leaving Kenya,
Mathu wrote to the Rev. R. G. Calderwood, CSM missionary and Secretary of the Missionary Council in
Kenya. In this letter he mentioned his wish to make
this visit:

> I sincerely hope that I will be
> privileged to visit Scotland. Having
> been brought up, so to speak, by the Scotch
> people, I naturally feel that it would be
> an honour to see something of their country
> and life during this time and to thank them
> at their native home for what they have done
> for me and my people directly or indirectly.[47]

Calderwood acted on this request, and in March 1939
Mathu spent three weeks touring and being entertain-
ed by Scottish churchmen. Dr. Arthur had returned
to Scotland by this time and wrote a lengthy report
of this tour which contains some valuable descriptions of Mathu. Perhaps the best of these is one
which he quotes in a letter by a Rev. Walter Calderwood, brother of R. G. and Rector of St. Marks Church
in Hawick, with whom Mathu spent three days:

> We enjoyed his visit immensely, and were
> genuinely sorry to part with him so soon.
> His command of English is amazing; so also
> are his courtly manners (almost Victorian).

In his dress and in his person, he is per-
fectly immaculate. When he changes his
suit, socks, tie, shoes, shirt, handker-
chief, scarf--everything changes to match!!
With the children in the S. S. (Sunday
School), he was no earthly use at all; so
much for his 6 months' study of Taching
[sic] Method. To the congregation in the
evening, he spoke <u>very</u> well indeed; very
softly and slowly, and a bit nervous; towards
the end, he forgot his nervousness and got
well away with it. He left a very good
impression; everyone sa ing [sic] 'Why
didn't he go on longer.' He had found the
Colour Bar less than he expected, he said
to Mr. Calderwood; of his views on Kenya,
he thinks by weight of numbers the African
is bound to throw off "white" suppression,
and rise to the top. On his last evening,
we had the Rector of Hawick High School and
the Secretary of the County Education
Committee, here to meet Eliud. They 'drew'
him on educational matters, and he excelled
himself--held the conversation throughout
the entire evening. The Rector was so
impressed that he actually invited Eliud to
visit the High School, and the Clerk
offered to take him to see some of the
village schools. Time did not permit. I
nearly fell off my chair in astonishment,
and show [sic] he made an unusually good
impression. Finally we were quite staggered
at how much farther on he was in civilization, education, and culture, than the
people among whom we have to work here in
Hawick. If george [sic] has a Kirk session,
composed of men like Eliud, then it is high
time that I stopped thinking of him working
amongst the primitive Africans, and equally
high time he began to think of me working
among the primitive Scots.[48]

Similar descriptions fill this report. They are of
interest not only because of what they relate about
Mathu but also because they illustrate the impact
that he had on British society. His poise and social
grace, his erudition, his avowed Christianity and his
"common sense" and "openmindedness" were all characteristics which set well both with the church hierarchy in Scotland and with the university acade-

micians. Most of these men were advocates of the
liberal cause in the colonies. They sought racial
equality and evolution toward an integrated society
built on western values. Mathu not only reflected
these ideals, he was also visible evidence of their
validity--an urbane, highly westernized African who
moved happily in an integrated environment. His
visit to Scotland strengthened the conviction of
Scottish churchmen that the efforts of their missions, which directed their energies toward such
liberal ends, deserved complete support.

During his year at Exeter, Mathu also made a
trip to Amsterdam which had two notable effects on
his outlook. He arrived in July 1939 as Kenya's representative to the World Conference of Christian
Youth. This was a time of great tension in Europe--
World War II was imminent. Approximately 1500 delegates from throughout the world gathered for this
Conference which had as its theme "Christus Victor".[49]
Because of the realization of impending world crisis,
an exceptional quality of urgency and religious fervor permeated the meetings. Consciousness was
heightened by the unusual circumstances, and members
manifested with great intensity the belief that
Christianity would prevail. "It was brought home to
us," Mathu relates in a letter to R. G. Calderwood,
"that the world cannot save itself, and that the only
salvation is to be found in Christ who has overcome
the world."[50] He experienced a sense of mission and
a greater confidence in his Christian values:

> The Christian Community must not stand
> back from and look on the problems that
> face the world today. Rather, the
> Christian Church in the world today must
> act as a whole so as to help solve these
> problems and make the world a better place
> for God's people.[51]

Mathu was also affected by his contact with the
other delegates. One of the significant elements in
Alliance teacher James Stephen Smith's description
of Mathu was the broad scope of Mathu's political
perspective. "Much like Tom Mboya," he relates,
"Mathu has a world view--unlike almost any other
politician in Kenya."[52] Certainly his wide travel
and multifarious experiences were an important factor in acquiring this quality. The Amsterdam Conference was one such experience which gave him

intense exposure to a great variety of peoples.
Seventy-one countries were represented here, and
Mathu explicitly noted the benefit he reaped from his
contact with them:

> It has been helpful to me to meet
> different people from all over the world.
> I have learned more than my geography ever
> taught me. The world to me now is not
> colours on maps--it is a place where human
> beings live. This has been a great lesson
> to me. To think internationally is now
> more than a possibility.[53]

This ability was to be of considerable benefit in
years to come. He could transcend the narrow ethnic
boundaries which restricted so many of his peers and
see a situation in a more comprehensive and constructive light. Thus this Amsterdam visit, though brief,
was a rich experience and made a definite contribution to his growth.

Following the completion of his education course
at Exeter, Mathu received a second grant to study
British Empire history, economics and government at
Balliol College, Oxford. The arrangements for this
further study were no more difficult than the earlier
ones had been, though there was opposition from Principal Murray to Mathu's leaving his institution.
Murray approved the idea of extending Mathu's stay
and even sought funds for this purpose from the
British Council.[54] But he disapproved the proposal
that the additional time be spent at Oxford. "I don't
really believe in Oxford for foreigners," he stated
in a letter to Grieve. "I think that Mathu's interest is rather to stay here as long as possible and
work out a definite programme under easy and friendly
conditions."[55] But Coupland wanted Mathu as his student and was able to organize the funds necessary to
make this happen. The British Council and Kenya
Government both agreed to renew their contributions,
and, because life at Oxford would be a greater expense, the Rhodes Trust also agreed to contribute
£150.[56] There was some initial doubt on the part of
the trustees of the Rhodes fund concerning the wisdom
of Coupland's request. They set as a condition that
Mathu should not concentrate wholly on the study of
economics, "which would probably turn him out a half-
baked and over self-confident socialist."[57] But
Coupland allayed their fears with the assurance that

he would "personally advise and supervise" the course of study.[58] The required funds were gathered, and Mathu moved into residence at Balliol College in September 1939.

As in his prior academic experience, Mathu performed well at Oxford. A three-term curriculum was arranged for him--one with Coupland studying colonial history; one with Perham on government; and one with John Fulton on economics. Because this was not a standard curriculum and was geared to no formal degree, Mathu might have had some difficulty establishing relationships with fellow students, but Balliol College had been chosen for him because of its tradition of accepting such special students, and his adjustment was made easier because he was not alone in this situation. The one criticism that was made of Mathu during this year was that he spent too much time on his studies and sacrificed certain social activities as a result.[59] But he had entered upon a new area of academic concentration and one which was directly relevant to his life in Kenya. Undoubtedly his intensive study resulted from these considerations. At the same time, the criticism is perhaps not wholly justified since Mathu did join the Youth Hostel Association of Great Britain and spent his holidays travelling to various parts of the countryside with other students.[60] In any case, his academic performance was successful. He completed his course of study and returned to Kenya in August 1940.

One final aspect of Mathu's experience in England which deserves examination is his association with the African community residing in London. The King's Cross section had developed as a center for African intellectuals who were studying, writing, exchanging ideas and structuring the groundwork for the re-emergence of the Pan-African movement. Kenyatta lived here for some time as did Kwame Nkrumah, George Padmore, I. T. A. Wallace-Johnson, Eric Williams, Paul Robeson, and Peter Abrahams at different intervals during the inter-war years. Their presence together in this common space and time is one of the remarkable phenomena of modern history. Mathu came to London on weekends and holidays over this two year period and shared in the activities of these men.

Because of the subsequent developments, it is particularly significant to consider the relationship

between Mathu and Kenyatta at this time. These were
years of flux in Kenyatta's life, and late in 1939 he
left London with Dinah Stock and lived in Sussex
where he farmed and began writing a novèl.[61] Before
this departure, however, he would put Mathu up on his
frequent weekend visits.[62] The two men clearly became friends. Ensuing events, such as Mathu's initiative in Kenyatta's return to Kenya and his appointment as Kenyatta's secretary, verify this. Nevertheless they were very different men, and as a result the depth of their friendship was limited.
Kenyatta was a charismatic, almost mystical, presence, living a bohemian expatriate existence in
English leftist circles, active in Pan-African politics, and convinced of his destiny to someday return
to Kenya and lead his people to freedom. He was intensely emotional and dramatic, sometimes highly ex-
troverted, in colorful costume, enjoying English pub
life and entertaining his friends with African tales.
At other times he was almost morose and would isolate
himself from everyone. Always he was a powerful and
independent personality, confident of his superior
abilities and highly critical of imperialism. At an
earlier time Mathu might have been strongly impressed
by Kenyatta's character, and the conservative values
in which he had been immersed at Alliance might have
been questioned. But he was now almost thirty, and
his identity was largely formed. He was highly
Anglicized, Christian, and politically moderate.
Like Kenyatta, he was by now highly sophisticated and
travelled easily in English society. But the circles
in which he was most comfortable were academic and
politically liberal, not the avant-garde, third world
society that had become Kenyatta's primary realm. In-
evitably there was some reserve on the part of both
men toward one another's values. Their common Kikuyu
roots bound them together and made them friends, but
their contrasting life-styles prevented them from
being genuine comrades.

     A number of political organizations were opera-
ted by members of London's African community, the
most important of which, with relationship to Mathu's
experience, was the International African Service
Bureau (IASB), which was founded by George Padmore
with an office on Gray's Inn Road. The focus of this
organization was on the "democratic rights, civil
liberties and self-determination" of the African
people with the ultimate objective of a united continent under African rule.[63] This Pan-African objective

was extreme, even revolutionary, for its time. But
the Bureau's leadership, i.e., Padmore, C. L. R.
James and Kenyatta, were realists, and their immediate concern was the dissemination of propaganda to
make the world aware of the grievances of the African
people against colonial government policies.[64]

Through Kenyatta's introduction, Mathu became
involved in the activities of the IASB. His recent
and first-hand knowledge of the Kenya administration's
activities was a rich source of explicit data which
could be used as the basis for articles published in
the Bureau's magazine, International African Opinion.[65]
Besides providing information for this publication,
Mathu also volunteered to spend his week-end after-
noons selling it on the London streets.[66] In addition to its own publication, the IASB also sought to
provide information on colonial grievances to sympathetic journalists of the major press. Mathu related useful material for articles on Kenya to the
Manchester Guardian and the New Statesman and Nation.[67]
He also assisted the Bureau by recruiting new members
from among London's African student population. Especially notable in this respect was his introduction
of a group of twenty premedical students from South
Africa, some of whom he had known at Fort Hare.[68]
Thus, although most of his time was spent in study or
in student related activities, during this two year
stay Mathu did have a degree of active involvement
with the African political movement in London.

One might question whether Mathu's connection
with the IASB was logically consistent with his social
and political philosophy and with his position as a
government financed student. In examining this question, certain themes emerge which will recur later in
Mathu's career. First, there is no evidence that
Mathu doubted the compatibility of his support of the
IASB with his personal values. Although the Bureau
was founded by Padmore, it was designed not to specifically mirror his views, but as a broadly based organization committed to acting in the general interest of African people. Padmore's belief in the
benefits of western culture for his people, and his
willingness to tolerate a gradual approach to extending their rights, did not imply that his ultimate
objective was anything less than the termination of
colonial rule. IASB officials welcomed Mathu's participation and recognized him as a valuable asset to
their cause. "He was preparing himself to return, we

knew, for an obviously important post as a teacher,"
noted T. R. Makonnen.[69]   Because of his attendance
at the most prestigious of English Universities,
Mathu was to receive special recognition from the
colonial administration and be in a unique position
to affect positive change. IASB leaders realized
that this advantage would only hold true if Mathu's
connection with strong anti-colonial protest never
became prominent. They consciously sought to shield
his image from too direct an involvement in their
cause. As an example, he was never mentioned in the
articles for which he furnished information.[70]   In a
sense, therefore, these men were also grooming Mathu
to play a role in the fulfillment of their aims. In
any case, it is evident that his cooperation with
their cause was genuine and remained low key, in part
at least, because of their own insistence. At the
same time, had Mathu been fervent enough in his participation in the Bureau, this insistence would not
have held. Clearly his commitment to these political
objectives was never great enough to supercede his
personal concern with his career. He involved himself in the Bureau's cause, but never intensely
enough to endanger his scholarship or his reputation
with his colonial patrons. It is another manifestation of his priorities and primary concern for his
individual well being. This was never so great that
he would abandon his principles. But it caused him
to employ caution in the methods he used to carry
them forward. The IASB leaders realized his position
and saw that it had a useful place in aiding their
missions--that Mathu could be of service from the inside of the colonial machine. But they had committed
themselves to be outsiders who to a much greater degree had given themselves over to their cause.

    Mathu left England in September 1940 consider-
ably enriched. While his objectives and outlook were
not fundamentally altered by his experience, he did
attain a wider perspective and more sophisticated
world view. The academic stimulus of his study at
Exeter and Oxford strengthened him intellectually and
gave him greater self-confidence. His successful
movement in urbane English society gave him polish.
Finally his contact with Kenyatta and his colleagues
increased his awareness of African political aims and
confirmed his decision to challenge colonial wrongs.
He returned to Kenya substantially broadened and
eager to incorporate his new experiences both into
his teaching career at Alliance and into involvement

in the colonial community.

Ironically the first few years following his return to Kenya were difficult, and culminated in a
crisis that forced Mathu to alter his total life
plan. Mathu continued his career in teaching at
Alliance and, considering his advanced study, seemingly should have found his position improved. But
the situation at Alliance had changed dramatically
while he was away, and in this new environment Mathu
never found the satisfaction he had known in former
years. A complex of difficulties developed and ended
in circumstances that resulted in his dismissal. An
association with a Kikuyu Karing'a Independent School
followed but never had time to develop very far because of his appointment to the Legislative Council.
In overview, in the period from 1940 to 1944, Mathu's
life was unsettled and shifting--his ambition was
temporarily thwarted, and his expectation for a
career in teaching was ultimately abandoned.

The altered conditions which Mathu found at
Alliance upon his return were almost wholly the result of one factor--the retirement of Principal
Grieve and his replacement by E. Carey Francis.
Grieve went on extended leave for reasons of health
in 1938. He returned to the school the following
year but had not fully recovered and decided it would
be wise to retire. The search for his successor finally focused on Francis, the Headmaster of Maseno
School, and he took charge at Alliance in August 1940,
just prior to Mathu's return. The effect was profound. Unlike Grieve, who worked through quiet and
subtle persuasion, Francis was an aggressive and
eccentric personality. He had an almost manic need
to feel himself in direct control of every facet of
the school's operation. He demanded rigid disci-
pline, strict moral standards and a kind of grateful humility from his students. "I like boys small--
without dignity," he wrote in 1939.[71] He posed a
sharp contrast with Grieve. Francis realized these
differences and prepared to make great changes upon
taking over. "I dislike the Alliance tradition," he
wrote from Maseno while considering the move. "I
should have, and should probably cause, revolutions".[72]
He did, indeed, initiate fundamental changes, which
brought to an end the comfortable atmosphere Mathu
had enjoyed in former years.

Among the most important of these changes was

Francis's replacement of the African staff with his
own former students from Maseno. It is probable that
Francis calculated this move from the start. He expressed skepticism as to the staff's ability even
before taking residence at the school:

> The things I have recently heard of the
> Alliance staff make me feel that the
> Africans are so slack and work such short
> hours that however carefully I attempt re-
> forms it is likely that they will all leave.[73]

After his first few months as Principal, Francis considered each untenured African teacher individually
and found reason why his replacement was required.
James Gichuru taught mathematics, and, while Francis
described him as "in character one of the best of the
staff," he did "not think he is the calibre to hold a
permanent post on the staff of this school."[74] Of
Joseph Otiende, who taught music and Swahili, he
wrote, "I do not feel that he has the personality and
the keenness on work for its own sake which we should
expect."[75] Even the school clerk, A. Cege, was replaced by a part-time employee. Part of Cege's function had been to teach typing. Dropping typing from
the schedule, Francis asserted that there was "doubt-
ful wisdom" in such instruction.[76] Within one year
of his arrival all these men had been replaced by
graduates of Maseno. Only Mathu, who was on permanent contract, remained.

There is a diversity of explanation for Francis's
replacement of these men. James Smith believes that
Francis's motivation was a basic dislike of the Kikuyu
people and a preference for Luo.[77] Besides his
hiring of Luo teachers, Francis also increased the
proportion of Luo in the student body at the expense
of Kikuyu.[78] But this argument fails to explain his
dismissal of Otiende who was Luhya. It is also questionable whether Francis would have considered accepting this position if such a prejudice were an important part of his makeup. Francis himself justified
his action by describing the men he replaced as lazy.
He saw the school as "over-staffed" and felt it was
corrupted by "luxuries."[79] He also disliked the political interest of the African staff. Gichuru and
Mathu had shown interest in the activities of the
KCA. Francis abhorred politics and facetiously referred to the "progressive Kikuyu type", describing
them as "impossible."[80] In this sense he found the

Luo more attractive, since they were further removed
from the center of political conflict and consequently less involved in political protest. With all
these things considered, however, it is probable that
Francis's main reason for making these changes was to
staff tne school with men he knew to be loyal--his
former students whose character he had helped mold.
The only non-Kikuyu, Joseph Otiende, had studied at
Kaimosi and thus was not a product of Francis's system.[81] The replacements, Messrs. Ojal, Akatsa and
Oriyo, were all Maseno "old boys" and more assuredly
trustworthy in Francis's eyes. He took this action
as part of his need to control every situation--his
need to play a paternal role both for his staff and
students. This would not have been possible with the
African staff he found on his arrival.

As with the other African members of the
Alliance staff, Francis also was dubious about Mathu's
value even before the two men had met. "While I
shall honestly try to get on with him," he wrote in
May 1940, "I do not disguise my misgivings."[82] This
negative attitude was clearly reached with no prodding from Mathu's educational associates in the colony. Grieve wrote Francis in March of that same
year concerning Mathu's return to let Francis know
that he thought "a good deal of him [Mathu] and that
he was sure that "he was looking forward to returning."[83] L. B. Greave, Education Adviser to Protestant Missions, wrote Francis later that year stating
that he felt Mathu would be "a great asset" to
Alliance and advising that Francis should "be reason-
ably generous and to act before he [Mathu] does" in
offering a position.[84] Calderwood wrote in a similar
vein, noting Mathu's "great potentialities" and arguing that "a Kikuyu of his ability, if he turned out
well, should be a tower of strength to the school."[85]
But Francis remained unimpressed. "If he regards the
work as a privilege," he wrote Grieve, "that is fine.
If he feels that he is being badly treated, comes as
a favour . . . then I think it would be better that
he should not come at all."[86] He reacted to Calderwood's recommendation that Mathu's starting salary
should be ₤180.[87] His influence was certainly a major
factor in the reduction of this figure to ₤150, which
Mathu received upon his return.[88] His skepticism
concerning Mathu's desirability resulted from the
same basis as his dislike of the other African staff—
he would be too independent of Francis's control, too
confident of his own ability and not sufficiently

deferential. But despite offers from the Department
of Education and the Law Courts, Mathu chose to return to the school. Because he was on permanent contract, Francis had no real option but to accept him.

The two years which Mathu spent at Alliance under Francis's Principalship were tense and marked by
a running series of disagreements between the two.
As a result of his year at Oxford, Mathu taught history and geography, and more and more, as his dissatisfaction grew, he incorporated political ideas
into his lessons. His study of empire under Coupland and Perham and his involvement with African politics in London were partially responsible for this,
but Francis's rigid paternalism was the primary cause.
Mathu's political consciousness was increasingly
heightened by this situation, while at the same time
his development in this direction only alienated
Francis even more. An ideological contest emerged
between them which the students followed with keen
interest. A principal floor for their debate was the
school chapel. It was an Alliance tradition that
staff members should conduct the morning religious
service, and Mathu and Francis used this opportunity
to express their opposing views. The situation is
described by Kipkorir:

> While Francis preached on services and
> obligations of servants, Mathu preached on
> the duties and responsibilities of masters;
> while Francis preached on humility, Mathu
> tackled maturity; while Francis talked on
> the Empire and explorations and the opening
> up of Africa and the good Christian work
> that resulted from it, Mathu discussed the
> exploitation of Africa.[89]

The approach was indirect, but no one was unaware of
its intention. Mathu's performance in these situations evidently impressed the students. In 1940
Francis questioned his seniors as to whom they considered best qualified to be the first African to
represent African interest in the Legislative Council, and their choice, to Francis's dismay, was
Mathu.[90]

During the same time, more direct confrontations
occurred. The first of these was a dispute over the
operation of the Old Boys Club. As earlier described, this organization was started by Mathu. The

headmaster was the Club's official patron, but, during Grieve's Principalship, he had not taken any
direct role in its activities. The Club membership
had grown steadily throughout the 1930s and by 1940
more than half of the school's alumni were enrolled.
But with Francis's arrival the situation changed. The
new Principal was not content to allow the Club to
function on its own. He sought involvement in its
business in a number of ways--most significantly in
the procedure for amending the constitution. While
Grieve had had no part in this process, Francis demanded that his approval be a preliminary to any
amendment proposal. His insistence alienated Mathu
and caused him to withdraw his participation.[91]
Francis thereafter altered the Club's structure significantly, changed its symbol and motto and established himself as a primary voice in all its decisions. Members' interest dwindled, and by 1948
Francis wrote, "Its activities seem to have ceased
entirely. I think it would be best to regard it as
dead."[92] A second conflict came in 1941 over the
arrangements for an inter-school sports competition
for the Kikuyu area. The staff supervision of this
event was structured so that no Africans were used
as judges. Mathu had been involved in Alliance
sporting activities since the beginning of his career
with the school and was offended by this situation.
To make his dissatisfaction known, he organized the
African teachers into a formal committee and wrote a
letter to the principals of the participating schools
calling the matter "humiliating." Predictably,
Francis reacted to this letter and accused Mathu of
"impertinence and disloyalty." [93] It is clearly from
these incidents that Mathu's presence at Alliance was
a major hindrance to Francis's need to feel himself in
control. It was crucial to this need that he be removed and replaced by someone more acceptable, i.e.,
less assertive.

Mathu's dismissal came in September 1942 as a
result of circumstances that violated the strict
moral requirements Francis had established at the
school. Despite the tension of his relationship with
the Principal, Mathu had no plan to leave. Earlier
the same year he had received approval from the Board
of Governors for an extension of two rooms on his
house. There were also negotiations in progress, as
a result of his request, for increasing his salary.[94]
But neither of these plans was realized. Francis was
away on leave for the first half of the year, and

during this time Mathu became involved with a girl in
the community. Restrictions were such under Francis
that single African staff were forbidden any entertaining of female guests in their homes. Mathu
violated this regulation, and Francis was quick to
use it as grounds for his dismissal. He returned to
Alliance in September and moved quickly to bring this
about. The Board of Governors accepted his recommendation, and Mathu's contract was terminated from
September 30.[95] Largely as a result of his refusal
to bend to Francis's will, Mathu's connection with
Alliance was ended. His departure put a final end to
the waning possibility of his original ambition for a
life-long career as a master at the school. He was
now forced to reorient himself, to establish new
plans and take some other direction.

        These final years at Alliance under Francis are
a further evidence of Mathu's acquired confidence and
of his basic commitment to principle. He could live,
even thrive, in the colonial atmosphere of Alliance
with its European administrators, separate salary
scales and housing based on race, etc., but only if
the philosophy of education which the school was employing was one that he could accept. Until Grieve's
departure this situation prevailed--the concept of
"Christian service" a la Hampton Institute and
Tuskegee. But Francis's blatant paternalism and his
outrage at any difference of opinion from his African
staff Mathu found intolerable. In these conditions
he was forced to speak out. The rewards of personal
security and recognition from his students and the
surrounding community were not equal to his contempt
for Francis's arrogance. It was a situation in which
his customary willingness to compromise would not endure.

        The two years between his dismissal from
Alliance and his appointment to the Legislative
Council Mathu spent as Principal of a Kikuyu Karing'a
School near Dagoretti. Peter Koinange had made a
similar move in 1938 when, after his return from
abroad, he rejected an offer from Alliance because of
the small salary offered.[96] Koinange took charge of
a Kikuyu Independent School at Githunguri. Mathu, on
the other hand, chose to teach in the more politically
oriented Karing'a system. However, this decision was
not primarily due to his support for the Karing'a
philosophy. Rather it was motivated by the school's
location in his home area and near Alliance. It was

an elementary school with approximately 250 pupils and was operating on an extremely slim budget.[97] Mathu's objective was to take charge and build it into an efficient and effective institution. He saw this as an opportunity to demonstrate the viability of the principle of self-help gleaned from Washington's writings and to create for his people a real alternative to European mission-dominated education. In this sense, and had he not left it for a political career, this school might have grown into Mathu's Tuskegee. Although he stayed less than two years-- not sufficient time to produce changes of great note--Mathu did bring about considerable development, especially in increasing public contributions and using the funds for building.[98] Beyond this, little can be said. His government appointment brought the project to a close, and from that time his energies were employed elsewhere. His involvement at the Karing'a School is mainly of interest as a "might have been"--an alternative he could have followed as a means of fulfillment.

In retrospect the years from 1934 to 1944 appear of vital significance to Mathu's future LegCo career. It was during this period that his social and political philosophy fully emerged. This development resulted from the experiences of his travel, and from the personal relationships he encountered both positively with Perham and Kenyatta, and negatively with Carey Francis. Also, despite the temporary displacement he faced at the end of this period, taken in perspective, this was a time of fulfillment in Mathu's life. He found satisfaction and some recognition in advanced study and, in the mid-30s, in his teaching at Alliance. In relation to his representation in the Legislative Council these were years of development and preparation; but in terms of his personal sense of achievement they were a time of rich experience and marked success.

CHAPTER FOUR

LEGISLATIVE COUNCIL REPRESENTATION I--1944-1951

Like a drop of water beating on a rock
unceasingly, you can make a hole.

Eliud Mathu, 1954[1]

As an aid in the successful analysis of Eliud
Mathu's career as a representative in the Kenya
Legislative Council, it is useful to make a chronological division and to examine the years from 1944
to 1951 as largely distinct from the latter years
which extended to May 1957. This division is by no
means arbitrary. While Mathu sought to pursue many
of his objectives throughout the whole of this thir-
teen year period, the Emergency in 1952 significantly altered the emphasis and effectiveness of his
efforts. In the years before this crisis, the colony's administration felt no great pressure to
accede to the demands of the African community. But
largely as a result of this situation, Mathu, as the
principal spokesman for these demands in the Council,
was free to function with minimal restriction from
government. It is during this earlier half of his
representative career that his broad program of reform is best seen. The specifics of this program are
all logical aspects of a general plan for Kenya's
future based on a conscious and definable political
and racial view.

Although Kenya's Africans and their political
allies had consistently agitated for direct representation in the colony's Legislative Council, Governor
Henry Moore's announcement of June 9, 1944, that an
African would be selected as the replacement for
H. R. Montgomery, retiring nominated Member for
African Interests, came as much of a surprise.
Kikuyu political organizations had African representation as one of its demands as early as 1921.[2] Even
the conservative Kikuyu Association listed this objective in a 1924 memorandum.[3] Throughout successive

years it was stated repeatedly by Africans as a political goal. In 1931 Jomo Kenyatta wrote to the Manchester Guardian as a representative of the Kikuyu Central Association and stated that "until this representation of Africans by Africans is justly settled, there can be no peace or prosperity in Africa."[4] In the British Parliament the question was periodically raised by Labour M. P.'s, and each time a rationale was given by the Government for delaying its inception. In 1938, for example, W. G. A. Ormsby Gore, the Secretary of State for the Colonies, replied to a question put by Ben Riley and argued that the appointment of an African would be "extremely difficult at the present stage when you have a great admixture of races. It is necessary you should have people who are familiar with very varied Native Conditions."[5] Ormsby Gore's position was that Europeans who had worked with Africans, either as missionaries or as government administrators, had a broader basis of experience and a more objective viewpoint and therefore could more effectively represent the Colony's African population in toto. There is evidence that Ormsby Gore's successor, Oliver Stanley, who held the office at the time of Governor Moore's announcement, similarly opposed the appointment of Africans to LegCo. In 1943 he wrote that while he realized such an appointment might be "a wonderful gesture," he held that any African so placed would "take very little part in the proceedings" and would "find difficulty in following arguments between Europeans." Stanley recommended "a more gradual approach" such as the expansion of African participation in Local Native Councils.[6] The indication is therefore that the decision to nominate an African to the Council in 1944 came with no pressure from Whitehall. Similarly, there was no unusual pressure for such an appointment from Kenya's African community. Since 1944 was an election year in the Colony, there was some intensification of the campaign for African representation as indicated by letters in the local press.[7] Also noteworthy is the publication of a government committee appointed by Moore in 1943 to study the problem of the reabsorption of returning troops into civilian society. Among the findings of this committee was the fact that the Africans interviewed "felt that there should also be Africans on the Legislative Council."[8] Given these factors, however, there is no evidence that Governor Moore's decision was forced upon him by popular coercion. It is probably that he saw it as a

preventive tactic to ease the readjustment of returning soldiers to the colonial situation. But in the
context of the circumstances operative in Kenya when
the announcement was made, there was general surprise
that such an action was taken.

At the same time that he announced this appointment, Governor Moore also stipulated the method by
which the representative would be chosen. There was
no alteration of the existing constitution required
by this innovation. The new African member would
simply fill one of the two unofficial seats provided
for representatives of African interests and traditionally held by Europeans.[9] Unlike the unofficial
representatives of other racial groups, all of whom
were popularly elected, these two members had always
been appointed by the governor.[10] The only variation
in the selection process to result from the appointment of an African was the decision by Moore to con-
sult spokesmen of the African community for suggested
candidates. "In order to secure that Africans themselves are closely associated in his selection," he
stated, "I propose to instruct the Chief Native Commissioner, after consultation with the Local Native
Councils, to submit a panel of names for my consideration."[11] The final selection remained in his hands.

There is some question as to the main reason why
Mathu was chosen to fill this seat. He was clearly
a prominent member of the small elite who had the
educational requirements necessary to function effectively in the job, but this does not explain why
he was selected over some other member of this group.
In keeping with Moore's instructions, Mathu was one
of three candidates, along with Peter Mbiyu Koinange
and Luo Chief Paul Mboya, whose names were submitted
by the Chief Native Commissioner from which the
Governor was to make his choice. Of these three,
only Koinange campaigned actively, traveling by car
to meet with members of the Native Councils to seek
their support. Mathu, on the other hand, did nothing
to directly influence these men. He describes the
circumstances of his inclusion as a candidate as
follows:

> I was on good terms with most of the
> chiefs, government officials, farmers,
> teachers, clergymen--these were the men
> who were serving on the Council--and so
> when the time came, they came to me and

said: "What about you, wouldn't you like
to be considered?" I said "Alright, [sic] if
you want to put forward my name, you can
have it." And I did not make any other
campaign.[12]

He attributes his popularity with these men to his
long connection with Alliance High School and explains:

I was in a peculiar position in this
thing, better than he [Koinange] was. I
had been attached to this very important
institution of higher learning, and these
boys, having left there, were in every
department, and they liked me. Whereas
he [Koinange] was away and just comes in
as a stranger more or less--he had been
away for ten years.[13]

In the same way, Mathu argues that his appointment
came about because he was better known by the administration.[14] He views his involvement with local
government and his committee activities as having
given him a special prominence which resulted in his
selection. This analysis would be disputed by certain scholars who see Mathu's nomination as a move
by the Governor to support the man "felt to be more
moderate."[15] The resolution of these conflicting
explanations remains speculative. Certainly Mathu
was highly qualified for the post, and the legitimacy
of his education, because it was wholly within
British schools, was better known to the administration than was Koinange's. Indeed, as has been seen,
Mathu had been specifically prepared for such a position by his tutors at Oxford. It is similarly true
that Mathu was better known by local officials simply because he had been present in the colony for a
longer time than Koinange. It may be that analysts
who argue that Mathu was considered more moderate
are employing historical hindsight, since only in
later years are Koinange's activities visibly more
militant than Mathu's constitutional approach. In
any case, Mathu was the Governor's choice, and his
appointment was announced on October 5, 1944.

With the exception of some minor reaction with
a tribal basis, the response of Kenya's African community to Mathu's appointment was positive. Kikuyu
reaction was uniformly favorable. Letters appeared

in the local press congratulating him on his success
and expressing support. James Gichuru, for example,
wrote as follows:

> The name of Mr. E. W. Mathu has not come
> as a surprise to many, for his ability and
> thoroughness are well known. . . We expect no
> miracles from him. But in him we have our
> confidence and reason to believe that the
> African viewpoints . . . will be properly
> presented to the Government. His supporters
> number millions, and he can face the task
> before him with confidence.[16]

Government reports for the year in Kikuyu areas similarly indicate an enthusiastic response. In Fort Hall
the appointment was described by the D. C. as "intensely popular,"[17] and in Nyeri as "warmly welcomed."[18] The Luo of Nyanza, however, reportedly expressed dismay. "A grave sense of inferiority" appeared, according to the Provincial Commissioner, and
"it was felt that the first appointment should have
been made from Nyanza."[19] But no organized resistance emerged in the province, and leaders of the Luo
community joined with Mathu in his establishment of a
political association. Among the African elite, the
predominant attitude was one of encouragement along
with the realization that this achievement merely
marked the beginning in a struggle for political
rights that was likely to continue for some time to
come.

No evidence is available on Jomo Kenyatta's response to Mathu's fortune. But it is probable that
he would have preferred another choice. The previous
year he replied to statements made on a radio discussion of colonial issues and gave his general opinion
on the requirements of African representation:

> Education is not the sole quality needed
> in a representative: it is essential that
> he should also . . . express their needs.
> If any African does this, the Europeans
> brand him an "agitator." On the other hand,
> if he conforms to the standard of compla-
> cency expected of him by the Europeans, he
> will hardly be doing his duty by his
> countrymen.[20]

As earlier noted, while Kenyatta had been friendly

with Mathu in London, there was a clear difference
in lifestyle and political attitude between the two
men. Kenyatta considered Mathu too cautious and
accommodating, and it is likely that he was not
wholly pleased with the appointment.

The policies that Mathu supported as a MLC were
all aspects of a broad political design which he intended as the basis for Kenya's future--a design
molded from the philosophy he had formulated during
his Alliance years. His willingness to exchange his
position as an educator for this appointment came
from his belief that it would improve his effectiveness in making inroads toward this goal. "I accepted this [nomination]," he related, "because it
fit [sic] in with my desire--my desire was to do
everything possible within the councils of state to
improve the lot of my people."[21]

His ultimate objective and the foundation of
his political program was the realization of an integrated multiracial society. "This country has a
tremendous opportunity," he argued, "in demonstrating
to the world that a multiracial community can develop
this country in harmony and for the benefit of all".[22]
He sought to create "an East African consciousness"
which would eliminate racial barriers and would
operate through a hierarchy chosen solely on the
basis of merit.[23] "We are here to develop as a community," he told his LegCo colleagues, "a Kenya
community, irrespective of the colours of the population."[24] He rejected the theory in Southern
Rhodesia that a partnership of separate communities
should be built and argued that "these plural
societies have existed and have not worked."[25] Virtually all of his activity in the Council was directed toward this end of inter-racial cooperation.

Within his general aim of seeking this integrated community, Mathu visualized some specific elements of its character. Culturally it would be
mainly western, based on the British prototype.
While he upheld certain particular African traditions,
such as <u>lobola</u> (bride wealth), in the face of criticism from colonial spokesmen, he nevertheless
preached to his people that "changes must come" and
urged that they "absorb the British way of life."[26]
At the same time he stressed the ability of the
African to adapt to these changes:

If there is a capacity for the African to
absorb the new institutions from Britain and
if the African absorbed the British way of
life, why take it gradually? I submit that
an African has absorbed it, he has absorbed
more than any other people I know in the
world in 50 years.[27]

As a logical application of these premises, Mathu
argued that the policies of the colonial government
should be devoid of racial distinction. Education,
welfare services, land ownership and social legislation, while all western innovations, should be common
for all. The African "wants everything that any
other person in the world wants," and, because of his
ability to assimilate these new institutions, there
should be no racial barriers to prevent him from ful-
filling his potential.[28] Within African society, too,
sectional legislation was undesirable. The African
people should not be viewed as a collection of separate ethnic groups but as part of the East African
community:

We should encourage harmonious development among all the African peoples in this
country,without accentuating their differences. As a matter of fact we should aim
at creating a nation out of them, which we
can.[29]

This did not mean that the cultural traditions of
Kenya's individual races and ethnic groups would not
continue to endure. Mathu simply argued that these
differences should not be emphasized and used as an
excuse for European domination. "There are differences in language, differences in customs and so on,"
he stated, "but those differences did not prevent the
present India from becoming a republic."[30] Moderni-
zation along western lines could occur, and ethnic
differences could continue to endure. India had
"made a nation out of a conglomeration of races" he
said, and Kenya could do the same.[31] The key was to
emphasize the fundamental similarity of all men and
a sense of common community would result.

Just as Mathu's position in the Council was consistent with his desire for a multiracial community,
so too was there consistency in the approach he employed to achieve his objectives. His policy was
humanistic, pragmatic and opposed to violence.

Certain arguments were an established part of his
logic and became associated with his name. Most
notable of these is the aphorism "Half a loaf is
better than nothing," which is linked with Mathu's
name even today and which he frequently incorporated
into his speeches in the Council. Reflecting on his
use of this phrase, Mathu noted:

>   This is a point on diplomacy because if I
> make a demand on the Government of the day
> for our people, there are two ways of doing
> it--we must have it 100% or we will kill
> you. The other approach, which was mine,
> was a more moderate one, and I think more
> diplomatic. It is this--if we don't get all
> what we want, we are grateful to that little
> thing you are going to give us. Having got
> that half, we are coming again for the other
> half. That was my approach and that is why
> I had to use that term because I had no way
> of enforcing my requests. We were power-
> less. We had no army of our own. We were
> all poor people. What can you do with that
> giant of the British people governing here
> from London? Therefore, half a loaf is
> better than no loaf.[32]

Predictably Booker T. Washington provided an historical precedent for Mathu in his employment of this
concept. Washington "had to approach it that way,"
Mathu related:

>   because . . . in those days nobody would
> have dared. But Booker T. Washington was
> clever to get something for the Black people
> in the States than to get nothing at all,
> and then use that to get more.[33]

In the same way, Mathu's approach also reflected
Washington's in its emphasis on self-help. Washington founded Tuskegee on the premise that American
Blacks must create their own opportunities for manifesting their ability. Similarly Mathu held that
Kenya's Africans must act for themselves, both
through private enterprise and by willingly contribu-
ting to the cost of public services to which they
could have access. During one debate in which he
supported the payment of fees for education, he re-
marked, "Well, some Africans who read what I have
said today would say that I am not acting in their

interests, but if their interests are to be spoon-
fed, I say no."[34] To these two ideas, generated by
Washington, Mathu added an emphasis on the common
humanity of all men and a rejection of violence.
Consistently in his confrontations with European
settlers he stressed the need to recognize the hu-
manness of the African. "They are not less or more
than human beings."[35] At the same time, and especially during the Emergency years, he warned his own
people against the use of violence as a tool for
change. Stating that "there is nothing good, self-
government or anything else, which can be achieved
by violence," he argued that confidence be placed in
change through constitutional means.[36]

These then are the primary tenets of the position Mathu put forth in his campaign to bring about
the community consciousness that was his goal. They
constitute a cohesive rationale which ideally and
logically called for the abolition of all racial
legislation, but which also incorporated a justification for the pragmatic compromise which was virtually inevitable given the political circumstances
under which he was forced to function. It was an
approach acquired from his series of associations
with Grieve, Jabavu, Perham and Coupland, and by his
study of Washington's work.

In the context of political consciousness in
Kenya in the 1940s. Mathu's position was progressive. The Europeans in the Council, both officials
and settler representatives, did not begin to advocate multiracialism until the mid-1950s.   Their
conception of Kenya in this pre-Emergency period remained that of a "white man's country" in which they
would retain a privileged status. Their consistent
pursuit of racially distinct policies, along with
their active recruitment of settlers and the majority
control of the Council which they maintained, are
adequate evidence of this fact. Despite the politically weak and constantly frustrating position from
which they were presented, Mathu's policies represented an ideological challenge to these men and were
a precursor of change to come.

In relationship to the African community, too,
Mathu's program was progressive. But the situation
is complex, and it is more difficult to generalize
than is the case with the Europeans. During the
1940s African politics in Kenya were in an excessive

state of flux. The heightened political awareness
which resulted from the wartime travel abroad of so
many young men was an important factor in producing
this volatility. As has been seen, these men gave
Mathu their support. But they also sought more direct involvement in producing change and were less
and less patient with the intransigence of the administration. Within the political organizations, especially the Kenya African Union, growing disagreement and factionalism occurred. The situation was
complex and is best examined in connection with
specific issues yet to be described. But in the
midst of this divisive and emotional climate, Mathu's
LegCo position was unique in that it offered an extensive and fully articulated program for change
which came to grips in a practical way with specific
grievances and at the same time placed them in a
broad perspective as part of an overall design for
Kenya's future. Despite the crises ahead in the
fifties, the multiracial approach which Mathu advocated in these years contained the fundamental
tenets which Kenyatta's government would apply with
independence.

Immediately following his appointment, Mathu set
about establishing a colony-wide African political
organization to give him support and to serve as a
channel for formulating his policies in the Council.
No such transtribal association existed in Kenya at
this time. Among the Kikuyu, Harry Thuku's Kikuyu
Provincial Association was the only formal body
operating legally.[37] Thuku recommended that it
should fill this role and offered Mathu the use of
the KPA offices.[38] But Mathu opposed tribal associations and for practical motives as well as reasons
of principle chose to form a wholly new association.
"I wanted an all-embracing political organization,"
he explained. "I would be representing the interests
of the whole country, so I had to have an organization to gather material for the LegCo from every walk
of life and every area."[39] To this end a meeting was
called in Nairobi in October 1944, and the Kenya
African Union (KAU) was formed.

Using the British party system as a model, Mathu
declined any official position in the association
when the appointment of officers was made. "I did it
by choice," he related, "because when the committee
of the KAU all over the country would produce material I would not have been directly involved so that I

can [sic] fight the case properly without having committed myself."[40] The officers who were appointed
included men from most of the colony's major tribes
among whom were Harry Thuku as Chairman, Francis
Khamisi from the Coast as Secretary, and Executive
Committee Members from Nyanza, Taita, Kamba, Gusii,
Masai and Luhya areas.[41] Mathu's encouragement was
instrumental in organizing this multi-ethnic leadership, but he himself remained technically a rank-and-
file member of the association.

Unofficially Mathu played a vital role in KAU
activities for the whole of its existence, and the
influence of his ideas on its policies is evident.
For example, the Union's constitution, which he
helped draft, states as primary objectives the following:

(a)   To unite the African people of Kenya.

(b)   To interpret African life and thought
      and to study and promote the advance-
      ment of the interests and welfare of
      the Kenya African by all legitimate
      means.

(c)   To cooperate with members representing
      African interests on the Kenya Legis-
      lative Council and to assist them in
      their work.[42]

He repeatedly stressed these aims in speeches at KAU
meetings and in articles in the association newspaper, Sauti ya Mwafrika (The African Voice). In
the first issue of this publication he wrote:

It is . . . a sacred duty of this Union
to keep a close watch with a view to en-
deavour to protect the African community
against the many evils that we meet within this land. These responsibilities may
be wide and farfetched--from our protection against thieves and burglars to our
protection against political domination by
any one race in Kenya.

These are the things that cannot be
fought for individually, but we must fight
them in a united front. And it is for
these big things that you and I are called

together to strengthen this united battle
front.[43]

Throughout its existence, as factions developed and
militancy grew, Mathu consistently stressed this
theme--a unified African effort to combat administration injustices through legal and constitutional
means--and it remained the dominant position of the
association.

Mathu's influence is also evident in the specific issues dealt with by the KAU in the petitions
which they submitted to the Government. Indeed,
often these documents could serve as precis of
Mathu's program in the Council. One of the most comprehensive petitions, which contains virtually all
of the major aspects of Mathu's LegCo position,was
prepared by W. W. W. Awori and James Gichuru in 1946
for presentation to the Secretary of State for the
Colonies. The two topics most heavily stressed in
this memorandum were education and land. The institution of compulsory education, beginning at elementary level, was given as "Priority No. 1." The argument that the introduction of modern concepts must
come slowly was decried and a willingness expressed
to pay higher taxes if a significant enlargement of
educational facilities would result. Concerning
land, it states that "there is a great need for more
and more land for the growing population of the
African" and argues that "since the European land-
holders were the sole beneficiaries of what we
Africans lost, it is they alone who must make good
the loss." In addition to these two central demands,
the document also calls for improved health services,
higher wages for African labor, increased African
representation in the Legislative Council, abolition
of restrictions on African trade and agriculture,
initiation of Africans into responsible administrative positions and the withdrawal of <u>kipande</u> (registration permits). It concludes with a statement on
self-government declaring that "the time is not yet
ripe" for such a system. The effort of the European
community to bring this about was "a South African
innovation" and not in the interest of the African.
A multiracial basis of government is called for in
which "both the African and European communities in
this country will participate." But the African
must have a leading role in its creation. "The
African people have a highly developed sense of
nationalism," it states, and "when the time will come

it will be the Africans themselves who will petition
His Majesty's Government to grant Self-Government to
Kenya."[44]   Such was the position of the association
and, as will be seen, it is indistinguishable from
that of Mathu in the Council. His influence on the
formulation of these petitions is clearly evident.

     While the position of the KAU might appear
moderate in the context of subsequent developments,
it was viewed with suspicion by the administration,
and measures were immediately taken to modify its
character. The principal criticism was against the
creation by Africans of an explicitly political organization. Similar associations of Europeans and
of Asians had existed in the colony for decades,
i.e., the Convention of Associations, the Electors
Union, and the East African Indian National Congress.
But it was argued by the administration that Africans
were not yet ready for such a union. They were not
yet sufficiently educated to cope responsibly with
political ideas. The position of the KAU required
tempering before it could be given government sanc-
tion. Its name was changed to the Kenya African
Study Union. The initiative for this alteration,
according to Mathu, came from his colleague in the
Council, Leonard Beecher. He was not unpopular with
Africans, and, indeed, his appointment in 1943 as a
LegCo Representative for African Interests had been
viewed as a significant boon to their cause.[45]   But
the introduction of direct African representation was
clearly an omen that his time on the Council was
limited, and, as a European, he was excluded from
active participation in the KAU. In the face of this
situation he advised the Chief Native Commissioner to
recommend to the Government that the word "Study" be
added to the Union's title, thus indicating that its
objective was more instructional than political.[46]
The association officers accepted this change. But
this agreement was clearly a placating tactic which
they saw as necessary if they were to obtain government approval. Two years later, after concern had
diminished, they returned to the original name.
Similarly, the newspaper was forced to drop the
phrase "A Political Monthly" from its mast-head and
to agree that the tone of its articles would be
"moderate to mild."[47]   After these alterations the
administration was reassured that the Union would not
threaten the colonial establishment and could be
safely sanctioned.

Despite Mathu's strong efforts to make the KAU
a genuinely colony-wide political organization, this
goal was never fully achieved. A number of factors
prevented this success, the most serious of which
was the omnipresent distrust between tribes. Among
the central officers, it had been noted, there was a
wide tribal representation. But this same multi-
tribalism did not extend to the rank-and-file. Only
in Central Province was there eventual success in establishing a broad general membership. In non-
Kikuyu areas, and especially among the Luo, opposition and/or apathy prevailed. The balance of correspondence to the press and the reports of district
officers on political rallies indicate this failure.
The Union was called by one Luo a "purely Bantu organization," and a separate Nilotic association was
sought.[48] District reports describe the campaign
for membership in non-Kikuyu areas variously as having "failed completely," having "negligible influence" and as being "met mainly with indifference."[49]
It is true that this evidence stems from colonial
sources. And while Mathu concedes the fact that
there was difficulty in extending membership outside
Central Province, he argues that the degree of this
failure was exaggerated in colonial reports as an
application of the tactic of "divide and rule."[50]
But whatever its extent, it is evident that there was
resistance to the KAU outside Central Province because of a feeling that it was Kikuyu dominated.

A second element of resistance came from members
of the legally proscribed Kikuyu Central Association
who considered the Union too conciliatory and wanted
to restore the KCA. The most vocal advocate of this
group was George Ndegwa, a Councilor of the Kiambu
Local Native Council, whose frustration over the administration's refusal to remove the ban on the KCA
led to his openly declaring himself the Association's
President in 1948, an action which resulted in his
imprisonment.[51] In Fort Hall District, KCA support
was especially strong, and the response there to the
KAU membership campaign was slow. Meetings were held,
but it was reported at the end of 1945 that "atten-
dances were not large, and there seemed to be little
enthusiasm for the Union in the District."[52] Initially one of the chief aspects of the KAU to which
KCA men reacted was the chairmanship of Harry Thuku
who since his release had not been especially critical of government policies concerning land. Yet in
1945 when Thuku resigned his position and was

replaced by James Gichuru, no remarkable rise in membership resulted.[53]

In 1946 a situation came about which Mathu was
able to use to strengthen the position of the Union
and stimulate the support of reluctant factions and
also to stabilize his personal relationship with
Jomo Kenyatta. This circumstance was the occurrence
of the Victory Parade in London to celebrate the conclusion of World War II. Each of the colonies sent
a delegation to these celebrations, and Mathu saw
this as an opportunity to aid his cause. The political position of the African could only be improved
through a united effort. The KAU was not successful
in its attempt to bring this about. A charismatic
leader, who could transcend any factional categoriz-
ing, was needed, and the only man likely to fill this
role was Kenyatta. Kenyatta was eager to return to
Kenya but there he would face prosecution by the
government for his membership in the KCA especially
since he had prominently participated in the 1945
Pan-African Congress at Manchester as KCA General
Secretary. But given the new British Labour Government and the holiday atmosphere of the celebrations,
Mathu anticipated the existence of a spirit of cle-
mency which might allow Kenyatta to return without
fear of arrest. The situation is best described by
Mathu himself:

> I suggested that we should get the
> Government to send us there, and I helped
> to draft the Royal Message and have it
> printed in gold, all my own suggestion.
> The then Chief Native Commissioner, he was
> called Colonel Merchant, was taken up by
> the idea. 'This is wonderful, Mathu's
> leading a royal delegation to England!'
> So I picked my men--chiefs, clergymen,
> teachers, people in business and govern-
> ment officials--a group of a dozen or so
> [there were seven]. We went, and we
> presented this Royal Address to the
> Secretary of State. . . . Now that was
> only a part of the story. The other part
> of the story . . . I wanted to go and get
> Kenyatta back. And I did. He couldn't
> return. There was a law against his return
> to Kenya . . . he had always wanted to re-
> turn but he can't [sic], and I couldn't
> rest this issue here. So I took all that

group to the Colonial Office to say how-do-
you-do to Mr. Creech Jones, the Secretary
of State then, and telling him that we have
also come to get your permission to get
Kenyatta back. . . .Before we went to the
Colonial Office, he [Kenyatta] had been to
our hotel. I had asked him to come there
to talk to these people, and I had asked
them to ask him whether he would like to
come back and he said: 'Of course I would
like to come back.' I didn't talk. I
only said that the chiefs would speak, and
the chiefs said: 'Well, of course we would
like to bring Kenyatta back, he is wanted
by everybody at home.' And we got Creech
Jones to telephone the Governor here to
lift the ban against Kenyatta. Governor
Mitchell, he had to, and we came the same
time. We came back together.[54]

The effect of Kenyatta's return on the KAU was
to remedy one difficulty but to bring another in its
place. He arrived in Kenya in September 1946 and in
June 1947 replaced Gichuru as KAU President. His
leadership of the Union encouraged the cooperation of
the KCA group. Membership did indeed grow, and the
Provincial Commissioner of Central Province reported
in that year that "for the first time Africans began
to hold vast meetings, numbering frequently as many
as 5,000 people."[55] But Kenyatta's presence was not
to be the panacea to the problem of cleavage among
Kenya's Africans. Membership outside Central Province continued to lag. Of more ultimate significance, as a result of the membership of the former
KCA men, a serious division began to grow within the
ranks of the association. The details of this development are best left as background to the emergence of Mau Mau.[56] But in the context of Mathu's
intention that Kenyatta might unite the African
people behind the Union, it must be noted that such
unity did not result in any real and sustained way.
Unity of this kind has never been a characteristic
of Kenya politics, and even today factionalism continues.

Despite its failure to develop into a country-
wide, homogeneous organization, the creation of the
KAU was a progressive achievement in Kenya's political advance. The KAU was the first organization to
seek to bring together the African people to work

directly with government representatives with the
purpose of stimulating political change through
legislative action.   It was the first African association to parallel the European Elector's Union and
the Asian East Africa Indian National Congress, and
in this sense it represented a new plateau in
African politics, indicative of the growing sophis-
tication of the African to the workings of the colonial political machine.   Put most simply it was the
legitimate precursor to the country's existing political parties.   It was clearly an innovative and constructive contribution to the development of nationalist politics among Kenya's Africans.

The specific issues with which Mathu was concerned in the Council are numerous and diverse, but
they can be viewed as elements of certain broader
areas of administration.   Even so categorized, however, the list is extensive, and a selective approach
must be employed to examine only the more significant
aspects of his representative career.   In virtually
every case the reform sought was compatible with his
political philosophy of multiracialism.   He applied
his efforts to achieve this type of social structure
in every possible field of legislation.

Mathu pursued these reforms from a most unpro-
pitious position in the Council.   The colony's
Governor in these years was Sir Philip Mitchell who
had replaced Moore in 1944.   Despite the local press
description of him as "a disciple of Sir Donald
Cameron," _Mitchell was typically paternalistic in
his views.[57]   He considered the concept of an independent Kenya controlled by Africans "fantastic."[58]
In a despatch to Creech Jones, he stated that:

> There is no "African nation," no purely
> African history or culture. . . . It is
> necessary to realize that history began
> for these African people about 1890, and
> that in the business in which we are
> engaged the unit of time is at present
> generations and not years.[59]

His task, he argued, was "to develop and civilize
this continent as part of what I may call Western
European civilization."[60]   Another dimension of his
attitude is indicated by the fact that at this time
he owned an extensive estate in South Africa and was
to purchase additional land in Kenya's highlands

before his administration had ended. But he cannot
be viewed completely as the settler's ally. If his
primary sympathies were in their camp, he was also
intent on sheltering the "lesser breeds" from ex-
ploitation. Quite simply, his position was characteristic of the dilemma of the traditional "dual
policy" which was the theoretical basis for Kenya's
development and which did not incorporate the possibility of an African-controlled, independent state.
Mitchell's position dominated the policy for the
official members of the Council who in 1944 held a
majority of 21 of the 40 seats. It was a position
practically manifested in a resistance to change but
tending to bend to the most vociferous force.

Even more obstructive to Mathu's efforts were
the European Elected Members of the Council. They
were 11 in 1944 and were supported in these years by
the recently formed Elector's Union. The Constitution of this association was representative of the
outlook of this group. Among its stated objectives
were:

> To work to safeguard the White Highlands
> as the permanent home of Europeans and their
> descendants in Kenya;

> To work to increase White Settlement in
> the Colony by every means possible.[61]

Their ultimate aim was to achieve self-government
with a settler-controlled Council. The most extreme
advocates of this policy were blatant racists. One
was Major A. G. Keyser, Member for Trans Nzoia, of
whom B. A. Ohanga states, "he would describe an
African in such a way that you would feel Africans
were really animals."[62] But even the most liberal
of these men were hardly allies of Mathu's cause.
S. V. Cooke, for example, the Member for the Coast
whom Mathu considers the least resistant of the
group, argued that to extend political power to the
African was in fact to give authority to men who
"need to examine the entrails of a goat before coming
to an important decision."[63] Nowhere among these representatives was there real support for strengthening the position of the African. Indeed, any success
by Mathu in this direction was viewed as a threat to
the European cause.

Mathu did find support on many issues from the

other non-European members of the Council, i.e., 5
Indian Elected Members and 1 Arab Elected Member.
But they composed a weak minority of the total membership, and some friction developed between Mathu
and the Asians because of his opposition to continued
Indian immigration. Generally, however, within the
Council these men were his best source of support.
If their backing was ineffectual in getting a measure
approved, it was a welcome boost to Mathu's morale,
given the hostile situation in which he had to function.

In such circumstances, it was almost predeter-
mined that a great many of Mathu's efforts to effect
constitutional change would end in defeat, yet his
persistence and ability to tolerate compromise did
produce a remarkable number of positive results.
Most of these gains required the application of the
"half a loaf" concept, but they were gains, nevertheless, and could be used as a launching point for more
thorough demands. It was not a case of acquiescing
to the official will of the Council. Rather it was
a matter of coping with the existing political
realities and continuing to press for change in spite
of them.

Educational Reform

Throughout his legislative career, Mathu predictably placed educational reform as his central
goal. "Education is the key to all progress,"[64] he
argued. "Without it no country in modern terms can
reach anywhere."[65] He dismissed the administration's
excuse that extensive expansion of educational services was too expensive. In his view such facilities
were so vital that their establishment should have
been provided "even at the expense of other services."[66] Like Booker T. Washington, he saw this
need in concrete terms, as the basis for advance in
specific fields:

> With a people well-trained in the science
> of agriculture, it is possible to improve
> our methods of agriculture and animal hus-
> bandry; with people who have been trained in
> the elements of building, it is possible to
> revolutionize our housing standards; with
> people trained in commerce, it is possible
> to build a successful trading community;

with people trained in medicine, it is
possible to raise the general standard of
health; with engineers and surveyors, it is
possible to have good roads and bridges.
And so on. Progress in any direction is
dependent on knowledge, education, training.67

It was a hard-nosed, practical outlook intended to
allow his people to function independently in a competitive world community.

As with most other issues on which he sought
change, on education Mathu presented an ideal situation which was his ultimate aim and, at the same
time, introduced many far less ambitious, specific
reforms. In keeping with his multiracial philosophy,
he sought a single system of schools open to all
races. "A school . . . should be a school for the
whole community, "he advised, "where all races come
together."68 But this was clearly an impossibility
in the circumstances at that time, and most of his
effort was directed toward accomplishing immediate
improvements within the existing structure. Of these
reforms, compulsory education was the most significant. It had been introduced for Europeans and for
Asians in urban centers in 1943. Mathu made repeated
attempts to have it extended to the African. Despite
Government objections that it would be too expensive,
he saw it as wholly feasible, and in 1946 he demanded
its introduction "next year, not 1952."69 These efforts proved unsuccessful, however, and only later,
near the end of his representative career, did he
succeed in getting the administration to undertake a
small pilot scheme of compulsory primary education
for Africans in Nairobi.70 In addition to this issue,
he campaigned for more secondary schools, increased
salaries for teachers, education of women, evening
classes for adults, more bursaries for study abroad,
recognition of Makerere degrees, and high posts for
Africans in the Department of Education. But none of
these efforts had any traceable immediate effect.

More directly influential than his attempts at
legislative reform of educational policy was Mathu's
function as critic of existing legislation. This
role had several aspects. In some cases he performed
as a kind of policeman, making sure that approved policy was carried out. A specific instance of this
was his pressuring to see that African primary and
agricultural schools were established in Embu and

Vihiga after funds had been provided for this purpose
in the Council.[71] At another level he worked through
the Fabian Colonial Bureau in London to see that
questions were raised in Parliament via Fabian M.P.S.
on issues such as Government scholarships for Kenya
students.[72] But perhaps most important was his criticism of the broad educational policy being applied
by the colonial administration. In 1946, for example
a comprehensive "Ten Year Plan for the Development
of African Education" was introduced which Mathu
immediately attacked as "niggardly" and as "a first
class example of inequality."[73] Although it cannot
be formally demonstrated, his outspoken opposition
to this plan was probably a primary cause for its
being replaced by more generous, though still highly
criticized legislation. Victories of this sort were
of a negative variety. They did not bring the same
satisfaction as, for example, the adoption of a constructive legislative proposal. But this role of a
critic was necessary, and, in the circumstances under which he was operating, it was one of the only
ways he could have real impact.

Ironically, while education was Mathu's prime
legislative concern, it was also the area in which he
had perhaps his most awkward Council experience. The
circumstances of this situation centered around his
membership in 1948 on an educational reform committee
with Leonard Beecher as chairman. The resulting
Beecher Report was in fact a new ten year plan for
African education. Mathu was the only African on the
committee, and he signed the report. Its provisions
were, indeed, somewhat better than the earlier plan.
They represented approximately a 25% increase in enrollment at most levels and a general upgrading of
standards.[74] But upon its publication it became
evident that certain core aspects of the report were
strongly opposed by the great majority of Africans.
The question of compulsory education, for example,
had been ignored. Also, there was popular disapproval of the recommendation that education remain in
the control of the missions. Finally, while the report placed a new emphasis on careful inspection of
standards, there was no provision that Africans would
be employed to do at least some of the inspecting.[75]
None of these criticisms were foreign to Mathu's educational policy. Nevertheless, in the spirit of compromise, he had approved it as a significant improvement over the earlier plan. The public rejection of the report was an embarrassment to his

position. The situation was most unwieldy. He had
helped to formulate it; now it was his responsibility,
in his capacity as leader of what was now a total of
four otherwise dissenting African representatives,
to express disapproval. He did, in fact, author a
written rejection of the report as spokesman for this
group.[76] But when the time came for debate on the
Council floor, he did not appear. Although the report was adopted, each of the African representatives
present at the debate spoke out against it.[77] The
episode was a trying one for Mathu and one case in
which his judgment was rejected by his people. It
represents a critical blunder on his leadership,
since the policies of this report endured throughout
the remainder of his LegCo career and the fact that
he had initially supported it was not forgotten by
his critics. The responsibility for its passage was
placed on his shoulders by his people, and he was
hard pressed to defend himself against such attack.
He had fluctuated badly in his position on this
issue, and, in the eyes of most Africans, compromised
too much.

National Registration and Kipande

The controversy in the Council over the proposal
to replace the long established kipande with a system
of national registration for all adult males was
among the longest and most emotional in LegCo history. In relation to Mathu, the developments relating to this question contain some of his most forceful and effective debate and most artful diplomacy.
In relation to the settler community, these developments include examples of the most pernicious racism
and inflexibility as well as one remarkable case of
a genuinely principled action. In the midst of this,
the official Government position emerges as indecis-
ive--seeking the least difficult solution. This trying issue vividly illustrates many of the most significant characteristics of the political climate of
these years.

The first stage in this dispute resulted from an
objection to the kipande system voiced by Mathu in
February 1946 during a debate over minor revision in
administering these permits. Mathu's objection led
to the Government's appointment of a Committee to review the issue in toto. Mathu sat on this Committee
with Francis Khamisi and five others.[78] His intention

was simply to have the system abolished with nothing
created in its place. A majority of the Committee
members rejected the kipande but recommended its replacement by a non-racial system of national registration via fingerprinting of all adult males.[79]
Mathu and Khamisi initially opposed this proposal and
submitted a minority statement calling for simple
abolition of the permits.[80]

    In 1947 the Committee's report was debated in
the Council, and a new ordinance was passed. At this
point Mathu and Khamisi agreed to go along with
national registration after they had "managed to ex-
tract assurance from the Government that a system of
registration will in toto be applicable to all races
in the Country" and that "registration would begin
with[the] European and Asian."[81] The Elected European Members were surprisingly acquiescent in this
debate. Two years later when a strong reaction developed, their spokesmen were unable to explain this
complacency and could only suggest "that pressure was
brought to bear which they were not strong enough to
resist."[82] But the tone of the 1947 debate gives no
indication of this. It is possible that part of
their passivity was produced by a sense of shame experienced when Mathu made public a letter he had received from a Nanyuki resident attacking him for his
role in this reform and describing him as "a nigger
. . . who mutters in LegCo all day."[83] In any case,
the debate was not volatile, and the new ordinance
was passed. Mathu's action had launched the developments leading to this passage, and the Chief Native
Commissioner credited him with "a personal triumph".[84]

    But complications ensued. The new ordinance was
due to come into force on May 16, 1949, and all fingerprinting was to have been completed by that time.
As this date drew near, however, an intense resistance developed in the European community. A Society
for Civil Liberties, formed to organize this opposition, published pamphlets to rally support. One of
these describes the adoption of national registration
as "only a form of appeasement to the sophisticated
or semi-literate Africans."   "The majority of
Africans have no objection to kipande," it argued,
"We are to be reduced to the level of the lowest
African in the Reserve."[85]

    The Government, apparently bewildered by this
situation, sought a solution by ignoring the pre-

scribed enforcement date and appointing a new Commission to explore a solution. This Commission was composed of one man, B. J. Glancy, a retired member of
the Indian Civil Service. His recommendations published in February 1950, devastated Mathu's accomplishments in the 1947 ordinance. Glancy advised
that registration be established but that an alternative to fingerprinting be provided for those able to
complete a written form in English. They were to
provide two identification photos. Secondly, he
urged the adoption of a voluntary kind of <u>kipande</u>
which would be attached to the registration cards of
Africans and would provide a record of employment.[86]
The holder was not obliged to keep this card, as he
had been in the past, but practical pressure from employers would obviously force most workers to do so.
In the debate, which immediately followed submission
of the report, Mathu's reaction to these proposals
was intense. As the debate drew on, however, he returned to his tactic of compromise and stated:

> I do know when it comes to the question
> to vote the non-Europeans will be united,
> but they will probably be voted down by the
> other members; but in order to give another
> chance I make another suggestion. If we
> are united and by the majority this Report
> is adopted, and Government amends the
> Registration of Persons Ordinance, I sug-
> gest this Report may not be acted upon for
> a period of three years, and during the
> three years the conscientious objectors to
> the fingerprinting should continue to be
> free from registration, but let the prin-
> cipal registrar go on registering all
> those people who think it is good, and if
> there is more than a handful at the end
> of three years who remain unfingerprinted,
> let us amend the law.[87]

But this proposal was ignored. Aware of how the
voting would go, he stayed away on the day when the
motion was passed.and remained absent for the rest of
the session. It is notable that, in this voting, one
European Elected Member, Derek Erskine, voted with
the Africans. He had spoken out strongly against
Glancy's recommendations, and as a result of the acceptance of the report, he resigned his seat in the
Council.

Although acceptance of the Glancy Report was a
tacit defeat for Mathu, the Government elected to ignore implementation with the result that neither registration nor kipande were enforced. There had been a
strong reaction from Africans and the Government chose
in action as the most viable way of avoiding the possibility of new strife. In February 1951 Major A. G.
Keyser presented a motion insisting that Glancy's recommendations be applied.[88] In the ensuing debate, exploiting the fear that a crisis might result, Mathu
responded by stating that "if this motion is passed
then we must question the genuineness of the Whites to
help Africans."[89] But the Government voted with the
non-European representatives to defeat the motion with
the stipulation that a new compromise registration
bill would follow. This bill, introduced just two
weeks later, accepted the 1947 provision for universal
registration by fingerprinting, but it maintained
Glancy's recommendation that a voluntary kipande be
introduced.[90] Because of this, Mathu opposed the
bill.[91] In the end, passage of the bill was a partial
defeat of Mathu's aim. Yet he had succeeded in remov-
ing the stigma of an identification system applying
solely to Africans. This achievement came only through
dogged persistence and forceful opposition to the
settlers' campaign.

Land Reform

Mathu ranked land reform just below education in
his priority concerns in LegCo and at the same time
today admits that he "hardly ever succeeded" in his
efforts in this regard.[92] The reason for this failure
is obvious. Because of its determination to maintain
a dominant European community in the colony with a
basis in agriculture, the Government was obviously
less receptive to demands for land reform than to any
other issue. Its commitment in these years was to
maintaining the status quo on the distribution of
land. The expansion of the area set aside specifically for settler farming halted with the Morris
Carter Land Commission Report in 1934. But territory
prescribed for settlement until this time remained a
private European domain with vast areas yet undeveloped, and the settlers were adamant that no encroach-
ment should be made on this acreage for African
reserves. The certain uproar that any attempt in this
direction would cause was another factor to dissuade
Government action. Maintenance of the highlands for

settlement was the one issue upon which no compromise
would be made.

Conversely Mathu realized that to the African
people it was this reform which was most vitally and
immediately sought. "It is on the land that the
African lives and it means everything to him," he
stated. "Without land the future of the African
people is doomed."[93] Steadily increasing population
pressure in the Reserve was producing a critical need
to expand. The ineffectiveness of Mathu's legislative
efforts to achieve this end was a precipitous cause
of Mau Mau.

Mathu's program for land reform in the Council
was multifaceted and aimed at furthering the realization of multiracialism. He sought the restoration of
at least part of the highland area to African ownership. "There are acres and acres of land lying in the
European areas, some of it undeveloped, some with one
person on it."[94] This land should be settled by
Africans. All such settlement, he argued, should be
done on an inter-tribal basis. This would not only
"relieve congestion" but would also "encourage
harmonious development among all the African peoples"
and diminish tribalism.[95] In connection with this,
the African tribal reserve system should be abolished,
and land should be individually owned as in European
areas. He emphasized the error in the administration's argument that communal ownership was an African
tradition and stated that an individual freehold
system existed among the Kikuyu "long before British
occupation."[96] Facetiously he proposed that a
communal structure might be acceptable if "done for
the country and not for one section of it.... it
should be not only among Africans but European farmers
too."[97] With regard to the agricultural activity on
African lands, Mathu urged that improvements be introduced. He sought removal of the restrictions on
the growth of cash crops, especially coffee and tea.[98]
He recommended Government financial assistance to
African farmers.[99] He called for the expansion of
instructional provisions to advance improved techniques of agricultural production.[100] He advocated
the creation of cooperative societies to allow the
African farmer a better opportunity to market his
goods.[101] And he called for the establishment of
irrigation schemes and roadways in the reserves as
additional benefits to production and marketing.[102]
But these suggestions met with little positive

response from the administration, and the economic
position of the African farmer remained static in
these years.

While the record of Mathu's LegCo speeches indicates that his pursuit of land reform was character-
istically patient, persistent and moderate in tone,
there are evidences that he was markedly frustrated
by his failure to make inroads. In 1947, although
normally prone to work within a policy-making body to
effect change, he resigned from a LegCo Commission on
African Resettlement because he "saw that the policy
was never to touch land in the Highlands for African
settlement."[103] Another indication of an emotional
response can be found in certain of his speeches at
KAU rallies which contain some of the most radical
statements of his career. In 1947 at about the time
of his resignation from the Resettlement Board, he
spoke at a Union meeting at Kakamega:

> We are the true inhabitants of Kenya.
> The land is ours completely. We were
> found here by the explorers. When God
> made man, he gave the people of each
> colour their own place to live, and we
> Africans were put here in Africa. It
> has been ours right from the word "go."[104]

Later, in 1951, he told a KAU gathering in Nairobi
that the African "would rather go naked and have his
land than be civilized."[105] Such speeches disturbed
the administration. After the latter statement, for
example, he was confronted by the Chief Secretary and
asked to explain his meaning.[106] But the rigidity of
the Government was producing this response--the
failure which confronted Mathu needed venting. Such
speeches provided this release and gave the administration warning that its refusal to grant reform would
not be tolerated.

Political and Representative Reform

From the beginning of his legislative career,
Mathu fought consistently to expand the African
position in the Council and to thwart settler attempts
at political domination. He had some success in both,
though his role more than in other areas of reform
must be viewed as one aspect in a broad African
campaign for political rights. From his seat in the

Council, he had a unique opportunity both to follow
the political schemes of the administration and
settlers and to campaign for a strengthening of the
African position. In these pursuits, he was tena-
ciously vocal.

Mathu's major goal in this area was to obtain an
increase in the number of African LegCo representatives. From the time of his appointment until the
declaration of the Emergency in 1952, the number was
expanded to six, and Mathu's efforts were an important factor in bringing about this increase. Predictably, he approached this issue in stages. He
began in 1945 by calling for the replacement of
Beecher with a second African representative.[107] This
aim was realized in 1947 when Beecher resigned and was
succeeded by a Luo, B.A. Ohanga. The following year
two more Africans were appointed in a general revision
of the legislative structure. Mathu called this increase "most welcome" but warned "that four seats will
not be sufficient, and that consideration should be
given in the near future to a higher number of
Africans."[108] The final increase of this period
occurred early in 1952 when two more African representatives joined LegCo. The legislation, of which
this increase was a part, was accompanied by the
appointment of Mathu to the Executive Council, where
he could participate with the Governor in policy-
making. These increases in the size of African representation mark a notable advance in furthering
their political position. Admittedly most of the men
appointed to these additional seats were weak and
showed little aggression. A simple examination of
the paucity of their involvement in debate gives
adequate evidence of this fact. Nevertheless the
victory was in winning the increase itself. As Mathu
notes: "It doesn't matter how they looked or whether
they were competent or not--it was a precedent."[109]
It was another step toward a greater African voice in
government.

In addition to helping advance African representation on the Council, Mathu endeavoured to open
lower level positions to his people. In 1947, for
example, he succeeded in winning government approval
of the appointment of Africans as Assistant District
Officers.[110] This was a significant step in the
Africanization of the provincial administration since
Assistant D. O.s normally graduated into higher posts.
Mathu sought such promotions and warned that to

educate an elite and deny them opportunities for fulfillment was dangerous business. "We should get these
people in the administration, give them higher posts,"
he argued, "and then they would feel they were part of
the machine to help run this country."[111] He also
campaigned for the advancement of African policemen
to the rank of Chief Inspector. On this issue the
Government tried placation by creating the position of
Senior Inspector, with a rank somewhat below Chief,
and making this subordinate post available to Africans.
While this was a minor defeat for Mathu, his reaction
is significant in that it illustrates his frustration:

> Sir, I do not think we can do very much
> more except to lodge this protest as
> vehemently as we can. We are in a minority
> and we will be outvoted but we would like to
> place on record that we consider that this is
> a grave injustice.... Africans always occupy
> subordinate positions in Government. 'Chief
> Inspector,' you say, 'will make him feel
> proud and swollen-headed, call him something
> lower.' That is the policy and that is the
> policy we attack and will continue to attack
> because it is not justified. And, Sir, the
> time has come when the Government must take
> the Africans into greater confidence, and
> the way to do it is to give them their right
> due.[112]

This intense response came at a time of growing violent protest and, although wholly speculative, it
is not unlikely that it was prompted by Mathu's realization of impending crisis and the knowledge that it
might be avoided if Government were to grant some
liberal reform.

Political reform was another area in which
Mathu's role as critic was significant for its tempering influence on administration policy which might
otherwise have yielded to settler efforts for self-
government. Throughout this period settler pressure
for this end steadily grew. The outcome of this
campaign might have been successful had it not been
for African reaction such as Mathu's criticism in
Council debate. The first crisis on this issue
occurred in 1945 when the Executive Council was opened
to European Elected Members. Mathu expressed his
suspicion that this was intended as "a start now with
self-government" and warned that "the African people

have fears, and Your Excellency and this Government will have to demonstrate that they are groundless by actual practical facts."[113] The legislation passed, however, with the support of the entire European membership, including Leonard Beecher.[114] In 1947 a second reform reduced the number of Official Members and created an unofficial majority. While there was no increase in the number of settler representatives at this time, and they could not control decision making, there was general anxiety among Africans that this reform might be merely the initial stage of a general plan to grant numerical dominance to the elected European bloc. Mathu responded to this possibility:

> Are we embarking definitely on self-government? If we are, I contend that it will be self-government of a minority in this country, and I should like to sound that as a warning....if that is the intention of His Majesty's Government in the United Kingdom, the attitude of Africans in this country would be entirely different from what it has been up to now.[115]

The revised legislative structure was adopted, but no increase in Elected European Member seats followed. The settlers launched a concerted campaign toward this end, introduced in 1949 with the publication of an Elector's Union pamphlet, "The Kenya Plan." But Mathu contained his criticism. This Kenya Plan had as its objectives, he charged, "the greatest possible executive control by the European community" as well as the establishment of "local government autonomy" for all areas outside "the native land units."[116] The proposals were "tantamount to a declaration of political war," and if they were accepted, the future of the African "would be doomed."[117] Mathu's protest, along with organized opposition by the KAU, was a significant factor in preventing the success of this scheme. There was a revision in the number of representatives in 1952, but there was no alteration in the racial balance and thus no benefit for the settler bloc. Mathu served as the leader in a holding action to prevent opposition gains, and in this role he was vigilant and effective.

Labor Reform

In his campaign to improve conditions for African
labor, Mathu often focused on broad issues rather than
specific reform. The core of his labor policy was the
establishment of a wholly integrated workforce. To
achieve this end, he recommended that Government
should take the initiative. "A Government department,
like the Public Works Department, should give the
lead," he stated, so that the commercial world, and
the various firms, could employ these Africans, as
the Public Works Department will have proved to them
that these fellows are capable of doing a very good
day's work."[118] He expressed the need for a change
in the colonial attitude toward employing African
labor. The existing mood, he argued, was "a psychology of disencouragement, a psychology of abuse."[119]
It was necessary to adopt a new confidence in the
African's ability to institute training programs for
their placement in skilled positions and to encourage
African employment on a wide scale.[120] He was especially concerned with the fate of returning soldiers
and repeatedly stressed the importance of their absorption into the economy.[121] He argued further that
these recommendations for increasing the African's
role in industry and commerce could be instituted only
if wages were increased. The standard wage, he argued,
was "absolutely below the subsistence level," and
until it was increased he felt "hesitant" about encouraging his people to seek employment.[122] Industry
had to abandon its tendency to see "the worker as a
machine," and had to appreciate his humanity. "His
wages and other conditions of work must be taken into
consideration with a view to enabling him to feel that
he is a human being."[123] Virtually all of these
appeals were aimed at affecting a general reorienta-
tion of the business community in favor of African
employment, and, because of this broad scope, it is
difficult to determine their success.

In his promotion of African business, Mathu
entered the realm of direct action. In 1945 he
sponsored a group of African merchants who sought
to purchase property for the establishment of a produce store in Nairobi's commercial section on Bazaar
Street. Until this time no African had attempted such
an endeavor. Mathu obtained Governor Mitchell's
approval of this purchase and by so doing established
a precedent for similar undertakings in the future.[124]

A second labor situation in which Mathu's direct involvement had decisive effect was in the resolution of the 1947 general strike in Mombasa. This was a complex incident in which there were rumors of the influence of Marxist ideology, and the involvement of black American seamen. In the support for this strike was expressed an unusual spirit of unity within the African community. Its origin was among railway and harbor employees, but it quickly gained momentum. By the time it actually began, January 13, 1947, it had grown into a general strike of virtually all Africans working in the Mombasa area. It was very well planned, with African leadership, a formal organizational structure called the African Worker's Federation, and a systematic method of collecting funds to keep it going. Its objective was to achieve a general wage increase for all African employees and improvements in living quarters for workers whose housing came with the job.[125] In the area of public transport especially, the strike had a debilitating effect. Ships waiting to be unloaded were glutting the ports, and rail and ferry services were cut. Prisoners and volunteers worked to fill essential needs, but the Government was clearly threatened and viewed this as a test of strength. "If there is any weakening on the part of the Government," wrote the Provincial Commissioner, "we British may as well pack up and go."[126]

The Government saw the strike as "illegal" and refused any discussion or negotiation of terms until work was resumed.[127] Pamphlets, scattered by airplane, declared this position and threatened prosecution of leaders. Hyde Clarke, Labour Commissioner, openly addressed the strikers and advised them that improvements would come only if the strike was ended. This effort had no effect. In a second attempt, Leonard Beecher, who was still on the Council, was flown to the coast to make a similar appeal. Like Hyde Clarke, he said that he "could do nothing to help" until work was resumed. He met with "downright refusal to return to work until wage increases [were made]."[128]

When the strike was into its tenth day, Mathu was sent to Mombasa by Government arrangement. He met with the leaders and attended a mass meeting of strikers "which gave him full authority to negotiate and bring settlement."[129] In this capacity, he met with Government officials and got their agreement to

institute wage increases "within three months."[130]
They agreed further that no reprisals would be taken
against the strike organizers and that employers would
be cautioned to take no action against their striking
workers. The following day, January 24, Mathu related
the terms. Work resumed on January 25, and a Government commission was appointed to institute the new
wage scale. Chege Kibachia, who led the strike,
commended Mathu for his "patience and perseverance."
"Our confidence in him made everything easy."[131] The
ultimate outcome of this incident was "an increase in
wages for nearly all workers in Kenya,"[132] and the
success of Mathu's role as intermediary had brought
about this peaceful resolution.

Social Reform

     Two aspects of social legislation were significant
concerns of Mathu in the Council. These were a desire
to expand and improve African social services and to
remove racial restrictions on free social movement.
Both objectives he persistently pursued.

     The social services on which he was most anxious
to institute reform were hospitals and prisons. He
sought an increase in hospital accommodations and
in out-patient dispensaries as well as expanded facilities for training of staff. He launched a Government
inquiry into the adequacy of medical services for
Africans in the Rift Valley[133] and supported a successful motion to license Makerere graduate who held
diplomas of medicine.[134] With regard to prisons,
Mathu argued for rehabilitation. "Crime," he stated,
"is essentially an aspect of social pathology." It
was necessary to look "into the social fabric" to find
its causes:

          Are we satisfied that our society pro-
     vides adequately for a decent living for
     all? I think the needs are not growing
     proportionately with the means. We are
     far from fulfilling our desire of "freedom
     from want." Our labour is still very
     cheap. Our housing conditions for labour,
     poor. Our education services inadequate.
     Our medical facilities insufficient. And
     so on. Instead of endeavouring all of us
     to improve these conditions for the African
     with a view to healing the colossal social

wounds, we seem to concern ourselves mainly
on the destructive side of things.[135]

Primarily, therefore, there had to be an effort at
creating a healthy community in which crime would be
a rarity. At the same time, existing prisons "should
aim at reforming the individual so as to make him as
useful a member of society as possible.[136] Mathu
raised this issued in Council on several occasions with
no immediate effect.[137] In related appeals, he
sought improved housing and an attack on the poverty
in the African reserves, but again no direct government action resulted.[138]

Mathu's campaign against racially exclusive
legislation extended into many areas. His one notable
success in this regard was in obtaining amendment of
the Native Authority Ordinance of 1937 which greatly
restricted the African's right to freedom of assembly.
The section of this ordinance which Mathu succeeded
in having repealed gave African headmen arbitrary
power to prohibit any public gathering in their area
on the grounds that it "might tend to be subversive
of peace and good order."[139] Mathu labelled this
"Darwinian legislation" and made a strong and pro-
phetic speech in the Council for its repeal. The
African tradition, he argued, was to hold meetings
"anywhere, everywhere, anytime, without restriction,"
and the effect of this legislation was seriously to
inhibit this "old freedom":

There is a feeling of hate and...inferi-
iority. They feel that they are not now
free; that they have to get permission; that
if they do meet they are prosecuted, they
are fired, they are imprisoned. There is
a feeling of frustration straight away.

Those who still cherish their former
freedom and common rights bitterly resent
having to apply for permission to meet
together for any purpose whatever.
Naturally, the law is evaded and they meet
at night behind locked doors with a sentry
outside; they meet in caves, in the depths
of banana groves or in swampy valleys away
from the habitations of their fellow men
to avoid detection. Yes, they meet together,
these "free, happy Africans" of His Majesty's
Colony of Kenya, like felons, with the

humiliating circumstances and methods
they are forced to adopt; whispering
and cursing the Europeans and their own
headmen who administer an oppressive and
unjustified Law. One day their repres-
sions are bound to burst out with the
usual unhappy consequences for all.

A society of any kind must be a functioning society. It must move, it must
live, but when there is a position like
this it leads to what I might call social
stagnation. In Kenya the position now
is that of complete social stagnation
in the African areas. All creative effort
is wasted; all constructive ideas are
rendered sterile in the end, with the
inevitable result that now the people
are sinking into a state of hopelessness
and bitterness.[140]

Prior to the LegCo speech, Mathu had written to the
Fabian Society to seek assistance through their
Parliamentary allies.[141] This appeal may have
brought some pressure on the Government. In any
case, he won his cause, and the Ordinance was amended
in January 1948.

The most obvious significance of this first
seven years of Mathu's legislative career lies in the
specific achievements of his efforts in the Council.
The founding of the KAU, the return of Kenyatta, the
establishment of national registration, the resolution
of the Mombasa strike and the amendment of the Native
Authority Ordinance are the most notable. While none
of these victories resulted in any profound advance
in the African's place in the colonial structure,
each brought some positive change and, in view of the
circumstances in which they were won, was a remarkable accomplishment.

In reference to Mathu's political philosophy,
these years have a second significance. They illustrate the practical application of his commitment to
the value of compromise and gradual advance. The
ideas assimilated in his years of study, travel and
teaching, he put to the test. It was a trying
process, riddled with frustration, and his ability to
persist was strengthened by his knowledge of the
historical basis for this approach.

Perhaps most notably, these years are also significant for the contribution they make to the broad
advance of African political independence. Mathu's
responsible leadership was clear proof to the reluctant administration that the African could perform effectively in the Council, and that his demands
for increased political power were practically justified. In the face of Mathu's obvious ability, it
was difficult for the Government to continue its
traditional characterization of the African as child-
like and in need of long years of colonial supervision. In the same regard, Mathu's criticism of
colonial policy in the Council was a useful deterrent
to the needless continuation of this rationale. Although he failed in many official efforts at reform,
his trenchant criticism of government policy certainly
had some impact on the conscience of the administration and stimulated a more careful evaluation of objectives. Conversely, his leadership provided a
foundation for the emergence of a modern structure
for African politics. The KAU was in actuality a
colony-wide African political party, the first in
Kenya's history. Its formulation of a platform and
its function as a supporting organization for the
African LegCo representatives created a system which
was to be maintained in later years. Similarly, the
broad aim of Mathu's LegCo efforts, the creation of
an integrated society devoid of racial barriers, was
to become the objective of the African dominated
government that came with independence. Here, too,
he established a foundation for later development.
His representation in these first seven years was a
signficant precursor for the future.

From a different perspective Mathu's representation in these years has a final significance as a
specific illustration of the factors responsible for
producing Mau Mau. Objectively the reforms which his
efforts achieved were small. While the attitude of
the colonial administration bore elements of paternalism and support for gradual Africanization over many
decades, its fundamental position stood behind sustained settler domination. The result was rigid
intransigence toward African demands especially on
the land issue over which Mau Mau specifically erupted. Mathu battled persistently to alter this situation but with little success. As an integral part
of the administration's system, he operated against
overwhelming odds. The quality and constancy of his
efforts could have little effect on instituting real

change. And without such change the parliamentary
approach was largely valuless. Mathu's representation has significance in its achievement of specific
minor reforms and, more importantly, as a foundation
for the defining of policies for utilization by later
African governments. But he was unable to bring
about major reform and alleviate the swelling frustration of his people which was imminently to be
given vent in the eruption of Mau Mau.

CHAPTER FIVE

LEGISLATIVE COUNCIL REPRESENTATION II--1952-1957

> We must restore law and order in this
> country, I entirely agree, but we must do
> our very best to cure the Kikuyu from the
> disease of land hunger, from ignorance by
> sound educational methods based on Chris-
> tianity; we must cure African homelessness
> in our urban areas; we must pay better
> wages so that workers can live decently
> as human beings; we must give the African
> real say and real responsibility in the
> affairs of his country.
>
> Eliud Mathu, 1952[1]

The change in Kenya's political climate resultant from the turn to violence by militant Africans
and the Declaration of the Emergency in October 1952,
placed Mathu in a precarious position as a representative of his people. Because the great majority of
the participants in Mau Mau[2] were Kikuyu, a growing
suspicion of all Kikuyu developed among the European
community, thus jeopardizing Mathu's credibility in
LegCo. At the same time, because he retained his
Council seat and directed his energies toward restor-
ing peace, Mathu lost the confidence of many of his
own people who supported the revolt. Despite these
difficulties, his commitment to change through constitutional reform endured. His efforts toward this
end were in fact intensified in these years. With
regard to Emergency legislation, he played a central
role. But in addition to the pursuit of this special
and temporary legislation, he continued his campaign
for reforms designed to improve his people's position
in the colony. Indeed he consistently emphasized the
cause and effect relationship between the need for
social, economic and political reform and the restoration of peace. For the whole of these Emergency
years, and until his electoral defeat in 1957, he
remained unquestionably the most aggressive and vocal
LegCo spokesman for African rights.

The determination of Mathu's position in relationship to Mau Mau, and more generally to the rapidly accelerating militant African politics of the
1950s, is a complex and multi-faceted process. For
the sake of perspective, it requires not only a
description of his own objectives, but a broader
analysis of the views of other influential individuals
and factions of the community. The range of attitudes
among Kenya's politically active Africans in this
volatile time was considerable, and within this
spectrum Mathu's position was virtually unique. At
the same time, and in spite of this variety of views,
there was surprising common agreement concerning the
basic goals of African political activity. Cleavages
occurred primarily because of disagreement over the
appropriate means to achieve these ends. The situation was complex, and an examination of some of its
aspects is essential for an understanding of Mathu's
activities during this second half of his representative career.

As background to this analysis, an examination
of a number of studies of African political leadership provides foundation for making some common sociological, psychological or cultural generalizations
about these men. A key element in most of these
works is the degree of accommodation by the African
to the western way of life. F. B. Welbourne labels
those who adapted most readily to the colonial culture as "Black Europeans" and describes them as
follows:

> They spoke English, wore European
> clothes. They adopted the material
> standards-- houses, motor cars, food
> and drink-- of the relatively wealthy
> Europeans who came to East Africa. They
> enjoyed European literature and music,
> even played cricket.[3]

The effect of these adjustments was fundamentally un-
satisfactory. "They became isolated from their
fellow Africans," Welbourne states, "without gaining
full acceptance by Europeans." Nevertheless they
often found a niche "through the Church or through
positions of authority in local government...which
provided all the satisfaction which they asked."[4]
Welbourne's description is that of a simple dichotomy
between those Africans who chose to accomodate themselves to the colonial culture and those who held to

their traditions. Among the Kikuyu in the 1950s this
breakdown needs qualification. As J. C. Carothers
points out in his 1954 text, "most Kikuyu men below
the age of...sixty years are persons who have lost
much of their conscious faith in native institutions
and beliefs"--due to their contact with and accommodation to the British presence. At the same time,
Carothers, too, describes a small elite of a "very
few" who had "acquired a solid foundation in the new
ways."[5] Thus a dichotomy did exist within Kikuyu
society, but unlike Welbourne's distinction between
the traditionalists and the colonized, it was a division between the great mass of men whose original
values had been shaken but not replaced by partial
accommodation and those who had successfully adapted
to a western life style. The crucial factor was each
individual's degree of accommodation and his ability
to find a satisfying existence within the colonial
setting.

The black elite of colonial Africa was by no
means a homogeneous community. Several categorizations of these men have been made,[6] the most applicable of which in relationship to late-colonial Kenya
is that of M. Semakula Kiwanuka.[7] This study is concerned with the political relationship between the
African elite and the colonial government and makes
three subdivisions along these lines. The first is
the Conservative group, composed mainly of chiefs who
were bound closely to collaborating with the colonial
regimes because, indeed, their chiefdoms often had
been created by and were upheld by colonial support.
Kiwanuka's second category is that of the Liberal Nationalists. "The Liberals," he states, "were constitutional and gradualist in their approach to the
independence of Africa....because of their education,
this group can rightly be described as intellectual in
its approach." Their objective was independence, but
they wanted to achieve it "without sacrificing cher-
ished European institutions and values."[8] The final
group in Kiwanuka's classification is the Radical
Nationalists. These were the militants who demanded
"self-government now," and who would not tolerate
compromise. They had no disagreement with the
Liberal's goal of independence but did reject their
gradualist tactics as Kiwanuka explains:

> The most outstanding difference between
> the Liberals and the Radicals was in the
> weapons they chose. The latter believed in

political organization, in the value of the
masses and in the countryside for that was
where the votes were. Another weapon chosen
by the Radicals but generally shunned by the
Liberals was inflamatory [sic] language.
For the moderates, theirs was the politics
of caution whereas the radicals did not shun
the "big lie." For this reason the Radicals
promised practically everything that would
win the support of the masses. Neither did
they shun violence. If violence was the
only weapon that would demonstrate African
determination to win independence, then
violence would be used.[9]

While Kiwanuka's study has relevance, there is
another factor that must also be considered in analyz-
ing African politics in colonial Kenya, i.e., race
consciousness. This concept is best defined by Colin
Legum as "the assertion by a people with recognizable
ethnical similarities of their own uniqueness; a
belief in their own special qualities, distinctions
and rights."[10] It was explicitly expressed in Africa
as early as 1881 by Dr. Edward Blyden,[11] and in more
recent times has been the foundation for the negritude
movement in the arts. Dr. B. A. Ogot considers it a
kind of "inverted racialism" which is fundamentally
destructive and probably transitory.[12] But however it
is judged, it clearly was a characteristic of many of
the black elite of colonial Kenya and is a useful
factor in distinguishing attitudes within this group.
Except in the case of the chiefs, where simple ex-
pediency explains their allegiance to the colonial
government, the degree of an individual's race consciousness was a telling characteristic in determining
his allegiance to a liberal or radical approach to
self-government. The "Black Europeans" were too
enmeshed in the English life-style to feel any strong
commitment to their "Africanness." The militants, on
the other hand, had not adopted colonial values to
this degree and were willing to tear down much of the
fabric of colonial culture to achieve their ends. As
a qualification of this thesis, it is important to
note that certain of these racially conscious militants were highly Anglicized and might easily have
been leaders in the liberal cause. But while they had
found intellectual satisfaction pursuing western culture, they had been thwarted by the colonial establishment and denied a meaningful position in the
community. Thus for these men, militancy and race

consciousness were defensive reactions more than positive assertions of genuine beliefs. In any case, the
degree of an individual's race consciousness was significant in deciding his political commitment at this
time.

How would Mathu be classified? If elaboration
were denied, his description would be that of a "Black
European" and a Liberal Nationalist with only a limited commitment to racial consciousness. But this is
merely an indicator of his character -- useful in a
general categorization of Kenya's black elite but
clearly requiring considerable expansion to achieve a
genuine portrayal of his role in pre-independence
politics. For while numerous others would fit this
same classification, Mathu was in fact virtually alone
in his position during these years. Description has
already been given of his political philosophy -- the
pragmatic change, constitutional reform, multiracialism and nonviolence.[13] It was an approach that
mirrors the liberal element in modern western societies
because Mathu was indeed largely a product of this
environment. He was perhaps the most westernized
black Kenyan of his day. He had found personal satisfaction in studying western culture, and he had
avoided the alienation and isolation of some others
who pursued this course because of the recognition
he found first at Alliance and then in the Council.
As a result, he wanted his people "to absorb the
new institutions from Britain"[14] and sought from the
government the right for them to share in these institutions at least on an equal basis with other races.
While he retained his respect for his native traditions,
e.g., lobola, circumcision, the relationship to the
land, and rejection descriptions of traditional
African society as primitive,[15] he preferred English
ways and sought to make them available indiscriminately to everyone in the Colony. Similarly, his
pursuit of self-government was a constitutional one
based on colonially-introduced LegCo procedures.

The outbreak of violence and the surge in militant
politics of the 1950s did not alter Mathu's attitude,
but it did create a difficult dilemma which he was
never able successfully to resolve. The leaders of
Mau Mau had a strong racial consciousness. Songs
connected with the movement consistently praised "the
House of Mumbi" and stated that "the Europeans will
be driven out," together with "those [Africans] who
say they prefer the Europeans."[16] Obviously this was

not compatible with Mathu's views, and this aspect of
the movement, together with its violence, prevented
him from giving it his support. At the same time, the
specific demands of Mau Mau were not unlike those for
which Mathu had been striving in the Council.   The
most crucial of these, and the catalyst which caused
this violence to erupt, was the administration's
intransigence on the land question.[17] The united
front presented by the settler community on this issue
via the 1949 publication of the Kenya Plan by their
Electors' Union, despite its rejection by the administration, was an important trigger to this development.
Land reform was among Mathu's primary objectives, and
the one on which he was least successful at getting
action.   Thus on this issue, as well as numerous
others advocated by radical spokesmen, Mathu was in
sympathy. As a result he was confronted with the
alternatives of either supporting the administration
and indirectly denouncing Mau Mau's goals, or joining
the movement and accepting its violent approach. He
could not in conscience clearly choose either and
throughout these years of necessity maintained a
middle course.

    Because of this dilemma confronting his poli-
tical sympathies, it is difficult to set down clearly
Mathu's place in the political spectrum of the 1950s
To describe him simply as a loyalist, as certain
writers have done,[18] would be a distortion. Indeed,
given the position of leadership which he held, it is
unlikely that he would have come through these years
alive had he taken a strong stand against Mau Mau.
Other prominent loyalists, such as Tom Mbotela and
Ambrose Ofafa, were assassinated, and Harry Thuku, who
supported the administration, was under constant guard
and was forced to go into hiding for a time.[19] Mathu
received a written death threat early in the Emergency[20] and years later was surprised and robbed in
his home by a forest gang.[21] But throughout these
years he lived with his family in Kiambu where
ambushes and violence were rampant, and he was never
attacked. Dame Margery Perham argues that this fact
is evidence enough that he was involved in some way
with Mau Mau.[22] Another indication of his divergence
with the loyalists, are the attacks that were made on
him by Africans who were clearly administration
supporters. The most notable of these was a criticism
in LegCo in 1954 by M. Okwirry, an official member.
After Mathu had questioned him on a statement he made
in a Council speech, Okwirry replied:

> If I were Mr. Mathu, I would not be in
> this hall at all. He is supposed to be a
> leader of the Kikuyu but who is he leading
> today? Is it those fellows in the forest
> or what?[23]

Mathu demanded and got an apology in this confronta-
tion, but it remains an indication of his estrangement
from the loyalist ranks. It might be argued that
these criticisms arose merely from Mathu's being
Kikuyu, but so too were fellow Council members,
Muchohi Gikonyo and Wanyutu Waweru, and neither of
them was so criticized. Gikonyo, in fact, was wounded
in an assassination attempt by a militant. It is more
likely that Mathu was criticized because his anti-Mau
Mau position was not sufficiently adamant. He attacked
the violence of the revolt and often led in instituting Emergency legislation when he felt it would
benefit his people and was not morely punitive. But
he never gave the government the uncritical support
necessary to place him distinctly in the loyalist
camp. To do this would have been to condemn his own
traditions. Loyalist literature is filled with such
denunciations. "If Europeans left the country today,"
writes one Kikuyu loyalist, "should we not go back to
the old tribal wars?"[24] Mathu had no strong racial
consciousness, but at the same time he did not reject
the African culture. He could not accept the loyalist's
total commitment to follow the administration's lead.

Just as Mathu's relationship with the loyalists
was ambiguous so too was his association with the
militants, but before this can be elaborated, it is
necessary to try to determine who these men were.
The key to this question lies in tracing developments
in the KAU between 1949 and 1953 when it was proscribed
by the administration. During these years the original moderate character of this organization was replaced by a new militant leadership. The transformation came in stages but began in 1949, the same year
that the settler community introduced their Kenya
Plan reasserting their intention to maintain European domination of the colony. In that year reports
began that former Kikuyu Central Association members
had infiltrated the Union, and, in the words of one
KAU member, "the Union was becoming a cloak for the
undercover activities of these people."[25] Perhaps
the most radical was Fred Kubai, a Kikuyu trade unionist earlier involved in the Mombasa General Strike.
Among his colleagues were Bildad Kaggia, Paul Ngei

and John Mungai. During 1950 the moderates, led by
Tom Mbotela, Ambrose Ofafa and Joseph Katithi, continued to dominate the organization. KAU resolutions
for that year consistently reflected the traditional
gradualist approach with such demands as an expansion
in African LegCo seats, African representation on the
Executive Council, and rejection of the Kenya Plan.[26]
But in spite of this moderate control, there were
repeated warnings, especially from Mbotela, of radical
activities carried out in the Union's name.[27] Perhaps
in part because of these warnings, an attempt was made
on Mbotela's life in March, and Kubai was one accused
of the crime. In late December of this same year a
major Union meeting was held in Nairobi. It was
dominated by Kenyatta, and, significantly, no African
MLC's attended. This was unusual, especially for a
Nairobi gathering, and the reason later given was that
the notice was too short.[28] This meeting may well
have marked a turning point in the Union's character.
Kenyatta described it as "one of the most important
ever held," and in his address to the members he
stated that an "ngoja kidogo (wait a while) policy
is no good because 'tomorrow never comes'."[29] From
this time on the influence of the radicals grew.

     The year 1951 was marked by crucial elections in
which the moderates were ousted everywhere. Kubai
was acquitted of the attack on Mbotela and became
Chairman of the Nairobi branch in June -- Mungai, Ngei
and Kaggia were his subordinate officers.[30] Earlier
James Beauttah, another militant, replaced Gideon
Macharia, who was supported by Mbotela, as Chairman of
the Fort Hall Branch.[31] These men then were the
leading militants with whom Mathu had contact, and
until their arrest and detention in October 1952, they
controlled the KAU.

     The details of their policy and the specifics of
their approach have been traced elsewhere and are
not directly relevant here.[33] It is sufficient to
note that they used oathing to link their cause with
the dissatisfied rural masses and they employed
violence as a tool. After their detention and until
three months before it was proscribed, the KAU continued to manifest an aggressive approach through the
leadership of Fanuel Odede and Joseph Murumbi. These
men were not of the same radical ilk as their immediate predecessors, but they did stress resolutions,
such as racial parity of representation in the Council
and common roll elections, which would lead automati-

cally to African domination of the colony's politics.
Odede was detained in April 1952, and the KAU's final
months were not notable. But by this time any militants were underground, and Mathu's relationship with
them was merely his position with regard to emergency
tactics--his position with regard to the phenomenon
of Mau Mau. The urban leaders with whom he had direct
contact had all been detained.

As a corollary to this description of radical
leadership, Kenyatta's role is special. It is generally agreed by most scholars that he was not the
driving force behind these men.[34] Rather he was
carried along by them and used as a symbol to attract
support especially in rural areas. Clearly this was
not without his consent. But his decision to accept
this role came almost reluctantly and was born more
out of frustration and even despair than out of any
positive involvement. He returned to Kenya intending
to find a responsible position from which he could
lead his people. This he was denied by the administration, and so he created his own realm at Githunguri. There is ample evidence that for several years
he followed a moderate line-- chiding his people for
idleness and wasted opportunity and supporting the
position of the liberals for constitutional reform.[35]
But his frustration grew. He was cut off from the
urbane comradeship and intellectual stimulation that
had become a vital part of his life-style in his long
sojourn abroad, and he saw little progress via the
gradualist tactics of the moderates. An interesting
insight into his situation is given by Peter Abrahams
who visited with him early in 1952. Abrahams describes
their first evening together at Githunguri:

> We sat on the veranda and drank steadily
> and in silence until we were both miserably,
> depressingly drunk.
>
> And then Kenyatta began to speak in a
> low, bitter voice of his frustration and
> of the isolated position in which he found
> himself. He had no friends. There was no
> one in the tribe who could give him the intel-
> lectual companionship that had become so
> important to him in his years in Europe.
> The things that were important to him--
> consequential conversation, the drink that
> represented a social activity rather than
> the intention to get drunk, the concept of

individualism, the inviolability of privacy--
all these were alien to the tribesmen in whose
midst he lived. So Kenyatta, the western man,
was driven in on himself and was forced to
assert himself in tribal terms. Only thus
would the tribesmen follow him and so give him
his position of power and importance as a
leader.36

Thus, he was driven to support the militants almost out
of desperation. The KAU meeting in Nairobi in December 1950 may well have been his declaration of this
decision. Even after this, however, there is evidence
of his reluctance to take this course. In October
1950 he and Mbiyu Koinange, with government approval,
launched the Kenya Citizen's Association--a kind of
forum intended to bring the entire Kenya community
together and end racial politics.37 Derek Erskine was
the organization's President, and Kenyatta took part
in its activities throughout 1951 and even into the
early part of 1952. But as was expressed in its statement of goals, the Association's objectives were "in
almost direct opposition to the whole trend of thinking and planning as it exists today,"38 and only the
most liberal members of the European community agreed
to take part. The effort failed. These various
evidences indicated, however, that Kenyatta did not
display the enthusiasm for radical politics shown by
younger men like Kubai. He was not the driving force
behind the movement.

Mathu's position in relationship to the militants
in some ways is not unlike Kenyatta's. Both were
highly westernized and at home with European values
and institutions. While their life styles differed,
both were African nationalists with the same basic
goals for Kenya's future, and both had a fundamental
objection to violent tactics. But Mathu had found
the satisfying social and professional niche which
Kenyatta was denied and which led the latter to support
the radicals. Mathu never took this step. To do so
would have not only violated his philosophy, but from
a practical point of view it would have meant the
loss of his Council seat and greatly diminished his
ability to influence administrative policy. As in his
association with the Pan-Africanists in London, this
fact was realized, respected and perhaps even taken
advantage of by the militants. James Beauttah, for
example, claims that of all the African MLC's in
office during the Emergency only Mathu was respected

by the radicals. He states further that they pur-
posely never sought his active involvement in their
activities because there was a kind of mutual understanding that he served as "a link" between them and
the administration.[39]

On two notable occasions Mathu's role as intermediary was public. The first of these was the
responsibility he was given by Kenyatta to provide
legal counsel for the Kapenguria trial.[40] Secondly,
with government approval, he met for a number of weeks
with representatives of the forest groups to negotiate
surrender terms.[41] But indications are that there
were other instances during the Emergency when he was
given information to convey to the administration from
the militants.[42] This is not to imply that he was an
ally in their cause. His cooperation in these situations was simply a manifestation of the dilemmas which
he was experiencing--his sympathy for their cause and
rejection of their tactics.

In addition to these occasions when he acted as
a liaison, Mathu also aided the militant cause indirectly early in its development by his silence
regarding their activities of which he was aware.[43]
J. F. Kanyua, who resigned from the KAU in 1950 because of the radical infiltration wrote in 1953 that:

> Mau Mau was developed within the ranks
> of the Kenya African Union. Those who have
> taken a leading part in the running of the
> Union since 1950 and who claim not to have
> been aware of this were either tools or
> fools.[44]

Mathu was not a Union officer, but he was in constant
touch with those who were. Yet, unlike Mbotela or
Ofafa, he never publicized his knowledge of militant
activities. Quite the contrary, in September 1952
while visiting England, he stated with Mbiyu Koinange:

> It has been claimed that there exists a
> secret organization called 'Mau Mau',
> allegedly supported by Kenya Africans, and
> especially by the Kikuyu. Up till now no
> convincing evidence has been produced by
> anybody to establish the existence of such
> an organization. The Kenya African Union
> and all African leaders have publicly
> denied any knowledge of it, and they have

also completely disassociated themselves
publicly from any subversive movements.
This was done, for example, at a recent
meeting at Kiambu attended by at least
30,000 Africans. It is interesting to
note that the word Mau Mau is not known in
any of the Kenya African languages. Should
it be proved, however, that such an organization does in fact exist, there is no
doubt that its significance can be only
minimal, and that its importance is being
exaggerated we fear for political and
economic reasons.[45]

In its details this statement was valid. There was
such a meeting in August at which Kenyatta denounced
Mau Mau and oathing. The phrase Mau Mau was of no
known African origin, and the specific existence of a
centralized organized subversive organization was also
questionable. Yet subversive activity was indeed
widespread at this time, and Mathu's statement denies
this. To accuse him of collaboration with the militants in his issuing this statement, as was later done
by the loyalists and Europeans, is to employ historical
hindsight. Mathu argues today that he minimized the
situation at this time because he did not anticipate
the oncoming violence and believed that to emphasize
these activities would indeed bring about unjustified
suppression of basic freedoms for his people.[46]
Nevertheless his underplaying the potential of the
situation and his earlier silence regarding KAU
activities did work to the advantage of the radical
cause. Despite his active participation and even
leadership in certain aspects of Emergency legislation
and his verbal attacks on the forest gangs, especially
in the earlier part of this period, there are links
and evidences of isolated cooperation between Mathu
and the militants.

A final group of Africans whose relationships
with Mathu during these years is significant is his
colleagues in the Council organized loosely as the
African Unofficial Members Organization. In 1952 the
number of this group was expanded from four to six,
and it remained so until the March 1957 election which
ended Mathu's Council career. Four of these representatives, i.e., W. Waweru, J. Tameno, M. Gikonyo and
J. Jeremiah, might be called backbenchers. Their
presence in LegCo was almost invisible. They introduced
no legislation and took little part in debate. Of the

others, B. A. Ohanga and W. W. Awori are most notable.
Both of these men were active participants in Council
activities throughout these years, and Ohanga became
the first African Minister (of Community Development)
in 1954. Except for a serious disagreement between
Mathu and Ohanga which resulted from this appointment
and which will be elaborated on in a later section,
relations between these men were generally agreeable.
They accepted Mathu's role as unofficial leader of
their organization, and all six usually voted as a
bloc. Nevertheless there were some significant differences in their points of view. The first involves
their relationship with the colonial community. Both
Awori and Ohanga were active in Moral Rearmament and
Capricorn Africa--organizations proposing multiracialism from different perspectives.[47] Mathu rejected such
membership--the former because it was "platitudinous"
and the latter "ingenuine."[48] Similarly all three
began as members of another multiracial organization,
the United Kenya Club, Mathu being one of its founders,
but he later resigned from this as well and describes
it as "humbug to divert us--eating with a few white
people."[49] The indication from this is that Awori
and Ohanga were more acquiescent to the administration.

This conclusion is supported by the second difference between them, i.e., their position in relationship to the Emergency and Kenya's future. While Mathu
supported much Emergency legislation, he always emphasized the need for constructive reforms to alleviate
the injustices which were its cause. The ultimate
reform in his view, especially in the 1950s, was
self-government. Neither Ohanga nor Awori took this
stand. With regard to the Emergency Ohanga argued
for "peace at any cost" and was willing to put off
reform legislation.[50] At the same time Awori criticized demands for self-government and focused solely
on economic and educational reform. He stated in 1955
that African dominated self-government at that time
would be equatable with giving "the steering wheel of
my car to a novice who has never learnt to drive."[51]
Thus it is clear that while there was general cooperation between African LegCo representatives, there
was basic differences between them, and Mathu was
not only the leader and most vocal of the group but
also the most critical of the administration.

Besides his relationship with these various
African elements, the effect of the Emergency on Mathu's
association with the European community is notable.

In toto there was a critical deterioration in this
relationship during these years. In part it was the
result of Mathu's refusal to support all aspects of
the administrations's Emergency policy. But this
factor was merely a consequence of the main cause.
Mathu was an articulate and aggressive critic of the
administration, and any means of limiting his effectiveness was welcome. The facts that he was Kikuyu
and unwilling to follow the government's lead on
Emergency legislation were welcome tools useful in
undermining his leadership. There were instances in
which his ethnic kinship with the rebels was recognized
as an asset by the government in their negotiating
efforts. As previously noted, he attended surrender
negotiations with gang representatives. He was the
only African on the Executive Council and for a time
was granted special permission to hold public meetings
in Kikuyu areas to organize the loyalists. There are
also cases when his position was publicly praised by
the European press. The most lavish praise came in
December 1952 after he had publicly denounced the
oathing and violence. The Mombasa Times stated that
this action "matches in boldness any deed performed
in the history of British rule in Africa." He was
described in this article as an "African patriot" dis-
playing "selfless courage."[52] Yet despite such endorse-
ments, the basic tenor of both settler and administration statements concerning Mathu was critical. Consistently he was accused of "hazy verbal evasion" and
clandestine support for the rebels.[53] Specifically
he was strongly criticized for his London statement
of September 1952 and even for having lost his gun to
the rebels when his house was raided. In March 1954
an unsuccessful motion was presented in the Council
by the settler representatives to ban Kikuyu representation "other than by chiefs or by Africans supported by local chiefs."[54] It was directed primarily
at Mathu. In this same year the appointment of the
first African Minister bypassed Mathu for the compli-
ant Ohanga. There is no doubt that, because his
stand against the rebels was not always consistent,
Mathu's status with the European community was significantly weakened.

The sum total of these various relationships
places Mathu in a unique position within Kenya's
African community in these years. His situation was
appreciated by one writer at the time who summarized
it as follows:

> Mathu has played a lone and difficult,
> not to say dangerous, hand. The settlers
> dislike him; the KAU resented his refusal
> to throw in his lot unreservedly with
> theirs; Mau Mau has threatened his life;
> and his own personal following is small.
> Yet he has an extraordinary kind of courage
> which has enabled him to retain his balance
> between conflicting forces which would have
> thrown almost anyone else.[55]

It did not throw him. But it did have a permanently
debilitating effect on his political leadership. He
was left with no real allies and with the paradoxical
stigma of having been both a loyalist and a revolutionary.

From October 1952 until at least late 1954, most
of Mathu's energies in the Council were directed at
legislation relating to the Emergency. In this role
he remained the most vocal not only of the African
representatives but perhaps of all the unofficial
Council members. He was also among the most successful at getting recommended legislation approved--some
of the major aspects of the administration's Emergency program were introduced by Mathu as Council
motions. Despite the personal unpopularity which
developed against him because of his refusal to accept
the government's hard line approach, he was able to
maintain an influential position on the Council and
steer this approach in a number of cases towards something more than merely a punitive purpose.

Unlike most members of the Council who viewed the
Emergency as an unprecedented crisis demanding harsh
reprisals, Mathu retained an historical prespective
and recommended his traditional solutions of constitutional reform and racial cooperation. This is not to
say that he regarded it as insignificant. On the
contrary, while many others saw it as a "return to
barbarism," he viewed it as a legitimate revolution
with numerous precedents in history. "The trouble we
have now is not the only trouble that human beings
have had in history," he argued. "The history of
Europe is the history of revolution."[56]

Despite this interpretation, he condemned the
revolt for its violence and experienced some guilt for
being of the same ehtnic background as its leaders.

"The Kikuyu have behaved abominably," he stated.   "I
have said that more than once, I have apologized in
this Council that I belong to such a people."[57]   Yet
he emphasized that his people must not be condemned en
masse and that the loyalist majority "have stood
against the Mau Mau more than anybody else."[58] He
stressed that, because of the particular plight of
these people, it was of special personal importance
to him that peace should be attained:

> It is my kith and kin who are suffering,
> who are dying by thousands as we have known
> in all ways, both from the security forces
> and from the Mau Mau end. There could be no
> other person who can feel more hurt by any
> measure that does not end this Emergency
> quickly than myself.[59]

The underlying cause of the revolt, in Mathu's
view, was the refusal of the European community to
embrace genuine multiracialism. Settler intransigence,
and the administration's failure to act against it,
had exacerbated African militants to violence.[60] The
solution, therefore, remained the adoption of cooperation between communities. He stated this in the
Council shortly after the Emergency was declared:

> I want to emphasize the words "as
> partners" because I think it is the positive
> principle that I am trying to impress on
> this Council-- that it must be a joint
> effort. The African and the European in the
> African areas in particular must work as
> partners for the good of the whole country:
> but if we fail...we shall have Africans
> feeling that they do not belong to the
> administration of this country: and the
> tendency would be for them to be a prey for
> those who want them to be subversive, and
> who want not peace, but violence.[61]

The means to this cooperative relationship was
extensive constitutional reform directed at improving
the social, economic and political position of the
African--the same reforms for which he had been working
before the violence began.[62] It was this aspect of
his approach to the Emergency that the administration
especially opposed. Government leaders argued, with
strong settler support, that to grant such reforms
in the midst of the Emergency would be to reward

violence with the result that the revolt would inten-
sify.[63] Instead they held that the restoration of
peace could be achieved only by military suppression.[64]
Thus much of the legislation debated in LegCo from
early 1952, months before the state of emergency was
formally declared, until late 1954 mirrored this view.
In these circumstances, Mathu's main role was to strive
to temper the harsher proposals and to introduce temporary measures relating specifically to Emergency procedures which he felt would have a constructive effect.

In his efforts at reducing the severity of
punitive legislation against the Kikuyu, Mathu had
little success. Many of these measures were adopted
in the months prior to the Emergency's declaration as
militant activity in Central Province became more
apparent. A 1930 Ordinance for collective punishment
was applied against demonstrations in Fort Hall in
February 1952. This was followed in July by new
measures including clan fines, simplified trial procedures, expanded requirements for identity certificates, and restrictions on the African Press. As this
wave of legislation began Mathu warned:

> In the case of emergency there is nothing
> to prevent us [from] using all the powers we
> have at our disposal. But to become so ruth-
> less...in my view is not going to solve the
> problem at all. In fact, it is going to
> worsen the situation.[65]

He described the administration's approach in these
matters as "patterned off of Machiavelli" and as "the
precursor of Mussolini and Hitler."[66] But his arguments had no impact, and all these proposals became
law. Realizing that this would happen, Mathu resorted
to his pragmatic tactic and tried to have this legislation apply only to Kikuyu areas. Recalling his
"half a loaf" argument, he stated: "If this principle
which we have opposed vehemently is to operate, we
would prefer it if it were operated in a restricted
area."[67] Nevertheless this compromise effort also
failed. In relationship to the reviving of the
collective punishment ordinance in Fort Hall, Mathu
introduced his own motion calling it "inequitable" and
requesting the government "only to punish the actual
offenders in appropriate cases."[68] He saw the application of the principle of collective punishment solely
against Africans as "indisputably racial" and rejected the sociological argument that it reflected

the communalism of African life.[69] This motion, however, was similarly defeated, and collective punishment endured as a common practice throughout the
Emergency. Thus Mathu's attempts to modify punitive
legislation against his people had no apparent success.

Where he did succeed was in a number of positive
recommendations for conducting certain aspects of
the Emergency, especially those concerned with the
treatment of the loyalists. He proposed four successful motions which were significant in easing his
people's plight. The broadest, and perhaps least
significant, of the four was a request from the administration for a clear statement of its policy toward
this group. His belief in the need for such statement is evident from the text of this motion which
read:

> Whereas statements have been made that no
> Kikuyu can be trusted and whereas other
> statements have also been made that the
> fight against Mau Mau shall be finished by
> the Kikuyu themselves and whereas the Kikuyu
> in large numbers are fighting, dying and
> losing their property including schools and
> churches in the battle on the side of law
> and order;
>
> Be it resolved that this Council requests
> the government to make a statement now in
> unequivocal terms of its present and future
> attitude toward the Kikuyu loyalists.[70]

The motion was carried, and reassurance by the administration of its confidence in the genuineness of
Kikuyu loyalists followed. It had no concrete effect,
but it did at least officially record a recognition by
the administration of the distinction between the
Kikuyu majority and the forest gangs.

More meaningful in terms of practical results was
the establishment of a Displaced Kikuyu Relief Committee to organize the resettlement of the masses of
Kikuyu labor evicted from the settler areas for
security reasons. This Committee was proposed by
Mathu in a Council motion in early 1953[71] and was
accepted by the Government. It brought about a systematic program of resettlement to replace the former
policy of collecting people at random and transporting
them indiscriminately and without previous provision

to the reserve. The Relief Committee provided food,
land, secondary transportation and medical services
and set up District Committees to work out detailed
arrangements at the local level. It was a clear
improvement over the previous chaotic situation.

Another of Mathu's successful motions which
directly benefited the loyalists and reduced the cost
of policing the countryside was his recommendation to
establish a Kikuyu Home Guard to patrol the reserve
areas and African locations.[72] Besides introducing
this proposal, Mathu, in conjunction with area herds-
men, took personal responsibility for the selection of
volunteers in his own Kiambu reserve.[73] Those selected
were neither paid nor armed, although Mathu tried to
win for them both these rights.[74] Nevertheless, they
were effective enough to be described by one settler
as "the eyes and ears of the Government."[75] Besides
aiding in the preservation of order, the establishment
of this force helped to advance confidence in Kikuyu
loyalty. This establishment also created a police
force with a better understanding of the community and
a less arbitrary attitude in maintaining the peace.

A final motion introduced by Mathu for the
benefit of the loyalists was only a partial success.
This was a proposal that "the Government should leave
the Africans to form and operate constitutionally a
colony-wide political organization."[76] It was one of
his favorite issues and was presented one month after
the proscription of the KAU. In his argument he
stressed his vital belief that the suppression of the
basic freedoms automatically produces subversion:

> When a people, like the Africans, who
> are six million strong, are left without an
> adequate and well-organized outlet for their
> political aspirations, that state of affairs
> will encourage those who are evil-minded and
> who want to go underground and we will have
> a double <u>Mau Mau</u> in the years to come, and
> we do feel, sir, that it is right and proper
> and it is a democratic right of the people
> in a British Colony, that they should be
> given encouragement to form, and operate, in
> a constitutional manner, an organization
> through which they can express their aspira-
> tions to the State.[77]

As with the establishment of the KAU, he insisted that

such an organization be multitribal--"that the African
people should have one united voice."[78] When he saw
that this was opposed, he sought partial success by
suggesting that the Kikuyu be excluded for the duration of the Emergency.[79] But this too was rejected,
and the most the Government would agree to was to
accept the original motion with the addition of the
phrase "that the present time is not opportune."[80]
Despite his dissatisfaction with this amendment, Mathu
had no choice but to accept it. It was first allowed
to operate, and then only on a local basis, in mid-
1955. This motion, along with the three others noted,
represents one of the contributions Mathu made to
improving the position of his people during the
Emergency.

A second area of Emergency legislation in which
Mathu was active concerned the conditions of the
detainees. While he introduced no motions in this
regard, he was active in debate arguing for humane
conditions in the camps and programs for rehabilitation. "If we do not want these people to commit a
crime again, to be antisocial when they are given
liberty," he argued, "we should equip them in such a
way that when they come out, they can earn a decent,
honest livelihood."[81] Some rehabilitant facilities
were provided by the Government, but the "hard core"
element was denied their use. Mathu criticized this
distinction and stated, "If these are the very bad
ones, surely they are the ones who want rehabili-
tating."[82] Consistent with his general philosophy
about the Emergency and its causes, he held that the
detention camps should not serve primarily as penal
institutions but as centers where individuals could be
restored productively to society.

Despite his generally liberal position on most
Emergency issues, there is one instance in which Mathu
took a hard line. It is merely a statement made in
debate as part of a borad budget speech, but it is so
intense and seemingly atypical of his position that it
is of special note. He stated:

If I saw "General Tanganyika" I would not
negotiate, I would shoot him on sight first
and then try and negotiate with him dead....
We must not dilly-dally in Nairobi and Thika
and other places, but we must go into the
forest whole hog and get these fellows shot
dead, bring the bodies and then burn them in

Nairobi. That is the only thing we can
do.[83]

Any explanation for the basis for this outburst must
be speculative. It came in mid-1954 and may merely
have been a manisfestation of frustration over the
inability to end the violence. In addition it is
probable that it was also an inverted argument to the
administration to reduce their attack on the locations
and open reserves and recognize the forests as the
area of focus. Viewed this way it is consistent with
his philosophy and is simply a dramatic presentation
of an argument intended to alleviate the suffering in
the reserves which he presented less forcibly at other
times.[84] Nevertheless it was harsh language and un-
characteristic of his traditional approach.

While the event of the Emergency seriously altered
the course of Mathu's legislative campaign and caused
the interruption of much of his fundamental program
of reform, it was not an unproductive time for him in
dealing with the particular aspects of this situation.
His efforts were important in aiding the loyalist
cause and also acted less successfully as a kind of
conscience for the administration, forcing it to consider the arbitrary character of many of its measures
and to reflect on their consequences. To a great
extent, he was virtually a lone wolf in this role.
Yet he remained highly vocal and consistent in his
cause despite its effect on his relationship with both
the Government and the revolutionaries.

Given his conviction that the means to ending
Kenya's violence was extensive legislative reform cul-
minating in true multiracialism, it was essential that
Mathu continue to pressure for these reforms in the
midst of the Emergency despite the administration's
intransigence. His basic rationale to the Government
in this endeavor was much like his argument for freedom of assembly--that it would strengthen the
African's confidence in the administration's good
faith and hence create a positive atmosphere and the
restoration of peace. In early 1954, for example, he
stated:

What are the loyalists going to do, what
is their objective if they know there is no
educational development, no agricultural
development, no medical services --the
loyalist is not going to fight because all

the things he wants-- in fact he is going
to say, 'what am I fighting for? Am I
fighting for something which is on paper,
that in future something will come for the
loyalist?' He loses heart and, therefore,
I say if we are to end the Emergency we
have got to get away from the idea that if
we do something good, something exceptional,
in the Kikuyu land we are appeasing the
Kikuyu tribe. We are not appeasing the
Kikuyu tribe-- we are doing the proper thing
to end the Emergency quickly....I think we
should encourage the Kikuyu to fight his
battle by doing positive constructive work
in Kikuyuland.[85]

As previously noted, the administration rejected this
argument. But Mathu never abandoned it even though
it brought him little success.

The specific areas of reform and the particular
changes sought by him in these years were indistinguishable from those pursued in his pre-Emergency
career, e.g., education, legislative representation,
land and agricultural reform, rights of labor, and
social welfare. The repetitiveness of his requests
for a number of changes was so constant that he saw
it as almost humorous. Demands for compulsory education for Africans, paved roads in the reserves,
appointment of Africans to superior Civil Service
posts, and removal of the restrictions on African
production of coffee, for example, he began to call
his "hardy annuals."[86] There were instances, nonetheless, when weariness set in, and he would question the
value of his presence in the Council. After one of
his motions had been rejected, for example, he stated
that perhaps it would be best if he were "to walk out
of this Legislative Council and then the Government
and those who supported them in this motion would feel
happier in running the affairs of this country."[87]
Overall, however, his faith in the legislative process
and in his own usefulness endured. On one occasion,
for example, after making an oft-repeated plea for
granting the African farmer the right to freely grow
coffee, he stated:

I repeated an example I have quoted here
many times, until I think it has tired many
honorable members, but I should like to say
that I do not apologize for repeating this

because my experience has been in matters
such as this in the Legislative Council one
has to persist over a number of years to
convince a person like the Director of
Agriculture that what one says, one says
with conviction.[88]

On this basis he continued his campaign despite the
paucity of success.

The one area of reform in which Mathu did score
a notable victory in this second half of his representative career was that of education, and there is
a special significance in this achievement. Education
had always been the field in which he felt action was
most needed. He persistently pushed for an expansion
of schools for his people. His success here came as
one of the final measures of the last session of the
Council of which he was a member, and it is the final
piece of legislation with which he was involved.[89]
Though it certainly was not foreseen by him as such,
it was nevertheless an appropriate conclusion to his
Council career. In its specifics it was also typical
of most of the measures with which he dealt. It was
an issue, that of compulsory African education, for
which he had argued since the first years in LegCo[90]
and which he deemed as one of the "hardy annuals."
When he did finally succeed in winning the administration's approval, it was a partial victory, the
product of compromise. The motion which he introduced
and to which the Government agreed was "to introduce
compulsory primary education for African children in
Nairobi."[91] It was limited, therefore, only to the
primary level and to this one area of Nairobi. But
at least the principle of compulsory education for his
people had finally been accepted, and there was an
understanding that it would later spread to lesser
towns and ultimately throughout the country.[92] It was
received by the African press as a major break-
through,[93] and Mathu received considerable acclaim
for this accomplishment.

In a second area, that of reform in the number
and selection process for LegCo representatives,
changes which would have profound consequences
occurred in these years, and while Mathu had no direct
role in initiating them, they significantly affected
his position. All these changes, from the increase in
the number of representatives in 1952 to the institution of a policy of direct elections established in

1956, were the result of the action of Whitehall. The
attitude of the Colonial Office concerning Mau Mau
differed from that of the local administration. Oliver
Lyttleton (Lord Chandos), Colonial Secretary, argued
that constitutional reform must accompany the military
effort.[94] The resulting alterations in the Council's
composition directly affected Mathu. Lyttleton visited
Kenya in March 1954 to discuss reform. Mathu joined
with A. B. Patel, the principal Asian leader, to use
this opportunity to dramatize their campaign for expanded non-European representation. They introduced
a motion "to enlarge Asian, African and Arab unofficial
membership" as well as their representation on the
Executive Council.[95] The motion was defeated, as they
must have expected, but it was referred to Lyttleton's
attention. The following week the Colonial Secretary
announced his proposals for a new constitution, the
principal aspects of which were the establishment of
one African and two Asian ministries and balancing
these three appointments with three European ministerial posts from the ranks of their unofficial membership so that the principle of "European parity" was
preserved. It is also notable that the single African
ministry, that of Community Development, was a minor
post which dealt only with matters relating to Africans.

The declared basis for Lyttleton's constitution
was multiracialism, but his conception of this principle was fundamentally different from Mathu's and
incorporated a system of representative balance
(parity) between Europeans and the combined non-European communities. Mathu saw multiracialism more
straightforwardly as simple cooperation between races
under a system in which ability would be the sole
qualifying determinant.[96] This was his ultimate objective, but in the meantime, while he was striving
in this direction, he accepted compromise when it
offered his people some positive advantage.

In the case of Lyttleton's reforms, however, he
did not initially take this course. He rejected them
as tokenism and planned a resistance effort. He resigned his seat on the Executive Council and attempted
to organize a boycott of the Council by the unofficial
African members which, had it worked, might have had
a similar effect to that staged in 1957 over the same
issues. In the early stages it seemed that he might
succeed. The African Unofficial Members issued a
public rejection of the plan:

We do not consider that the aim and objects of a multiracial society in Kenya can
be achieved by providing only one seat for
Africans in the proposed Council of
Ministers with a total of 16 seats.

The endeavours of one person, however
strong, have no chance of influencing
public policy. We had proposed three
ministers with portfolios, but during the
negotiations with the Secretary of State
we were prepared as a compromise to accept
two ministers with portfolios, or at least
one with and one without portfolio. This
was rejected.... the one portfolio, that of
Community Development, proposed for the
African Minister is so small that it can
hardly inspire confidence among African
communities in the new Government.[97]

All six members agreed to this statement, but
this unity soon collapsed. Mathu, despite his
seniority and obvious leadership of the African group,
was bypassed by the administration in its selection of
a candidate for the ministerial vancancy. His being
Kikuyu and less than enthusiastic about much of the
Emergency program, as well as his organization of the
AUMO against this constitution were certainly the
reasons for this. Instead Governor Baring sent the
Chief Native Commissioner in his private plane to
Kisumu to offer the post to Ohanga.[98] This proved
successful, and Ohanga broke from his original position and accepted the appointment. A second unofficial
African member, James Jeremiah, followed his lead and
accepted a post of ministerial rank as a Parliamentary
Under Secretary.[99] With these acceptances the new
constitution could go into effect, and the attempted
boycott collapsed. Mathu concluded that continued
resistance would be fruitless and resumed his seat,
although he did not return to the Executive Council.

A second aspect of Lytlleton's reforms was the
appointment of a commission to determine "the best
method of choosing African members of the Legislative
Council."[100] The resultant report, issued in January
1956 by W. F. Coutts, recommended a direct election
procedure with a qualitative voting requirement based
on age, education and position.[101] In the subsequent
debate, Mathu argued unsuccessfully to abandon these
restrictions. In defense of this argument, he cited

the traditionalist Suk, "men of tremendous common sense" who would be excluded by Coutts's qualifications. "They are the most ingenious, shrewd community that we have," he stated. "Even some of them are better than the university graduates in weighing and judging facts which are put before them."[102] But the Council approved the Report, and the election which was to end Mathu's representative career was set for March of the following year.

On a second objective he raised to this report, however, the Government compromised in his favour. This concerned the number of representatives to be chosen in these elections. Coutts recommended that the existing number of six be maintained. Mathu called for ten. The Government recognized his argument and agreed to raise the number to eight.[103] In all the debates on this new constitution, Mathu had taken an opposing position, but he stood virtually alone, and with this one exception, could not rally sufficient support to allow his efforts to succeed.

Of the numerous other measures which he proposed in these years, there were four of relatively minor note which were accepted. The first was a token grant by the administration to allow African farmers to grow a maximum of one hundred coffee trees on their shambas.[104] Mathu's goal was unlimited production of all cash crops and consistently after this limited success he continued to argue for this right. A second success was winning the removal of restrictions on the purchase and consumption of liquor by Africans.[105] As in most of his endeavors, this victory came only after much prodding and repetitious debate. He also succeeded in getting the Government to pay cash compensations to Sudanese farmers who had been displaced by the construction of railroad lines through their land.[106] Finally, he persuaded the Government to agree to the appointment of an African to the Pyrethrum Board, an agency of the Ministry of Agriculture which traditionally had wholly British members.[107] All of these were minor victories, but they are significant in that they illustrate the wide expanse of issues in which Mathu sought change. They were the "drops of water heating on a rock" which he believed would finally "make a hole."

Except perhaps for the success of his education motion, Mathu's campaign for multiracialism through constitutional reform suffered badly during the

Emergency years. In the face of revolt the administration was especially reluctant to consider his reforms, and his persistence at proposing them merely
annoyed them. They became less receptive to his
views, and his relationship with them noticeably
suffered. Nevertheless he persevered and, until the
end of his career, remained positive about the value
of his efforts.

Mathu's position in 1956 was quite different from
what it had been in 1952. The violent campaign for
change by a portion of his people had created for
him an impossible dilemma in which he was left with no
real ally. He condemned the punitive approach of the
administration against the revolt and was able to
bring some aid to the loyalists. But his attempts at
constructive reform of more permanent value were consistently defeated. Because of his persistence in
these efforts, as well as his being Kikuyu and un-
committed to an all out military campaign against the
militants, the administration soured against him. At
the same time his criticism of the violence employed
by the militants lost him the support of many of his
people. The effect of this situation was to be one
factor in his political demise in the 1957 election.

CHAPTER SIX

ELECTORAL DEFEAT--1957-1958

The Meru vote in Central Province is very vital.

Dick G. Gachui, 1957[1]

Mathu's fatal flaw was that he was a moderate.

James S. Smith, 1970[2]

Taken together the variety of factors responsible
for Mathu's defeat in the elections of 1957 and 1958
have the elements of a classical tragedy. It was not
his political philosophy that was responsible for his
failure but rather a combination of external circumstances which a dramatist might depict as a conspiracy
of the gods or as the unfolding of fate. Intrigue
has its place here, exploiting the emotions and preju-
dices of the people for a calculated end; so too has
generation rivalry and the blanket categorization of
the old order as passe. Certainly Mathu's role was
more than passive in bringing about his demise, but
here too fate was a key factor. In the face of the
particular political climate of the time, his legislative career was looked on not as useful experience
but as evidence of inability to get results. In these
circumstances he was condemned by his past. His objectives were misrepresented, but considering their
context this was virtually inevitable. He was largely
a victim of fate, and his defeat was mainly due to
factors which he had no real ability to control.

The primary cause of Mathu's defeat in the March
1957 election was the omnipresent tribalism of the
African electorate and the skill with which it was
exploited by a district official who sought this
defeat. Had this one factor been absent and all of
the other elements of the situation remained, there
is no doubt that he would have retained his seat.
But this was the first, and in a practical sense the

most crucial, of a series of circumstances responsible
for Mathu's political collapse.

Discounting this tribal prejudice, were a political analyst to have calculated Mathu's basic political potential at the time of this election, his
findings would have been inconclusive. By this time
there were a number of Central Province Africans,
e.g., Charles Njonjo, Gikonyo Kiano, Jeremiah Nyagah,
Bernard Mate, who had acquired outstanding educational
credentials, so that this was no longer Mathu's unique
domain. At the same time, none of these younger men
had any real political experience. Mathu's long
representative career was in some ways a political
asset. He was called baha mwenye nyumba (father of
the house) by many of his people3 and during the
campaign was repeatedly praised in the African press
for his leadership.4 It was also fortuitous that he
had success in the Council in 1956 with several of
his reform efforts, e.g., education, liquor purchase,
increased African LegCo representation, African membership on the Pyrethrum Board, and this brought him
favorable publicity. Unquestionably he was the most
dynamic of the African representatives and, in the
words of one analyst, was "the only one who can really
match the other races in debate."5 Yet his membership
on the Council was not wholly beneficial to his
campaign. It associated him with the old order at a
time when there was a strong innovative atmosphere,
an enthusiasm for change. But this was not a crucial
factor in the 1957 election and would only become
significant the following year. More relevant to this
first election was the effect of his Council position
toward the Emergency. Because of his middle road
policy on this issue, he lost support from both the
loyalists and those who sympathies were with the
revolt. More important, however, in relationship to
the practical business of getting elected, he lost the
full confidence of the Government. Because this was
the first direct African election and there were
restrictions on the right to vote, a thorough administrative campaign to enroll qualified voters was required. This was the immediate responsibility of
district officials, and since there was no precedent,
individual interpretations of the new law's stipula-
tions were inevitable. This was particularly true
in Central Province where there was an additional
requirement of a loyalty certificate issued by the
district officers. As voter registration progressed,
it was evident that circumstances were not favorable

to Mathu's candidacy. Had the Government acted
objectively, they would have taken some action to at
least question this unusual situation. But nothing
was done, and it is probable that their dissatisfaction with Mathu's attitude toward the Emergency was
the main reason for their silence. Thus Mathu's
political potential at the time of the election was
dubious--he had certain advantages over his opponents,
but these had to be weighed against other very real
handicaps.

The specific voting requirements established by
the administration for the African elections were a
modification of those recommended in the Coutts' Report, and a number of these alterations worked against
Mathu's campaign. The fundamentals of Coutts' plan--
for a direct election with a qualitative franchise--
were accepted, but adjustments were made regarding the
details of the qualifications. The requirements based
on education level, income, and government service were
generally expanded in the approved reform.[6] Most significant to Mathu's situation, Coutts' proposal that
Central Province voters be required to take a loyalty
oath was rejected, and instead all potential voters
in this region had to obtain a loyalty certificate
before their registration requests would be considered.
These certificates were issued by the District Commissioner who was "the sole judge of such loyalty."[7]
Also important was the Government's decision that
multiple votes for individuals with exceptional qualifications should be allowed in Central Province. This
too was a revision of Coutts' plan which approved
multiple voting everywhere except in this one province.
The net effect of these alterations, and the way they
would be applied, was to create unique difficulties
for Mathu's candidacy. They made possible the circumstances that resulted in his defeat.

Part of the explanation as to why these voting
restrictions worked against Mathu's election lies in
the tribal composition of his constituency in relationship to the slate of candidates who were his opponents.
Typical of all eight constituencies, Mathu's Central
Province was multitribal. The dominant communities
were the Kikuyu, Meru and Embu, and, while they had
much in common, there was, nevertheless, a certain
parochial cleavage separating them. This was especially true of the Meru who were relatively isolated
in the north and who took advantage of this isolation
during the Emergency to distinguish themselves from

their more rebellious southern neighbors. Indeed,
this separatist movement was so pronounced that in
February 1956 the Government officially announced its
recognition of Meru as an area "separate and self-
contained."[8] At this same time the restrictions
placed on the area because of the Emergency were
removed.[9] Thus while scholars sometimes group these
peoples anthropologically, they clearly saw themselves
as three distinct societies. This then was the tribal
factor with which Mathu's campaign had to deal. Its
potential divisiveness became real when the list of
candidates appeared. Of the total of five, three
(Mathu, David Waruhiu and Stephen Kioni) were Kikuyu;
one (Jeremiah Nyagah) was Embu; and one (Bernard Mate)
was Meru.[10] Besides their tribal difference, Mate and
Nyagah were also notable for their accomplishments.
Both had studied abroad, and Mate had done post-gradu-
ate study at Edinburgh.[11] They were clearly formidable
competition and made tribal allegiance an important
aspect of the campaign.

With these circumstances as the ingredients of
the election, it was their manipulation by the district
officers that was the real cause of Mathu's defeat.
In a straightforward contest, with tribal loyalty as
the primary determinant, Mathu would have easily won.
Tribalism was the main determinant, as in most other
constituencies, but the tribe with the largest population did not have the greatest representation at the
polls. The Kikuyu had overwhelming numerical dominance
in Central Province. They made up approximately
1,150,000 of that region's 1,750,000 inhabitants, while
the Meru numbered only 366,000 and the Embu 230,000.[12]
Thus, given tribal voting, on the basis of numbers
Mathu should have had a strong advantage. Waruhiu and
Kioni were minor candidates with only localized support. They did not offer any real threat to Mathu's
Kikuyu following. But he lost and on tribal lines.

This occurred because of the way in which voting
requirements were applied by the local officials. The
Meru District Commissioner, J. A. Cumber, launched a
personal campaign to swell the Meru vote and elect
Mate. He was motivated not by an enthusiasm for the
Meru candidate but by a dislike for Mathu. The two
men had met on one of Mathu's tours of the area in
1955 and had not gotten on. Cumber noted that Mathu
had not visited the region "for some years" and on
this visit had "arrived late and left early."[13] He
was also critical of the Emergency legislation that

Mathu had introduced--he opposed the idea of the Home
Guards, and was especially annoyed at a proposed resettlement scheme which would have brought Kikuyu into
the Kibirichia area of Meru.[14] Cumber's relationship
with the local people was good. He supported an indirect system of government through the unusually
strong Council of Elders, the Njuri Ncheke,[15] and he
used his relationship with these men to stimulate
voter registration and to encourage Mate's election.[16]
Loyalty certificates were liberally granted, and an
active campaign to recruit the electorate had stunning
success. As an obvious boon in this effort was the
fact that it occurred at a time when the Meru were
experiencing a heightened culture consciousness,
evidenced by their successful campaign for recognition
independent from the Kikuyu. It was a situation Mathu
could hardly hope to control. At the same time in
Kikuyu districts registration was restrictive. Loyalty
certificates were cautiously bestowed, and there was
no active recruitment via local chiefs.[17] The people
displayed only "mild interest," and rumors that registration was a trick to enlist soldiers or collect
income tax kept many away.[18] Altogether it was a
series of circumstances wholly unfortuitous to Mathu's
cause.

It is evident that the course that this election
was taking was realized while the campaign was still
in progress. The Assistant Supervisor of African
Elections, for example, noted the significance of
tribal loyalty late in 1956 and stated:

> One thing is pretty certain-- all the
> Meru will vote for a Meru and, if more
> than one Meru stands, will make up their
> minds well before the election as to
> which they will have and vote as a tribe.
>
> The same thing is true of the Embu
> divisions of Embu district. The only
> places where voting may be expected to
> have any appreciable element of indiv-
> idual choice are the Kikuyu districts.[19]

Mathu had misgivings about the disproportionate Meru
registration figures and requested an inquiry in a
November 1956 LegCo speech:

> If you count all the registered voters of
> all the Kikuyu, Embu and Meru outside the

Meru district, the Meru has [sic] the larger
figures than all those put together. It is
difficult to understand how a district of
200,000 people has more registered people
than all the other people in the whole
colony. It must be due to something --
either the election assurances for a particular people before it comes, or something.
Those doubts are there, sir, and I do think
that the Government should clear them by
convincing all those interested that there
is nothing "fishy" in the whole thing.[20]

But the administration took no action, and the anticipated results materialized.

Voter registration concluded in mid-January 1957,
and the final statistics are notable. Of the total of
35,644 registered in the Province, 21,145 were in Meru
District. An additional 3,983 were Embu registrants,
and the remaining 10,498 represented the five Kikuyu
districts of the Province.[21] Because of the multiple
voting policy, these figures do not indicate the votes
in each area but merely the number of individuals on
the rolls. The vote statistics, while still heavily
pro-Meru, were somewhat less disproportionate. A
total of 50,363 votes could be cast in the constituency, and 26,018 of these were in Meru. More Kikuyu
were qualified under the multiple vote rule, and
18,131 votes were possible in their districts. The
Embu had 5,414.[22] Thus while the Meru composed less
than 20% of the Province's population, they had more
than 50% of its votes and 60% of its voters.

To combat these unfavorable odds, Mathu devised
an unusual strategy. He was the only candidate in
the entire colony to focus a good deal of his campaign outside of his constituency. He held many of
his rallies in Nairobi.[23] The rationale for this was
to appeal to the more sophisticated "expatriate"
voters who were registered in Central Province but who
lived in the city. Many of these men had multiple
votes, and some of them were Meru. He reasoned that,
because they were more westernized, tribal loyalty
might not be such an important factor in their judgment, and thus he might win their support. He was
also the only candidate in his constituency to affil-
iate with an organized political group. He was responsible for the formation of the United Front, one of
three political "parties" that emerged during the

campaign.[24] The United Front was made up simply of
the eight existing LegCo representatives seeking to be
returned. The advantage of joining such an organization was largely economic. While individual candidates
had to rely primarily on public speeches to convey
their policies, a group of candidates with a common
platform could afford to pool resources and print
pamphlets. They were also likely to get greater coverage in the press. The United Front issued handbills
arguing that their Council experience was an important
asset and advocating a reformist policy much like that
demonstrated by their representative activities to
that point. It was a practical tactic to expand their
publicity and reach a larger audience--another aspect
of Mathu's plan to overcome his political disadvantage.

        While political ideology had almost no relevance
in Mathu's defeat in this election, it was responsible
for involving him in a much publicized clash with a
Nairobi candidate, C. M. Argwings-Kodhek, who led
another of the three political "parties," a group of
four candidates who supported what was simply called
the 'A-K' Plan.[25] Mathu's role in this dispute was
mainly defensive and centered in his support for the
United Front. As noted, this was a moderate organization which advocated multiracialism and a gradualist
approach to self-government. The specifics of its
platform are outlined in the following passage from
one of its publications:

        Colonial Office remote control must
    continue for the time being, but the first
    step must be to achieve an African majority
    on the unofficial side. In the Public
    Service, more Africans must be given a larger
    number of responsible posts. In the Judicial
    field the jury system should be extended to
    Africans....In Education, a considerable ex-
    tension of services has already taken place,
    but the aim should be to install compulsory
    primary education, and each African child
    should receive eight years teaching without
    interruption. Health Services should be
    extended with particular emphasis on mater-
    nity, welfare and the setting up of a school
    medical service. Trade Union activities
    should be encouraged, and trade unionists
    ought to play a prominent part on statutory
    boards and committees. Labour should be
    stabilized and the family taken as the unit

> when this was brought about. In the towns,
> there should be better Housing for Africans,
> and no racial discrimination. In Agricul-
> ture, there should be financial assistance
> for farmers, more land for Africans, and
> equal marketing facilities. Water -- supplies
> in arid places should be arranged. In
> Commerce and Industry, the African trader
> must be encouraged. In the Communications
> field, all-weather roads should be built in
> African areas, and the railway system ex-
> tended to them. The fight against Racial
> Discrimination would be continued with
> vigour. Unrestricted immigration would be
> fought against. Conclusion: As we have
> indicated above, we have not been successful
> in every case. If returned, we shall con-
> tinue to urge the Government to effect re-
> forms in matters that are still pending.[26]

It was a comprehensive reformist program, and a major
argument for its worth was that it had been formulated
by men who had experience in dealing with the Government. The 'A-K' Plan directly attacked this position.
In a speech at Pumwani Argwings-Kodhek described the
existing African MLC's as "so ill-equipped that they
are merely used as enlarged pictures on the wall."[27]
Later his district political organization, the Nairobi
District African Congress,[28] passed a resolution
demanding that these representatives resign unless
they agreed to submit all proposed motions for public
approval prior to their introduction in the Council.[29]
Mathu confronted these attacks. He labelled Argwings-
Kodhek "This Mussolini of Kenya" and advised other
United Front members to ignore the NDAC demands.[30]
The basis for this conflict was to some degree ide-
ological. Argwings-Kodhek was less patient than the
United Front. He explicitly demanded African occupation of the Highlands, for example, and told the non-
African population that "if they don't want to stay
here they know what to do."[31] Mathu, on the other
hand, was remarkable subdued in his campaign demands.
He cooperated throughly with the moderate platform
of the United Front and told his constituents that
he had "no moon to offer, no fantastic promises."[32]
But all of this was extraneous to the election. The
two men were in separate constituencies and none of
Mathu's opponents seriously confronted him on any
issues.

The election occurred on March 15, and the results
closely reflected tribal support. The turnout was
good, with 48,607 of the 50,363 political votes being
cast. Bernard Mate overwhelmingly won with 24,758
votes. Mathu followed with 14,774. The remaining
three candidates trailed far behind--Nyagah - 5,684,
Waruhiu - 2,026, Kioni - 1,365--and lost their
deposits.[33] While these results were predictable, it
is notable that Mathu succeeded in carrying the great
bulk of the Kikuyu vote. Post-election criticism
unanimously agreed that the Meru were responsible for
the outcome,[34] and the clearest evidence of this comes
from a statement by Gikonyo Kiano who would be Mathu's
opponent the following year. He writes:

> Eliud Wambu Mathu, who has been the
> leader of African members in the Council
> for years and who is greatly loved by
> most Africans, Kikuyu and non-Kikuyu
> alike, was unseated in an election that
> has caused a lot of grave misgivings. What
> happened was that while it was relatively
> easy for some [i.e., Meru] members of the
> constituency to get loyalty certificates and
> therefore qualify to vote, it was particular-
> ly difficult for everyone else in the
> constituency to get these certificates. The
> result was the Meru voters alone proved to
> be more than all the voters in the other
> districts put together. Tribalism and loy-
> alty certificates, therefore, defeated
> Mathu.[35]

Political circumstances resulted in another
election for African representatives in 1958 in which
Mathu was again defeated but for reasons that were
primarily political. In this contest his opponent was
also a Kikuyu so tribalism was eliminated as a factor.
Instead the voter was faced with a political choice
which, if viewed objectively, was fundamentally only
a difference in style. That it was seen as more than
this at the time was a result of the political climate.
Mathu's defeat came partly because of his failure to
gauge this climate correctly and partly because he was
unavoidably associated with the increasingly unpopular
concept of gradualism in the pursuit of political reform. However similar his specific political objectives may have been to those of the new African representatives, his political image and campaign style
were linked with the past. His defeat symbolized the

rejection of compromise politics by the new forces of nationalism.

The 1958 election was itself a result of pressure from this new nationalistic political force as manifested in the activities of the eight newly elected African representatives.[36] Their first activity upon entering the Council was to denounce the Lyttleton Constitution and refuse acceptance of ministerial office under it. In conjunction with this they further demanded an additional fifteen African elected seats. Tom Mboya emerged as the group's leader, and, together with Ronald Ngala, he visited London to plead for these revisions. This effort brought the Colonial Secretary, Lennox-Boyd, to Kenya in October, and he agreed to establish a new constitution which included six additional African elected seats and a second African ministry. It further included the creation of twelve new Specially Elected Members-- four each for Africans, Asians and Europeans--to be chosen on non-racial lines by the Council acting as a kind of electoral college.[37] These reforms were rejected by the African representatives who boycotted the sessions in which they were discussed. But they were approved, nonetheless, and the elections were set for the following March.

Because it meant going against this boycott, Mathu showed some hesitation about running in this election.[38] He had been shaken by his defeat and did not appear publicly for some months.[39] In late August he again began to attend political functions and speak on broad political issues.[40] The almost unanimous lamentations by the press at his absence from the Council and the nature of his defeat certainly encouraged him. Nevertheless he did not jump at the opportunity to enter this race. That he did finally agree was largely due to the fact that this aspect of the boycott had already collapsed. Dr. Gikonyo Kiano, an American educated Kikuyu from Fort Hall, announced his candidacy early in the campaign and, since he had close links with Mboya and the African representatives generally, there was no pressure from them to oppose these elections.[41] Mathu declared his candidacy on January 10th, and <u>Baraza</u>, the African newspaper, speculated that his campaign would be a success.[42]

The electorate viewed the campaign as a ideological contest. The six new representative seats were obtained by subdividing constituencies and

forming new ones. Central Province now was split three
ways, and Mathu's new constituency included only
Kiambu, Thika and Fort Hall, all Kikuyu areas.[43] Kiano
was his only opponent, so the element of tribalism
was wholly absent from the race. Instead it was seen
as a contest between tradition and change. Despite
the fact that he had thwarted the African boycott of
Lennox-Boyd by seeking election, Kiano was recognized
as belonging to the new breed of nationistic politicians. His close association with Mboya was reflected
in the similarity of his campaign objectives and the
stated policy of the African Elected Members' Organization (AEMO). Like this association, he emphasized
that Kenya was "an African country" and "must be ruled
by the majority of its inhabitants, namely the
Africans."[44] It was a more emphatic commitment to
African self-government than Mathu had ever made. He
argued this position articulately and with an unusually dynamic style. "I have never listened to more
forceful speeches," writes one reporter, "and never
been more adequately answered."[45] In addition, like
Mboya, he cultivated an African personality by adding
traditional embellishments to his costume and using
folk tales and anecdotes in his speech.[46] He was a
new political face, with a compelling appeal, an
impressive background and an aggressive approach to
change. Mathu, on the other hand, represented the old
guard. He was respected for his achievements but, at
the same time, was associated with the "half a loaf"
mentality which had little appeal in these nationalistic times. Similarly his elegant western dress and
erudite speech were a sharp contrast with the political
image employed by Kiano and the other new politicians.
Although he was not yet fifty, he was in some ways an
anachronism no longer in touch with the popular outlook of the time.

        Despite these contrasts, there is indication that
in the more conducive circumstances in which the AEMO
was functioning, e.g., their cooperative willingness
to stand together in their demands, their increased
number, the indirect influence of West African developments, the more amenable attitude of the Colonial
Office, Mathu would have been wholly agreeable to
their aggressive approach. Beyond their political
style, the main thing distinguishing their philosophy
from that which Mathu had employed was their views of
priorities. They argued that before they could begin
to deal with specific issues such as land or education,
they must first achieve constitutional change to create

an African majority. Mathu had this as his ultimate
objective, but he approached it piecemeal by dealing
with the specific issues while simultaneously seeking
constitutional advance. An evaluation of either
approach must clearly consider the circumstances that
existed in the colonial relationship at the time.
Given the advantages of the 1958 political climate
over Mathu's earlier situation, and considering Mathu's
pragmatic attitude and nationalistic aims, there is
little doubt that he would have cooperated easily as
a colleague of these new men. Indeed, their tactic
of constitutional boycott, as has been noted, was
first attempted by him in 1954 and failed because of
disunity in the AUMO. Similarly, the position of
AEMO members on specific reforms reflects many of the
arguments presented by Mathu during his Council debates.
Demands such as colonywide compulsory education, restricted immigration, abolition of the qualitative
franchise, opening up of the highlands and the eradi-
cation of the color bar are all virtually identical
restatements of Mathu's position.[47] A further evidence
that he would have performed more aggressively in the
new Council is the fact that in his campaign Mathu
promised to oppose the new constitution and swore that
he would not accept a ministerial post if it were
offered.[48] Though it is somewhat speculative, these
factors indicate that Mathu would have continued as a
parliamentary leader in the more aggressive political
climate that was developing.

That this was not recognized at the time of the
election was only slightly due to any flaw in Mathu's
campaign and was more the result of a general rejection
of all things associated with the colonial past. He
could not escape being categorized as a gradualist
even though the political circumstances under which
he was forced to cope had permitted no constructive
alternative. He was also a victim of his own jargon.
He had consistently advocated "multiracialism" and
while he defined this quite differently than the
Colonial Office, it became synonymous with the Lyttleton
Plan and was therefore anathema to the nationalist
cause. He was also too experienced in the bureau-
cracy of the colonial system to give himself over to
the sweeping enthusiasm that categorized the new
politicians and his campaign remained low-key. Neither
could he convincingly adopt an African look in his
attire without it being obviously calculated to attract
votes. He was, simply, a prisoner of the past, and there
was little he could do to alter his image.

Kiano won the election by a good margin. Voting
took place on March 24 using the same voting rolls
as in 1957. The campaign had reportedly been "very
desultory," and the limited coverage it was given in
the press upholds this description.[49] Voter turnout
was also small and was down about 25% from the previous
year. Kiano collected 6,684 votes to Mathu's 3,926.[50]
It was a solid victory for the younger man and Mathu's
final electoral defeat.

The collapse of his political career shook Mathu
badly and led him to a final pathetic attempt to
save himself. His method was to stand as a candidate
for one of the four Specially Elected Seats created by
the Lennox-Boyd reforms. This was a complete reversal
of his campaign position in his race against Kiano.
In his speeches during that campaign, he proclaimed
his rejection of the Lennox-Boyd proposals and promised that, if defeated, he would not seek to return to
the Council by accepting nomination as a Specially
Elected Member.[51] Yet less than a month after making
this statement he announced his decision to pursue one
of these seats. The basis for this behavior was more
pitiful than base. In his statement announcing his
candidacy one can sense the desperation of his desire
to stay in politics:

> I was the first African to enter the
> Legislative Council in November, 1944. I
> have nearly 12 years' experience in this
> work, working with other races, and I have
> achieved a lot for Africans and Kenya as a
> result of co-operating with other commu-
> nities. In order to endeavour to carry that
> policy further, I intend to offer myself as
> a candidate for one of the Specially Elected
> Seats.[52]

It is as much an attempt at self-justification as a
political appeal.

This final attempt at retaining his LegCo position stemmed largely from the difficulty Mathu was
experiencing in coping with his fall from political
prominence. The tenor of Kenya's political scene had
changed fundamentally in a few short years, and
Mathu's career was a casualty of this phenomenon. The
rapidity of this process was too much for him to
digest, and his floundering in this final attempt to
survive reflects the emotional crisis he was experiencing.

Since his teaching days his personal security was a
vital aspect of his make-up. He had thrived at
Alliance largely because of the secure social and
intellectual community atmosphere this environment
provided. Similarly, after being ousted from
Alliance, he had found a new niche in the Legislative
Council. This is not to say that his efforts at
legislative reform, or for that matter teaching, were
ingenuine or consciously secondary to his security.
Rather the security that had accompanied both of these
positions merely provided the foundation that allowed
him to operate effectively. The introduction of
direct elections and the subsequent loss of his LegCo
seat had shattered his security and driven him to this
embarrassing attempt to save himself.

Mathu quickly realized the disastrous effect of
his announcement. He was ridiculed in the press and
renounced by the members of the AEMO. Of all of
these reactions, perhaps the most notable is a letter
in the Standard which, though atypical because of its
comparison, does have merit because it views events
in perspective:

> We have been regarding Mr. Mathu with
> high esteem, his good record and long
> experience in the House gave him a special
> place. He was always known as a man of
> sober thought and integrity. But--in spite
> of his recent manifesto, still hanging on
> our walls--he has changed his mind.
>
> The reasons for Mr. Mathu's failure last
> year are well known. It was really un-
> fortunate, but Mr. Mathu knows as well as
> anybody else that all the Kikuyu were behind
> him and so were many well-wishers of all
> races. His failure last month was partly
> due to a normal human reaction to something
> new--we were all sorry for the veteran but
> the people wanted a change, for better or
> for worse.[53]

Within a week of the announcement of his candidacy,
Mathu conceded his mistake. He withdrew his name from
the nomination list and concluded his political
career.[54]

The tragedy was complete. Mathu departed from
the political scene in an atmosphere of humiliation

and scorn. His reputation had already suffered as a
result of his association with the tactics of compromise and reform. It was now further weakened by the
remembrance of his artless attempt to stay in LegCo.
While the result of momentary poor judgment stemming
from his troubled emotional state, this error caused
Mathu to suffer an embarrassing and ignominious exit
from political life.

In perspective Mathu's political collapse was
largely the result of forces beyond his control.
Tribal prejudice and the changing political climate
were the real causes. He had argued in Council for
the right of his people to direct elections and did
not anticipate that their fruition would be his
demise. That this was so was more the result of fate
than his own inadequacy.

CONCLUSION

With the election of 1958 Mathu's political
career ended. He was not yet 50--an age when most men
are reaching their prime. Though finished with politics, Mathu remained active and continues so today.
For most of the past eleven years he has served as
President Kenyatta's Private Secretary and as Comp-
troller of the Kenya State House. He has also served
on the United Nations' Economic Commission to Africa
and as Chairman of the Council of the University of
East Africa. Since 1958 he has had no direct role in
the policy-making of his country and no political
following among his people. He sees his era as having
passed, and, despite the fact that many of today's
leaders are of his own generation, he consistently
refers to them as "these new men" and manifests the
attitude of one whose political involvement has ended.
While speculative, it is probable that his experience
is used by Kenyatta as a source of political advice.
But however influential this role may be, it is indirect and remains fundamentally apolitical in relationship to his personal career. Thus in the context
of this study, Mathu's activities since 1958 have no
direct relevance. His significance as a political
spokesman involved in defining and directing Kenya's
legislative policies ended with the opening of the
first directly elected Legislative Council, and
simultaneously his view of himself as a politician
ceased. From that time until today he has remained on
the sidelines--representative of a former era and
acquiescent to his subordinate role.

The political contribution to the success of
Kenya nationalism made by Mathu during his Legislative
Council career is beyond question. In the most prac-
tical sense, this is evidenced by the specific accom-
plishments his activities initiated or helped to
advance. The creation of the KAU, the abolition of
Kipande, the return of Kenyatta, the expansion of
African LegCo representation, the inroads toward
African compulsory education, cash crop production and
civil service opportunities, and the tempering of
Emergency legislation are the most notable of these.
Beyond these particular achievements, however, there

is a more general political relevance to Mathu's
presence in LegCo in that his persistence and skill in
debate provided a foundation for his successors. This
is most obviously seen by the fact that his parlimentary ability was positive proof to the administration
of the African's capability to effectively self-govern.
He was an important factor in creating an administrative attitude receptive to Africanization. At the
same time, he introduced and pursued a program of
legislative reform which remained as the basis for
governing even after independence. He is in this
sense a political precursor who articulated the fundamental principles on which the new nation was built.
His consistent presentation of arguments in Council
gave those who followed him a precedent and, again,
prepared the administration's willingness to change.

     As an extension of this issue of his relationship
with the administration, Mathu's career also has significance as an illustration of the attitudes and
motives of particular factions within the colonial
community. Among Europeans, for example, specific
segments viewed Mathu in particular and telling ways.
For the liberals, such as Perham and Coupland, Mathu
represented a prototype for a kind of parliamentary
leadership they saw as guiding the African people on
a gradual evolution to ultimate self-government. This
process would be peaceful and slow and would reach
fruition when the mass of the population had absorbed
the foundations of western culture. In this context,
Mathu's electoral defeat represented more than his
personal demise but the failure of this grand design
as well. On the other hand, for the settlers and some
officials, Mathu's presence in LegCo was regarded as a
necessary annoyance, endurable because it acted as
placation to the African and, because of the numerical
compositon of the Council, was never a real threat to
continued colonial control. They resented having to
tolerate his speeches and balked when his efforts made
inroads. But generally they accepted his representation as a token means of satisfying the demand for
African rights. As previously noted, throughout
these years the administration as a whole was ambivalent
in its commitment. In these circumstances Mathu's
competence in Council represented for them an evidence
of the capability of Kenya's Africans to effectively
self-govern.

     For the African community Mathu was viewed during
most of his Council years as a major spokesman.

Kenyatta's return and later the outbreak of Mau Mau
altered this attitude to some degree. But he remained
a respected leader. Because of the dramatic course
Kenya's political history has taken in recent decades,
Mathu's former prominence is largely forgotten and
even denied. But during his parliamentary career,
even the most militant African leaders such as James
Beauttah held him in respect. While a combination of
unfortuitous circumstances led to his electoral defeat,
throughout his Council career he maintained a solid
political following.

In overview what does Mathu's parlimentary career
reveal of Kenya's political history? From one perspective it represents the failure of the liberal
colonial design. Political events moved much more
quickly and militantly than liberal theorists intended,
and Mathu's career was a casualty of this phenomenon.
In this same context it might be argued that the
liberal parliamentary approach was ineffective in
achieving practical results--that hard-nosed revolutionary tactics were essential to accomplish meaningful change. But this argument, though valid in
certain particulars, is basically deceptive. An
examination and comparison of Mathu's legislative
objectives with those of his successors reveals that
Kenya's political course has been mainly evolutionary.
The dramatic victories of Mboya and the AEMO in
winning self-government have led to a popular depic-
tion of the policies of these men as revolutionary and
fundamentally different from the past. Only in their
results is this argument valid--the rapid achievement
of African dominated self-government did indeed produce revolutionary change. But this success was pro-
foundly aided by the international circumstances of
the time. The policies themselves which were the
basis for AEMO demands were only minor variants of
those advocated by Mathu since 1944. The attainment
of independence is an exciting event in Kenya's political history but it must be seen in perspective and
linked with the efforts of the past. Mathu's legislative career was one of the important elements in
providing the foundations for this victory.

In a similar vein, an analysis of Mathu's legislative career also illustrates the danger of cate-
gorizing historical personalities as specific social
types. The historian's task is to transcend the
factual data which is his raw material and reach conclusions which contribute something to attaining a

broader understanding of the past. Dealing in general
political categorizations is an unavoidable necessity
in this endeavor. But to focus on these categories
and define them too narrowly leads to simplistic
stereotyping. Mathu's career manifests many of the
characteristics of the "Black European." He successfully adapted to western culture and found recognition
and fulfillment in the colonial community. But this
fact was lost with the rapid attainment of independence carried forth by his successors. The increasingly enthusiastic nationalism after 1956 was accom-
plished by an uncritical rejection of the colonial
past. Mathu's second electoral defeat was an expression of this, and his political reputation today is
still heavily tainted by this view. It is unjustified
and the result of the creation of historical stereo-
types such as the "Black European."

Finally Mathu's career illustrates the intellectual link between black American writers and the
growth of African political thought. The course of
Mathu's academic development was consistently connected with the influence of Booker T. Washington, and
Washington's ideas are vital as the philosophical
basis for his political approach. Mathu's pragmatism
and willingness to compromise were directly derived
from the study of Washington's career. Such connections are a boon to the development of black studies
in that they show the very real relationship that
exists between the history of the Black man in America
and the African continent.

From the time of his electoral defeat in 1957 to
the present, Mathu has been politically inactive primarily because he is viewed as a discarded political
opportunist whose prominence was the result of his
cooperation with the colonial regime. As Booker T.
Washington carried the Uncle Tom stigma in America
because of his compromise of principle in the racial
atmosphere of his day, so Mathu must endure a similar
reputation in his country because he worked within the
colonial administration. His "half a loaf" approach
is seen today as having been a disguise for abandoning
the rights of his people in return for a seat in LegCo
from the British governor. His refusal to commit himself fully to either side during the Emergency is
interpreted as a biding of time until the future was
clear and he could give his support to the victor.
These arguments prevail today, and Mathu's reputation
suffers. Nevertheless, his contribution endures, and

historical perspective will eventually restore a more objective balance to an evaluation of his career.

Mathu was no charismatic messiah, and the direct and immediate effects of his legislative achievements brought no profound change. Yet it would be wrong to see his contribution to Kenya's political evolution as insignificant. His campaign for African nationalism was a quiet one, but it was also vigorous, constant, intelligent, and dignified. Despite the fact that he had few tangible victories, his efforts paved the way for the success of later men. It is unlikely that African representative government would have grown as quickly as it did in the late 1950s had not the representation of men such as Mathu gone before it.

NOTES

CHAPTER ONE

1. Kiambu District Annual Report, 1917-1918, p. 12, DC/KBU/1/11, Kenya National Archives (hereafter referred to as KNA).

2. As a general source see Vincent Harlow and E. M. Chilver (eds.), History of East Africa, Vol. II, (Oxford: 1965). For colonial administrative history see M. Dilley, British Policy in Kenya Colony, (New York: 1927); also George Bennett, Kenya: A Political History; the Colonial Period, (London: 1963). For a history of the missions see Roland Oliver, The Missionary Factor in East Africa, (London: 1952). Settler history is traced in Elspeth Huxley, White Man's Country: Lord Delamere and the Making of Kenya, 2 Vols., (London: 1935). A specific analysis of the paramountcy question is available in Robert C. Gregory, Sidney Webb and East Africa: Labor's Experiment with the Doctrine of Native Parmountcy, (Berkeley and Los Angeles: 1962).

3. As an example see John Middleton, "Kenya: Changes in African Life, 1912-1945," Harlow and Chilver (eds.), pp. 335-395.

4. From oral evidence told to M. W. H. Beech, Assistant District Commissioner, Dagoretti, December 12, 1912 by Chief Gatonyo wa Munene, Dagoretti Political Record Book, 1908-1912, Vol. I, pp. 120-128, in DC/KBU/3/4, KNA.

5. The two clans settled in these ithaka were Gatonyo and Kangau. Ibid., p. 123.

6. Ibid., pp. 140-142

7. This estimate was given by Mathu in his first interview session on November 11, 1970. It might be noted, however, that in an article written by Mathu in 1930 he gives the specific date of June 1, 1908, for his birth. See Eliud Wambu, "Kikuyu Autobiographies-I. Eliud Wambu-A Teacher in an African High School," Kikuyu News, Vol. IV, No. 114 (December 1930), p. 5.

8. The specific geographical boundaries of Dagoretti Sub-District are given in administrative records as follows: "from the junction of the

Dagoretti Nairobi-Ngong main roads in Chief Kinyanjui's
Location on the south up to Kijabe Railway Station on
the north. On the east to the beacons demarcating the
Kikuyu-Masai boundary, and on the west to within 3
miles of Nairobi (farm No. 10, Mr. de la Pasture)."
Kiambu District Annual Report, 1913-1914, p. 1,
DC/KBU/1/5, KNA.
      9. Father C. Cagnolo, The Akikuyu: Their
Customs, Traditions and Folklore, (Nyeri: 1933),
p. 73; also Jomo Kenyatta, Facing Mount Kenya: the
Tribal Life of the Gikuyu, (London: 1953), pp. 205-
221.
      10. A circular from the Chief Native Commis-
sioners in 1920 contained the following statement:
"All Government officials in charge of native areas
must exercise every possible lawful influence to in-
duce able-bodied male natives to go into the labour
field. Where farms are situated in the vicinity of a
native area, women and children should be encouraged
to go out for such labour as they can perform. Native
chiefs and elders must at all times render all possible lawful assistance....District Commissioners will
keep records of the names of those who are helpful
and of those who are not." "Labour in British East
Africa," Oldham Papers, Edinburgh House (Hereafter
referred to as EH).
      11. See Kenyatta, Facing Mount Kenya, p. 298.
      12. Kiambu District Annual Report, 1912-1913,
p. 14, DC/KBU/1/4, KNA.
      13. By 1917 the number of Africans from Dago-
retti working as clerks, messengers and servants in
Nairobi was estimated at 500. Many more than this
were working on plantations. Dagoretti Subdistrict
Annual Report, 1916-1917, p. 39, DC/KBU/1/10, KNA.
      14. Dagoretti Political Record Book, 1913-
1919, p. 45, DC/KBU/3/5, KNA.
      15. Kiambu District Annual Report, 1912-1913,
p. 20, DC/KBU/1/4, KNA.
      16. Dagoretti Political Record Book, 1908-
1912, Vol. I, pp. 120-128, DC/KBU/3/4, KNA.
      17. Ibid., pp. 122-125.
      18. Ibid., p. 126.
      19. Ibid.
      20. Ibid.
      21. As examples see the following: Kiambu
District Annual Report 1917-1918, p. 28, DC/KBU/1/11,
KNA; Dagoretti Sub-district Annual Report, 1916-1917,
p. 43. DC/KBU/1/10, KNA.
      22. Dagoretti Political Record Book, 1908-
1912, p. 7, DC/KBU/3/4, KNA.

23. Kiambu District Annual Report, 1917-1918, p. 35, DC/KBU/1/11, KNA.

24. Ibid.

25. Dagoretti Sub-district Annual Report, 1916-1917, p. 39, DC/KBU/1/10, KNA.

26. Kiambu District Annual Report, 1917-1918, p. 12, DC/KBU/1/10, KNA.

27. Eliud Mathu, Interview, November 11, 1970, Nairobi.

28. Wambu, "Kikuyu Autobiographies," p. 5.

29. Ibid., p. 7.

30. Ibid.

31. Kikuyu Vocational School, Calendar for 1924, (Kikuyu: 1924), p. 4, Oldham Papers, EH.

32. Memorandum by J. W. Arthur sent to J. H. Oldham, 2 June 1930, "The Origins and Development of the Education of the Kikuyu in Kenya," p. 7, Oldham Papers, EH.

33. Ibid., p. 8.

34. Ibid.

35. Wambu, "Kikuyu Autobiographies," p. 8.

36. This is not meant to imply that Kinyanjui was a progressive chief or a Christian. He aided Mathu in this situation because it was his policy to provide the missions with students, and he selected them generally from poor families. His own sons, however, were not permitted to attend school. Eliud Mathu, Interview, November 11, 1970, Nairobi.

37. Ibid.

38. Wambu, "Kikuyu Autobiographies," p. 8.

39. Ibid.

40. Eliud Mathu, Interview, November 11, 1970, Nairobi.

41. Kikuyu Vocational School, p. 5.

42. Wambu, "Kikuyu Autobiographies," p. 8.

43. Eliud Mathu, Interview, November 11, 1970, Nairobi.

44. Ibid.

45. See Ohanga's "Forward" in Elizabeth Richards, Fifty Years in Nyanza, 1906-1956, (Maseno: 1956), pp. i-v.

46. A detailed account of the origins of Alliance High School is available in the doctoral dissertation of Benjamin Kipkorir, "The Alliance High School and the Origin of the Kenya African Elite," St. John's College, Cambridge, 1969.

47. "Proposed College at Kikuyu," 1925, Oldham Papers, EH.

48. "Alliance High School Board of Governors' Report," January 28,1926, Alliance High School Papers,

Presbyterian Church of East Africa Archives (hereafter referred to as PCEA).

49. Minutes of a Special Meeting of the Repre-sentative Council of the Alliance of Missions, 5 August 1926, Alliance of Missions Minute Book, 1918-1940, Christian Council of Kenya Archives (hereafter referred to as CCK).

50. Anon., "Mr. George A. Grieve," Kikuyu News, Vol. V, No. 139 (March, 1937), pp. 117-119.

51. The Hampton Normal and Agricultural Institute, Hampton's Story, (Hampton: 1912), p. 1.

52. Ibid., p. 5.

53. "Alliance High School Annual Report for 1930," January 27,1931, Alliance High School Papers, PCEA.

54. "The Alliance High School, Kenya," (Nairobi: 1928).

55. Ibid.

56. Letter from G. A. Grieve to Dr. J. W. Arthur, August 2,1926, Alliance High School Papers, CCK.

57. "Minutes of Meeting of Alliance High School Board of Governors," 9 December 1927, p. 3, Alliance High School Papers, PCEA.

58. Higher Education in East Africa: Report of the Commission Appointed by the Secretary of State for the Colonies, September, 1937, Col. 147, (London: 1937), p. 76.

59. Ibid., p. 77.

60. Letter from J. W. C. Dougall to J. H. Oldham, May 24,1931, Oldham Papers, EH.

61. Eliud Mathu, Interview, November 11,1970, Nairobi. It is noteworthy that when I arrived at Mr. Mathu's office for this first interview he was at work organizing a scholarship scheme which was initi-ated by him at Alliance High School in honor of Mr. Grieve.

62. "Alliance High School Board of Governors' Report," January 28,1926, Alliance High School Papers, PCEA.

63. "Alliance High School Annual Report for the Year 1926," January 25,1927, Alliance High School Papers, PCEA.

64. Kipkorir, The Alliance High School, p. 137.

65. He is the son of Senior Chief Koinange.

66. Wambu, Kikuyu News, p. 9.

67. James Stephen Smith, Interview, October 14, 1970, Nairobi.

68. Alliance High School, Results of Exit Exami-nation, January, 1928, Ed./1/1022, KNA.

69. Eliud Mathu, Interview, November 23, 1970, Nairobi.

70. Eliud Mathu, Interview, November 23, 1970, Nairobi.

71. Norman Leys, Kenya. (London: 1924), p. 287.

72. Ibid.

73. Memorandum by H. D. Hooper, "Development of Political Self-Consciousness in the Kikuyu Native," p. 7, Oldham Papers, EH.

74. Kenya Land Commission Report: Evidence and Memoranda. 3 Vols. Col. 91.1933, Evidence, Vol. I. p. 68.

75. Kiambu District Annual Report, 1917-1918, p. 1, DC/KBU/1/11, KNA.

76. Ibid.

77. Dagoretti Political Record Book, 1924, p. 76, DC/KBU/3/6, KNA.

78. Keith Kyle, "Gandhi, Harry Thuku and Early Kenya Nationalism," Transition, Vol. VI, No. 27, (Oct. 1966), p. 17.

79. "Memorandum of Grievances: Important Discussion Between Officials and the Kikuyu Association," Oldham Papers, EH.

80. "Memorandum Presented by the Kikuyu Association, Kenya Colony to the Members of the East African Commission, November 1924," pp. 76-82, Dagoretti Political Record Book, 1924, DC/KBU/3/6, KNA.

81. See Harry Thuku, Harry Thuku: An Autobiography (Nairobi: 1970), p. 18. Also letter from J. W. Arthur to Oldham, March 14, 1922, Oldham Papers, EH; Kikuyu District Annual Report, December 31, 1921, p. 13, PC/CP/4/5/1, KNA; F. B. Welbourn, East African Rebels: A Study of Some Independent Churches (London: 1966), p. 128.

82. "Resolutions of the East African Association, July 10, 1921," Oldham Papers, EH.

83. "Memorandum by the Kikuyu Association, Southern District of Kikuyu, for the Hilton Young Commission, 1928," Kikuyu Association, 1921-1931, PC/CP/8/5/1, KNA.

84. Ibid.

85. Jomo Kenyatta, Kenya: Land of Conflict (London: 1945), p. 11.

86. James Beauttah, Interview, February 9, 1971, Maragua.

87. "Members of the Committee of the Kikuyu Central Association" to Sir Edward Grigg, December 31, 1925, Kikuyu Central Association, PC/CP/8/52, KNA.

88. Ibid.

89. Ibid.

90. Kikuyu Central Association to Sir Samuel Wilson, May 30,1929, Kikuyu Central Association, 1928-1930, PC/CP/8/5/3, KNA.
91. James Beauttah, Interview, February 9, 1971, Managua.
92. Ibid.
93. Eliud Mathu, Interview, November 11, 1970, Nairobi.
94. Ibid.
95. Ibid.

CHAPTER TWO

1. Kikuyu News, Vol. IV, No. 122 (December, 1932), p. 15.
2. Maseno offered a practical course of study for students of secondary school age, but only Alliance offered a course leading to the secondary school certificate. James Stephen Smith, Interview, October 14, 1970, Nairobi.
3. Note the plight of Peter Koinange or Jomo Kenyatta upon their return from abroad later in this era.
4. G. A. Grieve to Director of Education, Nairobi, November 15,1927, Department of Education, 1/1021, Kenya National Archives (hereafter referred to as KNA).
5. G. A. Grieve to Acting Director of Education, Nairobi, October 11,1931, Department of Education, 1/1023, KNA.
6. Ibid.
7. U. E. Mathew (ed.), Black Belt Diamonds: Gems from the Speeches, Addresses and Talks to Students of Booker T. Washington (New York: 1898), p. 4.
8. Booker T. Washington, Working with the Hands (New York: 1904), p. 195.
9. "Alliance High School Annual Report for 1929," Department of Education, 1/1026, KNA.
10. James Stephen Smith, Interview, October 14, 1970, Nairobi.
11. "Annual Report for 1929," Alliance High School Papers, Presbyterian Church of East African Archives (hereafter referred to as PCEA).
12. Eliud Wambu, "Kikuyu Autobiographies - I. Eliud Wambu - A Teacher in an African High School," Kikuyu News, Vol. IV, No. 114 (December, 1930), p. 8.
13. Kikuyu News, Vol. IV, No. 122 (December, 1932), p. 16.

14. Wambu, "Kikuyu Autobiographies," p. 9.
15. "Alliance High School Board of Governors'
Report for 1926," May 26, 1926, Alliance High School
Papers, PCEA.
16. Wambu, "Kikuyu Autobiographies," p. 10.
17. Eliud Mathu, Interview, November 17, 1970,
Nairobi.
18. "Alliance High School Old Boys Club Constitution," Christian Council of Kenya Archives (hereafter referred to as CCK).
19. "Alliance High School Old Boys Club Constitution," PCEA.
20. Alliance High School Magazine, No. 1, June
1937.
21. Ibid.
22. Wambu, "Kikuyu Autobiographies," p. 9.
23. G. A. Grieve to Acting Director of Education,
October 11, 1931, Department of Education, 1/1023/KNA.
24. Minutes of a Special Meeting of the Representative Council of the Alliance Missions, August 15,
1932, Alliance of Missions Minute Book, 1918-1940,
Christian Council of Kenya Archives (hereafter
referred to as CCK).
25. Eliud Mathu, Interview, November 17,1970,
Nairobi.
26. Ibid.
27. Memorandum from Director of Education to
Chief Native Commissioner, October 7, 1931, Department
of Education, 1/1023, KNA.
28. G. A. Grieve to Acting Director of Education,
October 11, 1931, Department of Education, 1/1023, KNA.
29. Ibid.
30. E. G. Biss, Acting Director of Education to
Secretary of Joint Matriculation Board, Pretoria,
Transvaal, South Africa, December 12, 1931, Department
of Education, 1/1023, KNA.
31. H. S. Scott to G. A. Grieve, January 2, 1932,
Department of Education, 1/1023, KNA.
32. This money paid Mathu's tuition expenses.
The money he had saved paid the cost of his passage
to and from South Africa. See Wambu, "Kikuyu Autobiographies," p. 9.
33. "Minutes of Meeting of Kiambu Local Native
Council," January 18, 1932, Department of Education,
1/1023, KNA.
34. Ibid.
35. Memorandum from Director of Education to
Chief Native Commissioner, January 30, 1932, Department of Education, 1/1023, KNA.
36. Wambu, "Kikuyu Autobiographies," p. 9.

37. Alexander Kerr, Fort Hare, 1915-48: the Evolution of an African College (London: 1968), p. 10.
38. Eric Walker, A History of Southern Africa (London: 1957), p. 570.
39. Kerr, p. 10.
40. Ibid.
41. Ibid., p. 130.
42. Ibid., p. 129.
43. Ibid., p. 41.
44. Ibid.
45. Eliud Mathu, Interview, November 17, 1970, Nairobi.
46. Ibid.
47. Report from the Principal of South African Native College Re: Eliud Wambu Mathu, March 19, 1934, Department of Education, 1/1023, KNA.
48. Eliud Mathu, Interview, November 17, 1970, Nairobi.
49. See Clements Kadalie, Clements Kadalie, My Life and the ICU: the Autobiography of a Black Trade Unionist in South Africa (London: 1970).
50. D. D. T. Jabavu, The Life of John Tengo Jabavu, Editor of Imvo Zabantusundu, 1884-1921 (Alice, South Africa: 1923), p. 65.
51. Kerr, p. 45.
52. Eliud Mathu, Interview, November 17, 1970, Nairobi.
53. It is noteworthy that this friendship was strong enough and endured so that Jabavu paid Mathu a personal visit in 1949. Eliud Mathu, Interview, November 17, 1970, Nairobi.
54. Ibid.
55. Ibid.
56. Kadalie, p. 208.
57. D. D. T. Jabavu, The Black Problem: Papers and Addresses on Various Native Problems (Alice, South Africa: 1920), pp. 15-16.
58. Ibid., p. 80.
59. Ibid., pp. 62-63.
60. Ibid., pp. 15-16.
61. D. D. T. Jabavu, All Africa Convention: Presidential Address (Alice, South Africa: 1936), p. 11.
62. Jabavu, The Black Problem, p. 80.
63. Mathu himself feels that the Director of Education was responsible for the withdrawal of his bursary. Eliud Mathu, Interview, November 17, 1970, Nairobi.
64. Report from the Principal of South African Native College Re: Eliud Wambu Mathu, March 19, 1934,

Department of Education, 1/1023, KNA.
    65. Director of Education to G. A. Grieve,
March 21, 1934, Department of Education, 1/1023, KNA.

CHAPTER THREE

    1. "Report of Nairobi Conference," 4 January
1938, Kenya African Teachers' Union, Education 96,
Presbyterian Church of East Africa Archives (here-
after referred to as PCEA).
    2. "Report of Chief Inspector of Schools, 1936,"
Department of Education, 1/1020, Kenya National
Archives (hereafter referred to as KNA).
    3. This date is given by Mathu in interview,
November 17, 1970; also by Makham Singh, History of
Kenya's Trade Union Movement to 1952 (Nairobi: 1969),
p. 51.
    4. James Gichuru held a primary teacher's certi-
ficate from Alliance and taught mathematics up to
Form II level.
    5. Kenya African Teachers' Union, "Report of
Nairobi Conference," January 4, 1938, Education 96,
PCEA.
    6. Ibid.
    7. Ibid.
    8. Ibid.
    9. Maseno School began secondary school certi-
ficate classes in 1938.
    10. "Alliance High School Annual Report for
1938," Educational Records and Reports, 1929-1948,
Kaimosi Friends' African Mission Archives (hereafter
referred to as KFAM).
    11. Kipkorir, pp. 165-166.
    12. James Gichuru, Erastus Kinyanjui and A. Cege
(school clerk).
    13. The Kenya Missionary Council was a body
formed in 1924 of Protestant missionary societies in
Kenya to consider and advise on matters of common
interest to all societies. Christian Council on Race
Relations, Suggestions for a Council, I/D/6, PCEA.
    14. Christian Council on Race Relations, memo-
randum to all members, February 27, 1939, I/D/6, PCEA.
    15. Rev. M. G. Capon, Toward Unity in Kenya
(Nairobi: 1962), p. 47.
    16. F. Cavendish Bentinck to Mr. E. E. Biss,
Hon. Sect'y of Christian Council on Race Relations,
July 11, 1935, I/EA/127, PCEA.
    17. "Report of Sub-Committee appointed to con-
sider the Native Registration Ordinance, with

particular reference to the 'Kipande' System," I/191, CCK.

18. "Minutes of a Meeting of the Christian Council on Race Relations," May 18, 1938, I/D/6, PCEA.

19. "Report of a Special Meeting of the Christian Council on Race Relations," July 14, 1938, I/D/6, PCEA.

20. "Minutes of a Meeting of the Christian Council on Race Relations," July 20, 1938, I/D/6, PCEA.

21. Ibid.

22. Report from the Principal of South African Native College Re: Eliud Wambu Mathu, March 19, 1934, Department of Education, I/1023, KNA.

23. Eliud Mathu, Interview, November 17, 1970, Nairobi.

24. "Minutes of Meeting of Alliance High School Board of Governors," February 17, 1937, CCK.

25. This salary of ₤120 would increase ₤5 annually until ₤150. James Stephen Smith earned ₤400 to ₤600/annum.

26. Peter Mbiyu Koinange completed his B. A. one year before Mathu but had not yet returned to Kenya at this time.

27. Eliud Mathu, Interview, November 23, 1970, Nairobi; Dame Margery Perham, Interview, May 18, 1971, Oxford.

28. Dame Margery Perham, Interview, May 18, 1971, Oxford.

29. R. H. Wisdom, Acting Director of Education to Dr. J. W. Arthur, August 27, 1938, Alliance High School Papers, PCEA.

30. R. H. Wisdom, Acting Director of Education to G. A. Grieve, January 31, 1939, Alliance High School Papaers, PCEA.

31. "Alliance High School Annual Report for 1938," Alliance High School Papers, PCEA.

32. A notable difference in these negotiations was the fact that Perham was dealing with authorities in England who were often more receptive to African education than local officials.

33. Dame Margery Perham, Interview, May 18, 1971, Oxford.

34. Margery Perham to Master Lindsey of Balliol, February 1, 1938, Balliol College File on Eliud W. Mathu.

35. Margery Perham to Lord Lothian, Secretary of Rhodes Trust, August 21, 1939, Rhodes Trust File No. 2984, Rhodes House, Oxford.

36. A. J. Dawes, Head of the East African Department of the Colonial Office, to Reginald Coupland, March 30, 1939, Rhodes Trust File No. 2984,

Rhodes House, Oxford.
37. Ibid.
38. Reginald Coupland to Lord Elton, Secretary
of Rhodes Trust, April 30, 1939, Rhodes Trust File
No. 2984.
39. Ibid.
40. John Murray, Principal of University College
of the South West, Exeter, to Captain A. Sullivan,
British Council, no date, Alliance High School Papers,
PCEA.
41. Ibid.
42. Lord Lothian, Secretary of Rhodes Trust, to
Lord Elton, June 23,1939, Rhodes Trust File No. 2984.
43. Margery Perham to Lord Lothian, Secretary
of Rhodes Trust, August 21,1939, Rhodes Trust File
No. 2984.
44. Reginald Coupland to Lord Elton, April 30,
1939, Rhodes Trust File No. 2984.
45. Eliud Mathu, Interview, November 17, 1970,
Nairobi.
46. Eliud W. Mathu to G. A. Grieve, February 11,
1939, Alliance High School Papers, PCEA.
47. Eliud W. Mathu to Rev. R. G. Calderwood,
September 21, 1938, Alliance High School Papers, PCEA.
48. Report on Eliud Mathu's Scottish Visit,
April 18, 1939, Alliance High School Papers, PCEA.
49. Eliud Mathu to Rev. R. G. Calderwood,
August 2, 1939, Alliance High School Papers, PCEA.
50. Ibid.
51. Ibid.
52. James Stephen Smith, Interview, October 14,
1970, Nairobi.
53. Eliud Mathu to Rev. R. G. Calderwood, August
2, 1939, Alliance High School Papers, PCEA.
54. John Murray to Capt. A. Sullivan, December
16, 1938, Alliance High School Papers, PCEA.
55. John Murray to G. A. Grieve, February 7,
1939, Alliance High School Papers, PCEA.
56. Lord Elton to Lord Lothian, July 21, 1939,
Rhodes Trust File No. 2984.
57. Lord Elton to Lord Lothian, no date, Rhodes
Trust File No. 2984.
58. Ibid.
59. Lord Elton to J. E. W. Flood, Director of
Colonial Studies, Crown Agent for the Colonies,
January 29, 1940, Rhodes Trust File No. 2984.
60. Eliud Mathu, Interview, November 23, 1970,
Nairobi.
61. Jeremy Murray-Brown, Kenyatta (New York:
1973), p. 241.

62. Eliud Mathu, Interview, November 17, 1970, Nairobi.

63. Quoted in James R. Hooker, Black Revolutionary: George Padmore's Path from Communism to Pan-Africanism (London: 1967), p. 50 from George Padmore's "Hands Off the Protectorates" (London: 1938), Nairobi.

64. T. Ras Makonnen, Interview, January 14,1971, Nairobi.

65. Ibid.

66. Eliud Mathu, Interview, November 23,1971, Nairobi.

67. T. Ras Makonnen, Interview, January 14, 1971, Nairobi.

68. Ibid.

69. T. Ras Makonnen, Interview, January 14, 1971, Nairobi.

70. Extracts from the Minutes of Meeting of Alliance High School Board of Governors, February 23, 1938, Department of Education, I/1020, KNA.

71. E. Carey Francis, Personal Jottings, June 24, 1939, I/304, CCK.

72. Ibid.

73. E. Carey Francis to L. B. Greaves, May 29, 1940, I/304, CCK.

74. "Alliance High School: Staff," November 12, 1940, Alliance High School Papers, PCEA.

75. Ibid.

76. Ibid.

77. James Stephen Smith, Interview, October 14, 1970, Nairobi.

78. E. Carey Francis to L. B. Greaves, May 29, 1940, I/304, CCK.

79. Personal Jottings, June 24, 1939, I/304, CCK.

80. "Alliance High School Annual Report," 1940, A/8, CCK.

81. E. J. Kellum, Principal of Kaimosi School to Joseph Otiende, no date, Educational Records and Reports, 1929-1948, KPAM.

82. E. Carey Francis to L. B. Greave, May 29, 1940, I/304, CCK.

83. G. A. Grieve to E. Carey Francis, March 12, 1940, CCK.

84. L. B. Greave to E. Carey Francis, April 24, 1940, CCK.

85. L. B. Greave to A. Lacey, Director of Education, no date, CCK.

86. E. Carey Francis to G. A. Grieve, March 7, 1940, CCK.

87. L. B. Greave to E. Carey Francis, April 24, 1940, CCK.

88. "Minutes of Meeting of Alliance High School Board of Governors, Executive Committee Meeting," October 30, 1940, I/238, Church Missionary Society Archives (hereafter referred to as CMSA).

89. Benjamin Kipkorir, "The Alliance High School and the Origin of the Kenya African Elite," St. John's College, Cambridge, 1969, p. 321.

90. Ibid., p. 218.

91. Eliud Mathu, Interview, November 17, 1970, Nairobi.

92. E. Carey Francis to S. D., no date, Alliance High School Old Boys Club, I/294, CCK.

93. Quoted by Kipkorir, p. 334.

94. "Alliance High School Annual Report for 1941," I/238, CMSA.

95. "Minutes of Meeting of Alliance High School Board of Governors," 1943, Department of Education, I/1020, KNA.

96. James Stephen Smith, Interview, October 14, 1970, Nairobi.

97. Kiambu Annual Report, 1941, Department of Education, I/1098, KNA.

98. Eliud Mathu, Interview, November 17, 1970, Nairobi.

CHAPTER FOUR

1. Colony and Protectorate of Kenya, Minutes of the Proceedings of the Legislative Council (hereafter cited as MPLC), June 2, 1954, Col. 775.

2. See Chapter I.

3. Ibid.

4. Manchester Guardian, May 1, 1931, p. 6.

5. Parliamentary Debates, Commons, May 3, 1938, col. 1543.

6. Oliver Stanley to A. Creech Jones, April 30, 1943. Kenya Correspondence I. 1940-43, Mss. British Empire S 365, Rhodes House Library, Oxford.

7. East African Standard, June 9, 1944, Supplement A.

8. Colony and Protectorate of Kenya, Post War Employment Committee Report and Report of the Sub-Committee on Post War Employment of Africans (Nairobi, 1943).

9. The other representative for African interests was the Rev. L. J. Beecher, appointed by Moore in 1943.

10. Of the 41 seats in Legislative Council, 19 were held by unofficial representatives who were appointed on racial lines: 11 Europeans; 5 Indians; 1 Arab (all of who were popularly elected); and 2 nominated representatives for African interests. The rest of the members (22) were official members nominated by the government.

11. MPLC, June 9, 1944, col. 241.

12. Eliud Mathu, Interview, December 2, 1970, Nairobi.

13. Ibid. Koinange returned from study in the United States in 1938.

14. Ibid.

15. Fred G. Burke, "Political Evolution in Kenya," pp. 185-239, in Stanley Diamond and Fred G. Burke (eds.), The Transformation of East Africa: Studies in Political Anthropology (New York: 1966), pp. 185-239. Also George Bennett, Kenya: A Political History: The Colonial Period (London: 1963), pp. 108-109.

16. East African Standard, October 13, 1944, p. 7.

17. Fort Hall District Annual Report, 1944, PC/ CP 4/4/73, Kenya National Archives (hereafter referred to as KNA), p. 10.

18. Central Province Annual Report, 1944, PC/ CP 4/4/2, KNA.

19. Nyanza Province Annual Report, 1945, PC/ Nyanza 2/157, KNA.

20. Listener, August 26,1943, p. 3.

21. Eliud Mathu, Interview, December 2, 1970, Nairobi.

22. MPLC, November 21, 1951, col. 110.

23. MPLC, March 16, 1948, col. 102.

24. MPLC, July 23, 1947, col. 48.

25. MPLC, November 28, 1946, col. 448.

26. MPLC, January 12, 1949, col. 806; MPLC, February 21, 1952, col. 103.

27. MPLC, February 21, 1952, col. 105.

28. MPLC, December 13, 1946, col. 883.

29. MPLC, January 19, 1950, cols. 958-959.

30. Ibid.

31. Ibid.

32. Eliud Mathu, Interview, December 2, 1970, Nairobi.

33. Ibid.

34. MPLC, December 20, 1950, cols. 1042-1043.

35. MPLC, November 25, 1948, col. 117.

36. Times (London), December 2, 1952, p. 8.

37. Although the Kikuyu Central Association was proscribed in 1940, secret meetings continued to be

held up until and even after the establishment of the
Kenya African Union.

38. Eliud Mathu, Interview, December 16, 1970,
Nairobi.

39. Ibid.

40. Ibid.

41. See Carl Rosberg and John Nottingham, The
Myth of Mau Mau: Nationalism in Kenya (New York:
1966), p. 214.

42. "The Kenya African Study Union, Rules and
Regulations," DC/Fort Hall 3/256, KNA.

43. Quoted in Empire, Nov./Dec. 1945, p. 8.

44. Wycliffe W. W. Awori and James S. Gichuru,
Memorandum of the Economical, Political, Educational
and Social Aspects of the African in Kenya Colony,
1946, Mss. British Empire S 365, Rhodes House Library,
Oxford.

45. East African Standard, June 23, 1944, p. 2;
October 13, 1944, p. 7; Bennett, p. 96.

46. Eliud Mathu, Interview, December 16, 1970,
Nairobi.

47. Kenya Confidential Despatch No. 3, March
25, 1946, Office of the Colonial Secretary 8/1490,
KNA.

48. East African Standard, March 5, 1948,
Supplement A.

49. Londiani District Annual Report, 1947, Reel
41, Section I, in microfilm collection of the Kenya
National Archives at Syracuse University (hereafter
cited as KNA Mic.); Kitui District Annual Report,
1947, Reel 9, Section I, KNA Mic., Central Province
Annual Report, 1950, C. Q. 544/66, Public Record
Office, London (hereafter referred to as PRO).

50. Eliud Mathu, Interview, December 16, 1970,
Nairobi.

51. Kiambu District Annual Report, 1948, PC/CP
4/4/3, KNA.

52. Fort Hall District Annual Report, 1945, Reel
12, Section I, KNA Mic.

53. Fort Hall District Annual Report, 1946, p.
13, PC/CP 4/4/3, KNA.

54. Eliud Mathu, Interview, December 2, 1970,
Nairobi.

55. Central Province Annual Report, 1947, CO/
544/63, PRO.

56. See Chapter Five, pp. 129-135.

57. East African Standard, September 20, 1944,
p. 1.

58. Electors' Union, Kenya Plan (Nairobi, 1949),
p. 10.

59. Kenya Confidential Despatch, No. 16, May 30, 1947, Office of the Colonial Secretary, 8/1530, KNA.

60. Ibid.

61. Kenya Guardian, May, 1944, p. 2.

62. B. A. Ohanga, Interview, February 3, 1971, Nairobi.

63. East African Standard, April 21, 1950, Supplement A.

64. From speech delivered at Mwakinyunga, Teita Hills, January 6, 1947. Published in Pan Africa, June 1947, p. 10.

65. Eliud Mathu, Interview, December 2, 1970, Nairobi.

66. Pan Africa, June 1947, p. 12.

67. Ibid., p. 10.

68. MPLC, January 19, 1950, col. 930; MPLC, January 18, 1949, col. 1056.

69. MPLC, December 20, 1946, col. 1043.

70. See Chapter Five, po. 146-47.

71. East African Standard, October 11, 1946, p.3.

72. Dr. Rita Hinden to Eliud Mathu, August 30, 1946, Kenya Correspondence 1944-46, Fabian Bureau Papers, Rhodes House Library, Oxford.

73. Pan Africa, June 19, 1947, pp. 10-11.

74. See African Education in Kenya - Report of a Committee Appointed to Inquire into the Scope, Content, and Methods of African Education, Its Admin- istration and Finance and to Make Recommendations (Nairobi, 1949). Compare with A Ten-Year Plan for the Development of African Education (Nairobi, 1946).

75. African Unofficial Members Organization, Comments on Report of Beecher Committee on African Education in Kenya, 1949; July 11, 1950, Mss. British Empire S. 365, Rhodes House Library, Oxford.

76. Ibid.

77. East African Standard, August 25, 1950, p. 1; Interview with B. A. Ohanga, February 3, 1971.

78. Precis of the Report of the Sub-Committee Labour Advisory Board, October 29, 1946, Kenya Correspondence 1944-46, Fabian Colonial Bureau Papers, Rhodes House Library, Oxford.

79. Ibid.

80. Ibid.

81. Eliud W. Mathu, the Kipande Controversy, April 29, 1949, Labour Legislation, Registration of Persons Ordinance, 1947, 5/3, KNA.

82. The Society for Civil Liberties, "Finger- prints! Why?" (Nairobi, 1949).

83. MPLC, July 24, 1947, col. 433.

84.   MPLC, July 24, 1947, col. 472.
85.   "Fingerprints! Why?."
86.   B. J. Glancy, Report of a Commission of
Inquiry Appointed to Review the Regulation of Persons
Ordinance, 1947, and to Make Recommendations for any
Amendments to the Ordinance that He May Consider
Necessary or Desirable (Nairobi, 1950).
87.   MPLC, May 17, 1950, col. 155.
88.   Ibid., cols. 158-159.
89.   MPLC, February 13, 1951, col. 23.
90.   MPLC, February 15, 1951, col. 92.
91.   MPLC, February 28, 1951, col. 430.
92.   Eliud Mathu, Interview, December 2, 1970,
Nairobi.
93.   Speech in Nairobi at KAU meeting, May 1951.
Quoted in F. D. Corfield, Historical Survey of the
Origins and Growth of Mau Mau (London, 1960), p. 11.
94.   MPLC, January 8, 1948, col. 715.
95.   MPLC, January 19, 1950, cols. 958-959.
96.   East African Standard, December 17, 1950,
p. 10.
97.   MPLC, July 23, 1947, col. 47.
98.   MPLC, July 17, 1945, cols. 209-210.
99.   MPLC, March 15, 1948, cols. 74-75.
100. MPLC, November 30, 1949, col. 71.
101. MPLC, November 22, 1944, col. 117.
102. MPLC, November 30, 1949, col. 71.
103. MPLC, July 23, 1947, col. 44.
104. East African Standard, July 18, 1947, p. 6.
105. Times (London), March 2, 1951, p. 5.
106. Eliud Mathu, Interview, December 2, 1970,
Nairobi.
107. MPLC, July 17, 1945, cols. 127-128.
108. MPLC, April 16, 1947, col. 46.
109. Eliud Mathu, Interview, December 2, 1970,
Nairobi.
110. MPLC, January 31, 1947, col. 978.
111. MPLC, December 16, 1949, col. 539.
112. MPLC, May 17, 1951, cols. 19-20.
113. MPLC, July 18, 1945, col. 132.
114. Ibid.
115. MPLC, April 16, 1947, col. 47.
116. Kenya Plan, p. 14.
117. East African Standard, October 7, 1949,
p. 6.
118. MPLC, December 7, 1949, col. 268.
119. MPLC, November 28, 1946, col. 449.
120. Ibid.
121. MPLC, March 14, 1945, cols. 53-55; July 20,
1945, col. 166; November 28, 1946, col. 449.

122. MPLC, November 14, 1945, col. 149.

123. African Conference (Being a Conference
of Delegates from the Legislative Councils of the
British African Colonies and Protectorates) (London,
1948), p. 18. Mathu attended this Conference in
London in 1948.

124. Schedule of Land Purchase, May 15, 1945,
Lands Office Reports, 6270, KNA.

125. Railway African Staff to Labour Commissioner, January 10, 1947, Labour-Conditions and Inspection of Labour, Mombasa, 1947, 5/26, KNA.

126. Provincial Commissioner, Mombasa to
Attorney General, January 20, 1947, Labour-Conditions
and Inspection of Labour, Mombasa, 1947, 5/26, KNA.

127. "The Mombasa Strike and Its Implications,"
East African Background (no date), Labour-Mombasa
Strike, 1947, 9/1836, KNA.

128. Governor Mitchell to Secretary of State
for the Colonies, January 18, 1947, Labour-Conditions
and Inspection of Labour, Mombasa, 1947, 5/26, KNA.

129. Makham Singh, History of Kenya's Trade
Union Movement to 1952 (Nairobi: 1969), p. 143.

130. Singh, p. 143.

131. East African Standard, February 7, 1947,
Supplement B.

132. Singh, p. 151.

133. MPLC, November 7, 1945, col. 35.

134. MPLC, July 27, 1945, col. 267.

135. East African Standard, February 2, 1945,
p. 7.

136. Ibid.

137. MPLC, January 9, 1945, cols. 633-636;
MPLC, March 20, 1948, col. 310; MPLC, January 11,
1949, col. 767.

138. MPLC, November 28, 1946, cols. 450-451;
MPLC, March 20, 1948, col. 310.

139. MPLC, January 9, 1948, col. 750.

140. Ibid.

141. Dr. Rita Hinden to D. R. Rees-Williams,
M. P., House of Commons, Kenya Correspondence III,
1946-53, Mss. British Empire S. 365, Rhodes House
Library, Oxford.

CHAPTER FIVE

1. East African Standard, November 10, 1952,
p. 6.

2. The term "Mau Mau" is used with reluctance
for want of a more accurate alternative to describe

the revolutionary reaction by Kenya Africans to the
colonial regime between 1952 and 1956.

    3. F. B. Welbourne, East African Christian
(London, 1965), p. 194.
    4. Ibid.
    5. J. C. Carothers, The Psychology of Mau Mau
(Nairobi: 1954), p. 7.
    6. Benjamin Kipkorir, 'The Alliance High School
and the Origin of the Kenya African Elite', St.
John's College, Cambridge, 1969; Michael Chaput, "Education as an Index of Elite Status" in Michael Chaput
(ed.), "Patterns of Elite Formation and Distribution
in Kenya, Senegal, Tanzania, and Zambia" (Syracuse,
1968); F. P. B. Derrick, "African Politics in the
Central Province of Kenya," Mss. Afr. S. 525, Rhodes
House Library, Oxford.
    7. M. Semakula Kiwanuka, 'The Three Traditions
of African Nationalism: A Study of the Western
Impact on African Politics, 1900-1960', unpublished
paper presented at 1970 Universities of East Africa
Social Science Conference, Dar es Salaam, December
27th, 1970.
    8. Ibid.
    9. Ibid.
    10. Colin Legum, Pan-Africanism: A Short
Political Guide (London: 1962), p. 31.
    11. Ibid., Appendix 26, p. 264; Hollis R.
Lynch, Edward Wilmot Blyden: Pan-Negro Patriot, 1832-
1912 (London: 1967); Edwin W. Blyden, "Africa and
the Africans," Fraser's Magazine, August, 1878,
p. 188.
    12. Bethwell A. Ogot, "Racial Consciousness
Among the African: A Colonial Heritage" in Racial and
Communal Tensions in East Africa (Nairobi: 1966),
pp. 104-112.
    13. See Chapter Three, pp. 75-79.
    14. Colony and Protectorate of Kenya, Minutes
of the Proceedings of the Legislative Council (hereafter cited as MPLC), February 21, 1952, col. 104.
    15. MPLC, February 21, 1952, col. 106.
    16. Quoted at length in L. S. B. Leakey,
Defeating Mau Mau (London: 1954), pp. 59-71.
    17. The role of land in prompting "Mau Mau"
is best illustrated in Donald L. Barnett and Karari
Njama, "Mau Mau" From Within: An Analysis of Kenya's
Peasant Revolt (London: 1966).
    18. Peter Evans, Law and Disorder (London:
1956); Oginga Odinga, Not Yet Uhuru (New York: 1967).
    19. Harry Thuku, Harry Thuku: An Autobio-
graphy (Nairobi: 1970), p. 69.

20. Mombasa Times, January 23, 1953, p. 3.
21. Mombasa Times, March 21, 1955, p. 3.
22. Dame Margery Perham, Interview, May 18, 1971, Oxford.
23. MPLC, May 20, 1954, col. 230.
24. Quote of Titus Wakabi, Agriculture Department employee, Mombasa Times, July 10, 1953, p. 2.
25. Quote of J. F. G. Kanyua, Nakuru Municipal Council Member, Kenya Weekly News, June 26, 1953, p. 21.
26. For examples of these resolutions see: "Resolutions Passed by the Kenya African Union in the General Meeting at Kaloleni Hall, February 5, 1950," Mss. Bt. Emp. S 365, Rhodes House Library, Oxford; Tom Mbotela, Vice President of KAU to DC, Ft. Hall, DC/Ft. Hall 3/256, Kenya National Archives (hereafter referred to as KNA).
27. Tom Mbotela to DC, Nyeri, September 23, 1950, DC/Ft. Hall 3/253, KNA; F. D. Corfield, Historical Survey of the Origins and Growth of Mau Mau (London: 1960).
28. East African Standard, December 29, 1950, p. 5.
29. Ibid.
30. Carl G. Rosberg, Jr. and John Nottingham, The Myth of "Mau Mau": Nationalism in Kenya (New York: 1966), p. 269.
31. Provincial Commissioner, Central Province to the Hon. Chief Secretary, Nairobi, September 12, 1951, Adm. 29/5, KNA.
32. Corfield, pp. 60-61.
33. Rosberg and Nottingham, Chapter 7.
34. Ibid.; Peter Abrahams, "Nkrumah, Kenyatta and the Old Order" in Jacob Drachler (ed.), African Heritage (New York: 1963), pp. 131-144; George Delf, Jomo Kenyatta: Towards Truth About the Light of Kenya (New York: 1961); Jeremy Murray-Brown, Kenyatta (New York: 1973).
35. For examples see: Jomo Kenyatta, Suffering Without Bitterness (Nairobi: 1968), p. 44; Venture: Journal of the Fabian Colonial Bureau, February 1949) p. 8; Empire: Journal of the Fabian Colonial Bureau, August 1948, p. 8; Fort Hall District Annual Report, 1947, PC/CP 4/4/3, KNA.
36. Abrahams, p. 141.
37. "Kenya Citizens Association - An Analysis of Its Purpose," 1952, Office of the Colonial Secretary 8/535, KNA.
38. Ibid.
39. James Beauttah, Interview, February 9, 1971,

Maragua, Kenya.
    40. Eliud Mathu, Interview, February 15, 1971,
Nairobi.
    41. Sir Michael Blundell, So Rough a Wind: The
Kenya Memoirs of Sir Michael Blundell (London: 1964),
p. 190.
    42. Eliud Mathu, Interview, February 15, 1971,
Niarobi.
    43. The notable exception to this is his 1949
Council statement quoted in pages 118-119 of Chapter
Four--but this information was disclosed as part of
his argument to win freedom of assembly.
    44. Kenya Weekly News, June 26, 1953, p. 13.
    45. Eliud Mathu and Mbiyu Koinange, 'The
Situation in Kenya,' Mss. Bt. Emp. S 365, Rhodes House
Library, Oxford.
    46. Eliud Mathu, Interview, February 15, 1971,
Nairobi.
    47. For Moral Rearmament see: Peter Howard,
Frank Buchman's Secret (London: 1961); for Capricorn
Africa see J. H. Oldham, New Hope in Africa (London:
1955).
    48. Eliud Mathu, Interview, February 15, 1971,
Nairobi.
    49. Ibid.
    50. Mombasa Times, September 25, 1954, p. 2.
    51. Baraza, July 16, 1955, p. 3.
    52. Mombasa Times, December 4, 1952, p. 1.
    53. See: Kenya Weekly News, July 10, 1953, p.
20; February 6, 1953, p. 20; Comment, March 24,
1955, p. 8; Christopher Wilson, Kenya's Warning: The
Challenge to White Supremacy in Our British Colony
(Nairobi: 1954); Ione Leigh, In the Shadow of Mau
Mau (London: 1954).
    54. Mombasa Times, March 25, 1954, p. 3; MPLC,
February 25, 1954, cols. 296-315.
    55. D. H. Rawcliffe, The Struggle for Kenya
(London: 1954), p. 123.
    56. MPLC, February 18, 1955, col. 134.
    57. MPLC, July 31, 1953, col. 318.
    58. MPLC, March 4, 1954, col. 517.
    59. MPLC, October 20, 1954, col. 270.
    60. East African Standard, October 7, 1949,
p. A.
    61. MPLC, November 27, 1952, col. 471.
    62. East African Standard, November 10, 1952.
p. 6.
    63. For examples of this position see: Mombasa
Times, November 20, 1952, p. 5; Kenya Weekly News,
May 22, 1953, p. 21; Leigh, p. 215; Wilson, pp. 66-70.

64.   A distinction must be made here between the
local administration in Kenya and the Secretary of
State for the Colonies. The colony's Governor, Sir
Evelyn Baring (1952-1959) and his administration
certainly held this view. See Corfield, pp. 274-275.
The Colonial Secretary, Oliver Lyttleton's position is
described on p. 147 of this chapter.
65.   MPLC, July 11, 1952, col. 300.
66.   MPLC, September 20, 1952, col. 15.
67.   MPLC, September 26, 1952, col. 90.
68.   MPLC, February 20, 1952, col. 57.
69.   Ibid.
70.   MPLC, March 2, 1954, col. 374.
71.   MPLC, February 17, 1953, col. 7.
72.   MPLC, December 5, 1952, col. 684; Times
(London), December 6, 1952, p. 6.
73.   Mombasa Times, December 10, 1952, p. 3.
74.   For recommendations to arm the Home Guard
see: MPLC, May 14, 1953, col. 285; MPLC, July 24,
1953, cols. 119-20; MPLC, February 18, 1954, col. 65.
For recommendations for salaries see MPLC, February
18, 1954, col. 65.
75.   Sir Michael Blundell quoted in United
Empire, Jan-Feb., 1955, pp. 27-31.
76.   MPLC, July 30, 1953, cols. 265-66.
77.   Ibid.
78.   Ibid. col. 269.
79.   MPLC, July 31, 1953, col. 318.
80.   MPLC, July 30, 1953, col. 276.
81.   MPLC, October 8, 1953, col. 118.
82.   MPLC, September 29, 1954, cols. 58-9.
83.   MPLC, May 27, 1954, col. 532.
84.   For example see MPLC, October 13, 1953, col.
211. Mathu here describes those in the reserves as
"small fry" and argues that the screening of these
areas by the administration was "terrorizing the
common man, the Kikuyu in the land units, for doing
nothing." He insists that the area of concentration
to capture terrorists must be the forests.
85.   MPLC, February 18, 1954, col. 66.
86.   MPLC, October 20, 1955, col. 946.
87.   MPLC, February 20, 1953, col. 270.
88.   MPLC, November 24, 1954, col. 659.
89.   MPLC, November 16, 1956, col. 133.
90.   See Chapter Four, pp. 88-92.
91.   MPLC, November 16, 1956, col. 133.
92.   MPLC, November 22, 1956, col. 334.
93.   Baraza, December 1, 1956, p. 1.
94.   Oliver Lyttleton to Kenya Administrator,
April 15, 1954, Kenya Official Gazette, Supplement

No. 18 (Nairobi: 1954), pp. 226-29.
        95.   MPLC, March 3, 1954, col. 464.
        96.   See Chapter Three, pp. 75-77.
        97.   East African Standard, March 12, 1954, p.
31.
        98.   Eliud Mathu, Interview, February 15, 1971,
Nairobi.
        99.   James Jeremiah, Interview, February 14,
1971, Teita, Kenya.
        100. Kenya Official Gazette, Supplement No. 18
(Nairobi: 1955), pp. 226-29.
        101. Report of the Commissioner Appointed to
Enquire into Methods for the Selection of African
Representatives to the Legislative Council (Nairobi:
1955).
        102. MPLC, February 24, 1956, col. 211.
        103. Ibid.
        104. MPLC, December 10, 1954, col. 876.
        105. MPLC, February 24, 1956, col. 212.
        106. MPLC, December 14, 1954, col. 1028.
        107. MPLC, February 28, 1956, col. 284.

                        CHAPTER SIX

        1.   New Comment, February 8, 1957, p. 13.
        2.   James Stephen Smith, Interview, October 14,
1970, Nairobi.
        3.   Baraza, March 2, 1957, p. 1.
        4.   For examples see Baraza, February 23, 1957,
p. 4.
        5.   Silvanus Robinson, "Men and Ideas in Kenya
Today" in the Bow Group, Race and Power: Studies of
Leadership in Five British Dependencies, pp. 57-74
(London: 1956), p. 70.
        6.   For specifics of this reform see Colony and
Protectorate of Kenya, Sessional Paper No. 39 of
1955/56 (Nairobi: 1956).
        7.   R. D. F. Ryland, "African Elections: Com-
pilation of Electoral Rolls," DC/Ft. Hall 3/250,
Kenya National Archives (hereafter referred to as
KNA).
        8.   East African Standard, February 24, 1956,
p. 23.
        9.   Africa Digest, May-June, 1956, p. 26.
        10. Minutes of Proceedings at Nyeri on
Nomination Day, January 22, 1957, DC/Ft. Hall 3/251,
KNA.
        11. Meru District Annual Report, 1956, Reel
16, Sect. I, in microfilm collection of the Kenya

National Archives at Syracuse University (hereafter referred to as KNA Mic.).

12. East African Statistical Department, Quarterly Bulletin, March 1957, p. 10. These statistics are based on 1948 census figures to which 1 1/2% annual increase has been added.

13. Meru District Annual Report, 1955, Reel 16, Sect. I, KNA Mic.

14. Meru District Annual Report, 1952, Reel 16, Sect. I, KNA Mic.; Eliud Mathu, Interview, February 15, 1971, Nairobi.

15. For an analysis of the special influence of the Njuri Ncheke in Meru see H. C. Lambert, "Disintegration and Reintegration of the Meru Tribe," Afr. S. 1380, Rhodes House Library, Oxford.

16. Baraza, July 9, 1955, p. 3; African World, May 1957, p. 21; Eliud Mathu, Interview, February 15, 1971, Nairobi.

17. District Officer, North Teita Division to District Commissioner, Fort Hall, November 3, 1956, DC/Ft. Hall 3/251, KNA.

18. Baraza, November 24, 1956, p. 3.

19. "Progress Report for September, African Elections," October 13, 1956, DC/Ft. Hall 3/250, KNA.

20. MPLC, November 15, 1956, col. 104.

21. Assistant Supervisor of African Elections, "Analysis of African Registered Voters for the Central Province," January 16, 1957, DC/Ft. Hall 3/251, KNA.

22. Ibid.

23. G. F. Engholm, "African Elections in Kenya, March 1957," in W. J. MacKenzie and Kenneth Robinson (eds.), Five Elections in Africa: A Group of Electoral Studies, pp. 394-454, (London: 1960), p. 440.

24. Colony-wide political organizations were forbidden. District organizations were permitted everywhere, but in Central Province. To get around this candidates issued common platforms. There were three such unions--The United Front, The Capricorn Contract, and the 'A-K' Plan.

25. Besides Argwings-Kodhek this group included Arap Towett, J. Ole Tameno, and Oginga Odinga. Only Odinga succeeded in being elected.

26. Engholm, p. 430.

27. "The Nairobi District African Congress - Outline of Policy," May 13, 1956, Mss. Bt. Emp. S. 365 120/1, Rhodes House Library, Oxford.

28. This was the district political organization founded by Argwings-Kodhek with the administration's approval.

29. Baraza, October 13, 1956, p. 1.

30.   Africa Digest, November-December, 1956,
p. 95.
31.   East African Standard, January 25, 1957,
p. 5.
32.   New Comment, February 8, 1957, p. 13.
33.   Baraza, March 16, 1957, p. 1.
34.   See for example: Nyeri District Annual
Report, 1957, KNA Mic., Reel 14, Section I; New
Comment, March 15, 1957, p. 3; African World, March,
1957, p. 22; East African Standard, April 5, 1957,
p. 3.
35.   Africa Today, May-June, 1957, p. 6.
36.   These eight men were: Tom Mboya, Oginga
Odinga, Bernard Mate, Ronald Ngala, Masinde Muliro,
Daniel Arap Moi, L. G. Oguda, and J. N. Muimi.
37.   For details of these reforms see Kenya:
Proposals for New Constitutional Arrangements, Cd. 309
(London: 1957).
38.   Baraza, January 3, 1958, p. 1.
39.   Baraza, August 23, 1957, p. 3.
40.   Baraza, September 6, 1957, p. 5.
41.   Baraza, January 3, 1958, p. 1; Oginga
Odinga, Not Yet Uhuru (New York: 1967), pp. 153-54.
42.   Baraza, January 3, 1958, p. 1.
43.   Central Province Annual Report, 1958, Reel
5, Sect. I, KNA Mic.
44.   Africa South, June, 1958, p. 72.
45.   Kenya Comment, April 4, 1958, p. 15.
46.   Kenya Comment, May 30, 1958, p. 5.
47.   See sample policy statements by Mboya,
Odinga and Kiano in the following: Tom Mboya, The
Kenya Question: An African Answer (London: 1956);
Mombasa Times, May 14, 1956, p. 1; African World,
February, 1957, p. 21; New Comment, March 22, 1957,
p. 5; Kenya Comment, May 30, 1958, p. 5.
48.   Baraza, February 28, 1958, p. 1.
49.   Central Province Annual Report, 1958,
Reel 5, Sect. I, KNA Mic.
50.   Ibid.
51.   East African Standard, February 27, 1958,
p. 5.
52.   East African Standard, April 10, 1958, p. 1.
53.   East African Standard, April 16, 1958, p. 4.
54.   East African Standard, April 16, 1958, p. 7.

A NOTE ON SOURCES

The major source for the core of this study --
the analysis of Eliud Mathu's legislative career --
was the Minutes of the Proceedings of the Legislative
Council of Kenya Colony. These debates were available
on microfilm at Syracuse University as well as in
their original published form in the British Museum
and at the Macmillan Library in Nairobi. Archival
records, especially those of the government depart-
ments and districts of colonial Kenya contained in
the Kenya National Archives were also an essential
source of data on Mathu's Council years. Further
useful unpublished material was found in the Colonial
Office Records on file in the Public Record Office,
London. Finally the Fabian Colonial Bureau Papers and
numerous other relevant manuscript materials in the
Rhodes House Library Collection, Oxford, were of
significant use.

For Mathu's earlier years the mission archives
of the Presbyterian Church of East Africa in Nairobi
and at Edinburgh House, London, were of major importance. These were supplemented by the records of the
Church Missionary Society, London, and of the
Christian Council of Kenya and the Kaimosi Friends
Africa Mission, both made available to me in Kenya.
Considerable material on Alliance High School's early
years and on the negotiations for Mathu's studies
abroad was also found in the Kenya National Archive's
Department of Education files. In addition, limited
but essential information was contained in Mathu's
personal files at Balliol College and at the Rhodes
Trust.

The interviews conducted with a number of persons
were vital both as a source of new data and as a
basis for amplification of written evidence. Mr.
Mathu was more than generous with his time, especially
considering the many responsibilities connected with
his position as Personal Secretary to the President.
Indeed the most serious difficulty confronted in
researching was in trying to arrange interviews.
Various individuals who might have had much to relate, today hold important posts and did not find

time to meet for an interview session. Others were
admittedly inhibited by the political theme and chose
not to talk. In any case, this aspect of the research was often frustrating and consumed considerable
time -- often without results. Those interviews that
were given were useful and are appreciated. Regarding
these interviews, it is noteworthy that those that are
listed in the "Summary of Sources" are formal sessions.
There were also countless informal conversations with
knowledgeable individuals in Kenya which added much
to a better understanding of the subject. Taken
together these oral sources, once successfully obtained, provide an invaluable supplement to the
written record.

SUMMARY OF SOURCES

A. UNPUBLISHED SOURCES

I.   In the United Kingdom.

a. Public Record Office, London
Colonial Office Records.

Series C.O. 533   515 volumes. Original corres-
pondence, East Africa Protect-
orate/Kenya, 1903.
Series C.O. 542   38 volumes. Government Gazettes,
from 1908.
Series C.O. 543   7 volumes. Miscellanea, from
1901.
Series C.O. 544   58 volumes. Sessional Papers,
East Africa Protectorate/Kenya,
from 1905.
Series C.O. 630   14 volumes. Acts, East Africa
Protectorate/Kenya, 1901-40.

b. Edinburgh House, London.
Of the manuscript collections held at the Church
of Scotland Mission Archives, the following are
specially relevant:

Alliance High School Papers.
The papers of J. W. Arthur.
The papers of J. H. Oldham.

c. Church Missionary Society, London.

Alliance High School Papers.

d. Rhodes House Library, Oxford.
The most relevant manuscripts in this collection
are the following:

Fabian Colonial Bureau Papers.
The papers of Elspeth Huxley.
The diaries of Edward J. Scott,
1949-62.

Of special note are the following papers:

Clive, John Horace: 'Kenya Administration, 1920-47'.

Derrick, F. P. B.: 'African Politics
in the Central Province of Kenya'.
Lambert, H. C.: 'Disintegration and
Reintegration of the Meru Tribe'.

e.   Rhodes Scholarship Files, Oxford.
File No. 2984   Eliud Mathu.

f.   Balliol College Files, Oxford.
Eliud Mathu.

g.   Cambridge University Library.
Kipkorir, B. E.: 'The Alliance High School
and the Origins of the Kenya African
Elite, 1926-62'. Ph.D., 1969.

II.   In East Africa.

a.   Kenya National Archives, Nairobi.
The most relevant records in this collection are
those of the following:

Christian Council of East Africa
Church Mission Society
Constitutional Developments
Department of Education
Department of Lands
District Reports
Kikuyu Central Association
Local Government
Labour
Ministry of Community Development
Office of the Colonial Secretary
Political Record Books
Provincial Reports

b.   Christian Council of Kenya Archives, Nairobi.

Alliance High School Papers
The papers of L. J. Beecher, 1951-52.

c.   Presbyterian Church of East Africa Archives,
Nairobi.

Alliance High School Papers
Christian Council Race Relations'
Committee Papers, 1930-44.

d.   Kaimosi Friends Africa Mission Archives, Kaimosi,
Kisumu.

Alliance High School Papers
Jeanes School Correspondence, 1929-39.

e. University of Nairobi Library.
Odhiambo, J. E.: 'Independent Schools in
Nyanza: A History', B.A., 1968.

f. Universities of East Africa Social Science Con-
ference, 1970, Dar es Salaam.
Kiwanuka, M. Semakula: 'The Three Tradi-
tions of African Nationalism: A
Study of the Western Impact on
African Politics, 1900-1960'.

B. INTERVIEWS

Beauttah, James, Maragwa (Feb. 9, 1971).
Jerimiah, James, Teita (Feb. 14, 1971).
Khamisi, Francis, Nairobi (Jan. 10, 1971).
Makonnen, T. R., Nairobi (Jan. 14, 1971).
Mathu, Eliud, Nairobi (Nov. 11, 1970; Nov.
17, 1970; Nov. 23, 1970; Dec. 2, 1970;
Dec. 16, 1970; Feb. 15, 1971).
Muhoya, Cyrus, Embu (Jan. 5, 1971).
Ohanga, B. A., Nairobi (Feb. 2, 1971; Feb.
3, 1971; Feb. 10, 1971).
Perham, Dame Margery, Oxford (May 18, 1971).
Smith, James Stephen, Nairobi (Oct. 14,
1970).
Vasey, Sir Ernest, Nairobi (Dec. 10, 1970).
Wood, A. Michael, Nairobi (Feb. 9, 1971).

C. LEGISLATIVE DEBATES

Colony and Protectorate of Kenya: Minutes of the
Proceedings of the Legislative Council of Kenya
Colony, 1943-58.

D. OTHER PUBLISHED MATERIALS

I. Books.

Aaronovitch, S. & K.: Crisis in Kenya, London (1947).
Altrincham, Lord: Kenya's Opportunity: Memories,
Hope & Ideas, London (1955).
Barnett, Donald L. and Karari Njama: Mau Mau from
Within: Autobiography & Analysis of Kenya;
Peasant Revolt, London (1966).
Bennett, George: Kenya, A Political History: The
Colonial Period, London (1963).

_____and Carl Rosberg: The Kenyatta Election: Kenya
   1960-61, London (1961).
Blok, H. P.: A Swahili Anthology, London (1948).
Blundell, Michael: So Rough a Wind: The Kenya
   Memoirs of Sir Michael Blundell, London (1964).
Capon, M. G.: Toward Unity in Kenya, Nairobi (1962).
Carothers, J. C.: The Psychology of Mau Mau, Nairobi
   (1956).
Cooke, David (ed.): Origin East Africa: A Makerere
   Anthology, London (1965).
Cromwell Hill, Adelaide and Martin Kilson (eds.):
   Apropos of Africa: Sentiments of American Negro
   Leaders on Africa from the 1800's to the 1950's,
   London (1969).
Delf, George: Jomo Kenyatta: Towards Truth About the
   Light of Kenya, London (1961).
Desai, Ram: Christianity in Africa as Seen by
   Africans, Denver (1962).
Easton, Stewart C.: The Twilight of European
   Colonialism: A Political Analysis, London (1961).
Farson, Negley: Last Chance in Kenya, London (1949).
Fazan, S.: History of the Loyalists, Nairobi (1961).
Gerth, Hans C. and C. Wright Mills: From Max Weber:
   Essays in Sociology, New York (1968).
Gicaru, Muga: Land of Sunshine: Scenes of Life in
   Kenya Before Mau Mau, London (1952).
Goldthorpe, J. E.: An African Elite: Makerere
   College Students 1922-1960, London (1965).
Greaves, L. B.: Carey Francis of Kenya, London (1969).
Groves, C. P.: The Planting of Christianity in
   Africa, Vol. IV, London (1958).
Hatch, John: A History of Post War Africa, London
   (1965).
Hill, M. F.: The Dual Policy in Kenya, Nakuru (1944).
Hodgkins, Thomas: Nationalism in Colonial Africa,
   London (1956).
Hooker, James R.: Black Revolutionary: George
   Padmore's Path From Communism to Pan-Africanism,
   London (1967).
Howard, Peter: Frank Buchman's Secret, London (1961).
Howe, Russell Warren: Black Africa: Africa South of
   the Sahara from Prehistory to Independence, London
   (1967).
Hussey, E. R. J., H. S. Scott and Right Rev. J. J.
   Willis: Some Aspects of Education in Tropical
   Africa, London (1936).
Huxley, Elspeth and Margery Perham: Politics in
   Kenya, London (1944).
Jabavu, D. D. T.: All African Convention: Presiden-
   tial Address, Lovedale, South Africa (1936).

___ The Black Problem: Papers & Addresses on Various
Native Problems, Lovedale, South Africa (1920).
___ The Life of John Tengo Jabavu, Editor of Imvo
Zabantusundu 1884-1921, Lovedale, South Africa
(1925).
___ Native Disabilities in South Africa, Lovedale,
South Africa (1932).
___ The Segregation Fallacy & Other Papers: A Native
View of Some South African Inter-Racial Problems,
Lovedale, South Africa (1932).
___ What Methodism Has Done for the Native, Lovedale,
South Africa (1923).
Jones, Thomas Jesse: Education in Africa, New York
(1922).
Kadalie, Clements: My Life and the ICU: The Auto-
biography of a Black Trade Unionist in South
Africa, London (1970).
Kenyatta, Jomo: Facing Mount Kenya: The Tribal Life
of the Gikuyu, London (1938).
___ Suffering Without Bitterness: The Founding of the
Kenya Nation, Nairobi (1968).
Kerr, Alexander: Fort Hare, 1915-48: The Evolution
of an African College, London (1968).
Lavers, Anthony: The Kikuyu Who Fight Mau Mau,
Nairobi (1955).
Leakey, L. S. B.: Defeating Mau Mau, London (1954).
Legu, Colin (ed.): Africa: A Handbook, London (1961).
___ Pan Africanism: A Short Political Guide, London
(1962).
___ Must We Lose Africa?, London (1954).
Leigh, Ione: In the Shadow of the Mau Mau, London
(1954).
Lubembe, Clement K.: The Inside of the Labour Move-
ment in Kenya, Nairobi (1968).
Lynch, Hollis R.: Edward Wilmot Blyden: Pan Negro
Patriot 1832-1912, London (1967).
MacMillan, W. M.: The Road to Self-Rule: A Study in
Colonial Evolution, London (1959).
Madjalany, Fred: State of Emergency: The Full Story
of Mau Mau, London (1962).
Mansergh, Nicholas: The Commonwealth and the Nations:
Studies in British Commonwealth Relations, London
(1948).
Mataamu, Bwana: The Beautiful Nyakiemo: Origin of
the Kikuyu-Masai, London (1951).
Mboya, Tom: Freedom and After, London (1963).
___ The Kenya Question: An African Answer, London
(1956).
McGregor, Ross W.: Kenya From Within: A Short Poli-
tical History, London (1927).

Mitchell, Sir Philip: African Afterthoughts, London
    (1954).
Mockerie, Parmenas Githendu: An African Speaks for
    His People, London (1934).
Murray, A. Victor: The School in the Bush: A Crit-
    ical Study of the Theory and Practice of Native
    Education in Africa, London (1938).
Murray-Brown, Jeremy: Kenyatta, New York (1973).
Nyabongo, H. H. Prince Akiki K.: Africa Answers Back,
    London (1936).
Odinga, Oginga: Not Yet Uhuru, New York (1967).
Oldham, J. H.: New Hope in Africa, London (1955).
Oliver, Roland: The Missionary Factor in East Africa,
    London (1952).
Padmore, George: Africa and World Peace, London
    (1937).
___ How Britain Rules Africa, London (1936).
Perham, Margery: Colonial Sequence, 1949-69, London
    (1970).
Rawcliffe, D. H.: The Struggle for Kenya, London
    (1954).
Richards, Elizabeth: Fifty Years in Nyanza, Maseno
    (1956).
Rosberg, Carl G. and John Nottingham: The Myth of
    "Mau Mau": Nationalism in Kenya, New York (1966).
Singh, Makham: History of Kenya's Trade Union Move-
    ment to 1952, Nairobi (1969).
Smith, Edwin W.: Aggrey of Africa: A Study in Black
    and White, London (1929).
Stoneham, C. T.: Mau Mau, London (1953).
___ Out of Barbarism, London (1955).
Taylor, Sidney (ed.): The New Africans: A Guide to
    the Contemporary History of Emergent Africa and
    Its Leaders, Nairobi (1967).
Thompson, Vincent Bakpetu: Africa and Unity: The
    Evolution of Pan-Africanism, London (1969).
Thuku, Harry: Harry Thuku, an Autobiography, Nairobi
    (1970).
Walker, Eric A.: A History of Southern Africa, London
    (1957).
___ The South African College and the University of
    Cape Town, Cape Town (1929).
Welbourn, F. B.: East African Christian, London
    (1965).
Wells, A. W.: Southern Africa: To-day and Yesterday,
    London (1939).
Wight, Martin: The Development of the Legislative
    Council, London (1947).
Wills, Colin: Who Killed Kenya?, London (1955).
Wilson, Christopher: Kenya's Warning: The Challenge

to White Supremacy in Our British Colony, Nairobi, (1954).
Wiseman, E. M.: Kikuyu Martyrs, London (1958).
___ The Story of the C.M.S. in Kenya, London (1960).

II. Articles.

Abrahams, Peter: "Nkrumah, Kenyatta and the Old Order," in African Heritage, Jacob Drachler (ed.), New York (1963), pp. 131-44.
Alport, C. J. M.: "Kenya's Answer to the Mau Mau Challenge," United Empire, XLV (Sept./Oct., 1954), pp. 173-76.
Beck, Ann: "Some Observations on Jomo Kenyatta in Britain, 1929-30," Cahiers D'Etudes Africains, VI (1966), pp. 308-29.
Beecher, Rt. Rev. L. J.: "Christian Counter-Revolution to Mau Mau," in Rhodesia and East Africa, F. S. Joelson (ed.), London (1958), pp. 82-92.
___ "The East African Prospect," United Empire, XXXVII (July/August, 1946), pp. 161-66.
___ "Missionary Education in Kenya," The East and West Review: An Anglican Missionary Quarterly Magazine, V (Oct., 1939), pp. 322-32.
Bennett, George: "The Development of Political Organizations in Kenya," Political Studies, V (June, 1957), pp. 113-30.
___ "Imperial Paternalism: The Representation of African Interests in the Kenya Legislative Council," in Essays in Imperial Government, Kenneth Robinson and Frederick Madden (eds.), Oxford (1963), pp. 141-69.
___ "Kenyatta and the Kikuyu," International Affairs, XXXVII (Oct., 1961), pp. 477-82.
Benson, T. G.: "The Education of the East African Native," Journal of the Royal African Society, (Oct., 1936), pp. 470-89.
Burke, Fred G.: "Political Evolution in Kenya," in The Transformation of East Africa: Studies in Political Anthropology, Stanley Diamond and Fred G. Burke (eds.), New York (1966), pp. 185-239.
DuBois, W. E. Burghardt: "Of Mr. Booker T. Washington and Others," in The Souls of Black Folk: Essays and Sketches, W. E. Burghardt DuBois, London (1965), pp. 29-38.
Engholm, G. F.: "African Elections in Kenya, March 1957," in Five Elections in Africa: A Group of Electoral Studies, W. J. Mackenzie and Kenneth Robinson (eds.), London (1960), pp. 394-454.
___ "Kenya's First Direct Elections for Africans,

March 1957," Parliamentary Affairs, X (1957),
    pp. 424-33.
Faris, J. T.: "James Stewart of Lovedale," Missionary
    Review of the World, XXXIII (Jan.,.1910), pp. 46-9.
Goldthorpe, J. E.: "An African Elite," British
    Journal of Sociology, VI (March, 1955), pp. 31-47.
Henderson, J.: "Industrial Training in Africa: The
    Situation in South Africa," International Review
    of Missions, III (Feb., 1914), pp. 336-46.
Kerby, Michael H.: "The Unhappiness of the Kikuyu:
    or the Seeds of Mau Mau," East African Medical
    Journal, XXXIV (Oct., 1957), pp. 529-32.
Kiano, Dr. Gikonyo: "Political Trends in Kenya,"
    Africa South, III (1957), pp. 69-76.
___ "Victory for Democracy: Elections in Kenya,"
    Africa Today, I (May, 1957), pp. 3-6.
Loram, Charles T.: "Dissertation on the Education of
    the South African Native," Teachers College Record,
    XVII (May, 1916), pp. 268-73.
McGlasham, Neil: "Indigenous Kikuyu Education,"
    African Affairs, LXII (Jan., 1964), pp. 47-57.
Mair, Lucy: "New Elites in East and West Africa,"
    in Colonialism in Africa, 1870-1960, Vol. III,
    Profiles of Change: African Society and Colonial
    Rule, Victor Turner (ed.), Cambridge (1971), pp.
    167-92.
Mungeam, G. H.: "Masai and Kikuyu Responses to the
    Establishment of British Administration in the
    East African Protectorate," Journal of African
    History, XI (1970), pp. 127-43.
Nagenda, John: "Kenya," in Africa: A Handbook,
    Colin Legum (ed.), London (1961), pp. 109-16.
Ndungu, J. B.: "Gituamba and Kikuyu Independency in
    Church and School," in Ngano: Studies in Tradi-
    tional and Modern East African History, B. G.
    McIntosh (ed.), Nairobi (1969), pp. 131-50.
Nkumbula, H. M.: "Mission Education in Africa,"
    Makerere, I (May, 1947), pp. 58-9.
Ogot, Dr. Bethwell A.: "Racial Consciousness Among
    the Africans: A Colonial Heritage," in Racial and
    Communal Tensions in East Africa, East African
    Institute of Social and Cultural Affairs (pub.),
    Nairobi (1966), pp. 104-12.
Oldham, J. H.: "Christian Education in Africa,"
    Church Missionary Review, LXXV (1924), pp. 305-14.
Orr, J. R.: "Education in Kenya Colony," Church
    Missionary Review, LXXIII (1922), pp. 232-35.
Padmore, G.: "Blackman's Burden: The Story Behind
    Mau Mau," United Asia, V (Dec., 1953), pp. 336-41;
    VI (April, 1954), pp. 83-9.

Patel, A. B.: "Kenya's Future: An Asian View,"
Commonwealth Challenge, III (Oct., 1954), pp. 23-7.
Robinson, Silvanus: "Men and Ideas in Kenya Today,"
in Race and Power: Studies of Leadership in Five
British Dependencies, The Bow Group (eds.), London
(1956), pp. 57-74.
Scott, H. S.: "Some Aspects of Native Education in
Kenya," in Some Aspects of Education in Tropical
Africa, E. R. J. Hussey, H. S. Scott, and Right
Rev. J. J. Willis (eds.), London (1936), pp. 46-79.
Ward, Major R. E. K.: "The East African Political
Scene," African Affairs, VL (July, 1956), pp. 136-
52.

III.   Pamphlets and Publications of Organizations

Africa Bureau: Future of East Africa, London (1955).
African Unofficial Members Organization: Method of
Electing African Members of Kenya Legislative
Council, Nairobi (1955).
___ Statement of Policy, Nairobi (1953).
Alliance of Missionary Societies of British East
Africa: The Representative Council of the Alliance
of Missionary Societies of British East Africa,
Nairobi (1940).
Beecher, Rev. L. J.: The Kikuyu, London (1953).
Bennett, George: Kenyatta and the Kikuyu, London
(1961).
Brockway, Fenner: Why Mau Mau? An Analysis and a
Remedy, London (1953).
Capricorn Africa Society: The Aims, Objects and
Programme of the Capricorn Africa Society,
Salisbury (1954).
___ The Capricorn Africa Society Handbook, Salisbury
(1955).
___ Education for Nationhood, Nairobi (1958).
Church of Scotland Foreign Mission Committee: Mau
Mau and the Church, Edinburgh (1953).
Cullen, A. D.: Precis of the East Africa Royal Com-
mission 1953-55 Report, Cmd. 9475, Nakuru (1955).
Electors' Union of Kenya: European Electors' Union's
'Kenya Plan' and 'British East African Dominion,'
Nairobi (1949).
___ General Election, 1948-Nairobi South, Nairobi
(1948).
___ The Kenya Land Question, Nairobi (1952).
___ Kenya Plan, Nairobi (1949).
Fabian Colonial Bureau: Domination or Co-operation?
Report on a Conference on the Relationship Between
the British and Colonial People, London (1946).

___ Kenya Controversy, London (1947).
Federal Independence Party: The General Policy of the
    Federal Independence Party, Nairobi (1954).
Hampton Institute: Hampton's Story, Hampton, Va.
    (1912).
Inter-Territorial Commission on Higher Education: The
    High College of East Africa, Entebbe (1938).
J. H.: African Advancement: How the African Has
    Benefited from British Administration and Settle-
    ment in Kenya Over the Last Half-Century, Nairobi
    (1954).
Joint East African Board: Memorandum on Post-War
    Problems in East Africa, London (1943).
Kenyatta, Jomo: Kenya: The Land of Conflict, London
    (1945).
Kikuyu Central Association: Correspondence Between
    the Kikuyu Central Association and the Colonial
    Office, 1929-30, no date.
___ Memorandum of the Kikuyu Central Association, Fort
    Hall, to be Presented to the Hilton Young Commis-
    sion, no date.
Kikuyu Independent Schools Association: Report and
    Constitution, 1938, Nyeri (1938).
Kikuyu Provincial Association: Rules and Regulations,
    Nairobi (1939).
Koinange, Mbiyu and Achieng Oneko: Land Hunger in
    Kenya, London (1952).
Mbotela, Tom: Implementation of the Universal Decla-
    ration of Human Rights, Nairobi (1946).
Mitchell, Sir Philip: Current Affairs in East Africa,
    London (1947).
Moral Re-Armament: The Forgotten Factor, London
    (1952).
The Society for Civil Liberties: Remember, Nairobi
    (1949).
___ Why?, Nairobi (1949).
United Conference of Missionary Societies: Report of
    the United Conference of Missionary Societies in
    British East Africa, Kikuyu (1918).
United Country Party of Kenya: Statement of Policy,
    Nairobi (1955).
The Voice of Kenya: A General Survey, Nairobi,
    (1953).
___ Historical Background, Nairobi (1953).
___ The Kikuyu Tribe and Mau Mau, Nairobi, no date.
Wiseman, E. M.: The Story of the C.M.S. in Kenya,
    London, no date.

IV.   Government Documents (Arranged Chronologically).

a.   United Kingdom Publications.

Report of Kenya Land Commission, Cmd. 4556, 1934.
Report of the Commission on Higher Education in East
    Africa, col. 142, 1937.
Higher Education in East Africa: Report of the Com-
    mission Appointed by the Secretary of State for
    the Colonies, September, 1937, col. 147, 1937.
Inter-Territorial Organization in East Africa, col.
    191, 1945.
Labour Conditions in East Africa: A Report by Major
    G. Orde-Brown, col. 193, 1946.
Inter-Territorial Organization in East Africa: Re-
    vised Proposals, col. 210, 1947.
African Conference (Being a Conference of Delegates
    from the Legislative Councils of the British
    African colonies and Protectorates), col. 1176,
    1948.
Land and Population in East Africa: An Exchange of
    Correspondence Between the Secretary of State for
    the Colonies and the Government of Kenya on the
    Appointment of the Royal Commission, col. 290,
    1952.
Report to the Secretary of State for the Colonies by
    the Parliamentary Delegation to Kenya, January,
    1954, Cmd. 9081, 1954.
Kenya: Proposals for a Reconstruction of the Govern-
    ment, Cmd. 9103, 1954.
Report of the East Africa Royal Commission, 1953-55,
    Cmd. 9475, 1955.
Despatches from the Governors of Kenya, Uganda and
    Tanganyika and From the Administrator, East Africa
    High Commission, Commenting on the East Africa
    Royal Commission, 1953-55 Report, Cmd. 9801, 1956.
Commentary on the Despatches from the Governors of
    Kenya, Uganda and Tanganyika and the Administrator,
    East Africa High Commission, on the East Africa
    Royal Commission, 1953-55, Cmd. 9804, 1956.
Kenya: Proposals for New Constitutional Arrangements,
    Cmd. 309, 1957.
Kenya: Despatch on the New Constitutional Arrange-
    ments, Cmd. 369, 1958.
Historical Survey of the Origins and Growth of Mau
    Mau, Cmd. 1030, 1960.

b.   Kenya Publications.

Post-War Employment Committee Report and Report of
    the Sub-Committee on Post-War Employment of Afri-
    cans, 1943.

Proposals for the Reorganization of the Administra-
    tion of Kenya, Sessional Paper No. 3 of 1945.
Land Utilization and Settlement: A Statement of
    Government Policy, Sessional Paper No. 8 of 1945.
Post-War Settlement in Kenya: Proposed Schemes, 1945.
Sessional Paper No. 1 of 1947, 1947.
Report on Native Affairs, 1939-45, 1947.
Report on the Economic and Social Background of
    Mombasa Labour Disputes, 1947.
Report on African Labour Census, 1947, 1948.
A Ten Year Plan for the Development of African Educa-
    tion, 1948.
African Education in Kenya: Report of the Committee
    Appointed to Enquire into the Scope, Content and
    Methods of African Education, Its Administration
    and Finance and to Make Recommendations, 1949.
Report of a Commission of Inquiry Appointed to Renew
    the Registration of Persons Ordinance, 1947, and
    to Make Recommendations for any Amendments to the
    Ordinance that He May Consider Necessary or
    Desirable, 1950.
Proposals for the Implementation of the Recommenda-
    tions of the Report on African Education in Kenya,
    Sessional Paper No. 1 of 1950.
African Education: A Statement of Policy, 1951.
Report of the Planning Committee, 1951.
Report of the Committee of Inquiry into Labour Unrest
    at Mombasa, 1954.
Report of the Commission on the Civil Services of the
    East African Territories and the East Africa High
    Commission, 1953-54, 1954.
Report of the Committee on African Wages, 1954.
Report of the Commissioner Appointed to Enquire into
    Methods for the Selection of African Representa-
    tives to the Legislative Council, 1955.
Report of the Commissioner Appointed to Enquire into
    Methods for the Selection of African Representa-
    tives to the Legislative Council, 1956.

V. Newspapers, Periodicals and Journals.

Africa Digest, 1954-58.
Africa South, 1957-58.
Africa Today, 1957-58.
African Affairs, 1944-57.
African World, 1944-58.
African World Annual, 1951-57.
Baraza, 1944-58.
Church Missionary Review, 1922-25.

Comment, 1949-58.
The Crisis, 1910-40.
East Africa and Rhodesia, 1944-58.
East Africa News Review, 1944-49.
The East Africa Command Fortnightly Review, 1945-46.
East African Annual, 1950-58.
East African Standard, 1918-58.
Empire: Journal of the Fabian Colonial Bureau, 1944-48.
Information Digest, 1953.
Journal of African Administration, 1949-58.
Kenya Comment, 1958.
Kenya Notes, 1953.
Kenya Weekly News, 1944-58.
Kikuyu News, 1927-46.
The Listener, 1943.
Makerere, 1946.
Manchester Guardian, 1930, 1953, 1955-58.
Mombasa Times, 1952-58.
The Mount Kenya Observer, 1951-52.
Mwalimu Annual, 1945-6.
New Comment, 1956-57.
New Commentary, 1957.
New Commonwealth, 1955.
New Statesman and Nation, 1936, 1956-58.
Pan-Africa: Journal of African Life and Thought, 1947.
The Roundtable: A Quarterly Review of British Commonwealth Affairs, 1944-58.
Sekanyola, 1921.
The Southern Workman, 1925-40.
The Sunday Post East Africa Review, 1942-43.
South African Outlook, 1923-25.
The Times (London), 1944-58.
United Empire, 1944-58.
Venture: Journal of the Fabian Colonial Bureau, 1949-50.
The Voice of Kenya, 1953-55.

INDEX

Abrahams, Peter, 59, 115
Administration, colonial,
  in Kenya, see Legisla-
  tive Council and indi-
  vidual governors by
  name
Advisory Council on
  African Education, 19
African Elected Members
  Organization (AEMO),
  144, 151
African Inland Mission
  (AIM), 6, 14
African Unofficial Mem-
  bers Organization
  (AUMO), 118-19, 130-31
African Voice, The, 80
African Worker's Federa-
  tion, 101
Aggrey, J.E.K., xv, 27
Agriculture, 132, 149.
  See also Land
Akatsa, W.B., 65
'A-K' Plan, The, 140-41,
  178.
All-African Convention,
  40
Alliance High School, 28f,
  32-34, 41-44 passim, 62,
  111, 147; Board of
  Governors, 33, 48-52
  passim, 67-68; Charac-
  ter, 14-18 passim, 30,
  36-37; and Mathu, 14,
  30-31, 43-52 passim, 60-
  68 passim, 73; Old Boys
  Club, 33-34, 66, 67
Alliance of Protestant
  Missions, 14

Arab Elected Member, 88
Argwings-Kodhek, C.M.,
  140-41, 178.
Armstrong, General
  Samuel C., 16
Arthur, Dr. John W., 9-
  11 passim, 29, 55-56
Awori, W.W., 81-82, 119

Balliol College, Oxford
  58-59, 66
Baraza, 143
Baring, Sir Evelyn (Gov.
  1952-59), 131, 176
Beauttah, James, 26-27,
  114-17 passim, 151
Beech, M.W.H., 4
Beecher, Archbishop
  Leonard J., 20f, 82,
  90-91, 97-101, passim,
  167
Beecher Commission, 90-
  91
Biss, Evan, 35-36
Black education in
  America, see individu-
  al educators by name
"Black European," 108-
  10ff, 152
Blyden, Dr. Edward, 110
Britain, xiv-xvi passim,
  1, 30, 111; Colonial
  Office, 53, 71, 85-86,
  129-30, 143-46, 176;
  Kenyatta in, 59-62
  passim, 84-85; in Ki-
  kuyuland, 1-4 passim;
  Koinange in, 117-18;

Mathu•in, 51-63, 172;
    Parliament, 71, 104
British Council, 52, 58
Brooke-Popham, Sir Robert
    (Gov. 1937-39), 50

Calderwood, Rev. R.G.,
    55-57ff, 65
Calderwood, Rev. Walter,
    55-56
Cameron, Sir Donald, 86
Cape African Teachers'
    Association, 46
Cape Native Voter's As-
    sociation, 40
Capricorn Africa, 119,
    178
Carothers, J.C., 109
Cege, A., 64
Central Province, 1-2,
    46, 83, 123, 135-37
    passim, 144, 178
Chandos, Lord, 130, 176.
    See also Lyttleton Con-
    stitution
Chipembere, Henry, xv
Christian Council on Race
    Relations, 49-51
Christian Missions, see
    individual missions by
    name
"Christian Service," 16ff,
    31f, 37, 68
Church of England Mission
    Society (CMS), 6, 14,
    27
Church of Scotland Mis-
    sion (CSM), 5-14 pas-
    sim, 19, 25, 32
Civil Service reform, 97-
    98, 128, 149
Colonial Office, see un-
    der Britain
Commissions, see individ-
    ual commissions by name
Commission on African Re-
    settlement, 96
Compulsory education for
    Africans, 89, 129, 145,

149
Constitutions, see indi-
    vidual constitutions
    by name
Convention of Associa-
    tions, 82
Cooke, S.V., 87
Council of the University
    of East Africa, 149
Coupland, Sir Reginald,
    52-54, 58-59, 66, 78,
    150
Coutts, Sir Walter, 131-
    32
Coutts Commission, 136
Crisis, The, xv, 26
Cumber, J.A., 137-38

Dagoretti, see under
    Kiambu District
Dawes, A.J., 56
Displaced Kikuyu Relief
    Committee, 124-25
Dorobo people, the, 2
Du Bois, W.E.B., xiv f
    26

East African Associa-
    tion, 23
East African Indian Na-
    tional Congress, 82,
    86
East African Red Cross,
    14-15
East African Standard,
    147
Education: Department of,
    35, 42; reform, 2, 81,
    88-91, 128f, 135, 145,
    149
Elders, Meru, 138
Elections: for Legisla-
    tive Council (1957),
    134-42; (1958), 134,
    142-46
Electors' Union, 82, 86f,
    99, 112
Eliot, Sir Charles, 1

Embu District, 89, 136-39
  passim
Emergency, the, 97, 107,
  112f, 119-27, 135-36,
  149-52 passim
Erkshine, Derek, 93, 116
European Elected Members
  Organization, 50, 87,
  92, 98-99
Executive Council, 97ff,
  120, 130f
Exeter University, 52-58
  passim

Fabian Colonial Bureau,
  90, 104
Facing Mount Kenya, 13
Female circumcision, 27
Fort Hall District, 74,
  83, 114, 123, 143f
Fort Hare, South African
  Native College at, 30-
  33 passim, 46, 55, 61;
  character of, 34-37
  passim, Mathu at, 34-
  43, 45, 51
Francis, E. Carey, 18, 63-
  69
Fulton, John, 59

Gachui, Dick G., 134
Gandhi, Mahatma, xiv
Garvey, Marcus, xv, 26, 38
Gatonye, "Chief," 4-5, 22
Gatonyo Clan, 155
German East African Cam-
  paign, 22
Gichuru, James, 46, 64,
  74, 81-85 passim, 163
Gikonyo, Muchohi, 113, 118
Githunguri, 68, 115
Glancy, B.J., 92
Glancy Commission, 92-94
Gospel Missionary Society,
  14
Greave, L.B., 65
Grieve, George Andrew, 20,
  52; as Alliance High

School principal, 15,
  34, 48-49, 58, 63, 67;
  background of, 12-16
  passim; and Mathu, 18-
  19, 29-36 passim, 65,
  78; philosophy of, 16-
  18, 28
Grigg, Sir Edward (Gov.
  1925-30), 15, 26

Hampton Institute, 16,
  21, 30, 34ff, 68
Hayford, Casely, xv
Herzog, James B., 40
Hilton-Young Commission,
  25
Hodgkin, Thomas, 14
Hut tax, 3ff, 22
Hyde Clarke, E.M., 101

Imperial British East
  Africa Company, 3
Imvo Zabantusundu, 39
India, 76
Indian Elected Members'
  Organization, 88
Industrial and Commer-
  cial Workers' Union,
  38
International African
  Opinion, 61
International African
  Service Bureau (IASB),
  60-62

Jabavu, Davidson D.T.,
  38-46 passim, 51, 78,
  162
Jabavu, John Tengo, 39
James, C.L.R., 61
Jeremiah, James, xii,
  50, 118, 131
Jones, A. Creech, 85-86
Jones, T. Jesse, 15
Josiah, Chief, 36

Kadalie, Clements, 38
Kaggia, Bildad, 113f
Kaimosi District, 65
Kakamega District, 96
Kamau, Johnston, see
  Kenyatta, Jomo
Kamba people, the, 48-49
Kamenju, Grant, xii
Kamwengi, Mathu, 7, 10
Kangau Clan, 155
Kanti, Benson, xii
Kanyua, J.F., 117
Kapenguria, 117
Kariuki, Jesse, 27
Katithi, Joseph, 114
Kenya African Study Union
  (KASU), 82. See also
  Kenya African Union
Kenya African Teacher's
  Union (KATU), 46
Kenya African Union (KAU),
  79, 104, 149, 169;
  establishment of, 79-
  86; and "Kenya Plan,"
  99; militant domination
  of, 96, 113-17 passim,
  125; as political party,
  105
Kenya Citizen's Associa-
  tion, 116
Kenya Missionary Council,
  49, 55, 163
"Kenya Plan," 99, 112ff
Kenyatta, Jomo, 25, 69,
  104, 149; in Britain,
  59-62 passim, 84-85;
  and Mathu, 11, 27, 59-
  60, 116-17; and mili-
  tants, 85, 114-17; po-
  litical philosophy of,
  13f, 71-74
Kerr, Alexander, 35f, 43,
  51
Keyser, Major A.G., 87,
  94
Khamisi, Francis, 80, 91-
  92
Kiambu District, 23, 112,
  125, 144; boundaries of,
  2f, 155-56; Local Native

Council, 35-36, 42,
  49, 83
Kiano, Dr. Gikonyo, 135,
  142-46 passim
Kibachia, Chege, 102
Kikuyu Association, 23f,
  70
Kikuyu Central Associa-
  tion (KCA), 50, 64,
  71; and KAU, 83-84,
  113-14; origins of,
  26-27; proscribed,
  168-69
Kikuyu Home Guards, 125,
  138
Kikuyu Independent
  Schools, 68
Kikuyu Karing'a Inde-
  pendent Schools, 63,
  68-69
Kikuyu Mission Volun-
  teers, 6
Kikuyu News, 32
Kikuyu people, the, 107;
  at Alliance High
  School, 48-49, 64-65;
  culture of, 5-7, 31,
  109, 155; and land, 2-
  7 passim, 22, 95; and
  Mau Mau, 83, 107, 122-
  24 passim, 176; ori-
  gins of, 2; and poli-
  tics, 1-2, 73-74, 136-
  39 passim, 147
Kikuyu Provincial Asso-
  ciation (KPA), 79
King, Martin Luther, xiv
Kinyanjui, Paramount
  Chief, 2f, 7-10 pas-
  sim; 23, 27, 157
Kioni, Stephen, 137, 142
Kipande, 24, 81, 91-94,
  104, 149
Kipkorir, Benjamin, 19,
  66
Kisumu Province, 131
Kiwanuka, M. Semakula,
  109-111
Koinange, Peter Mbiyu,
  32, 117-18; education

of, 18-22, passim, 51,
164; and Kenyatta, 116;
and Mathu, 34; as poli-
tical candidate, 72-73;
returns from abroad,
68, 160, 168
Kubai, Fred, 113-16 pas-
sim

Labor: Mombasa General
Strike, 101-4 passim,
113; reform, 100-102,
128
Land, 3, 23, 81; govern-
ment policy toward, 25,
81; reform 2, 25, 94-
96, 112, 128, 145
Leader, The, 27
Leakey, Canon Harry, 23
Legislative Council, 22,
44, 66-69 passim, 79,
111, 149f; composition
of, 168; and KAU, 80f,
114; and Kikuyu organi-
zations, 25-26; Mathu's
appointment to, 53, 63,
70-75, 147. Mathu's
reform efforts in:
civil service, 102-4,
128; education, 88-91,
128; Emergency legisla-
tion, 121-27; labor,
91-94, 128; land, 94-
96, 128; representation,
96-99, 128, 132-35,
passim
Legum, Colin, 110
Lennox-Boyd, A., 143f
Lennox-Boyd Constitution,
146
Lincoln, Abraham, 21
Lothian, Lord, 54
Lovedale CSM School, 37
Loyalists, 112-13
Loyalty Certificates,
135-38 passim
Lugard, Lord, 3
Luhya people, the, 64
Luo people, the, 48-49,
64-65, 74, 83
Lyttleton constitution,
130-32, 143-45 passim
Lyttleton, Oliver, 130,
176

Macharia, Gideon, 114
Makerere College, 17, 34
Makerere Commission, 49
Makonnen, T.R., 62
Manchester Guardian, 61,
71
Masai people, the, 2-7
passim, 22
Maseno School, 63ff
160-63 passim
Mate, Bernard, 135-37
passim, 142, 179
Mathu, Eliud Wambu:
origins, 2ff, 7f, 11-
13 passim, 21-27,
155-57 passim; and
Booker T. Washington,
xiii-xv, 18-19, 48,
77-78; Christian prin-
ciples of, 8ff, 32,
57, 107; "half a loaf"
concept, xiv, 77, 88,
123, 152-53; political
philosophy, xiii ff
13-14, 27, 44, 75-79
passim, 108-111, 116-
17; at Alliance, 15,
18-20, 31-34, 45-49
passim, 63-68, 158,
164; in South Africa,
34-43, 51, 161-62; in
Britain, 51-63, 172;
visits Amsterdam, 57;
heads Kikuyu Karing'a
School, 68-69; member-
ship in organizations,
46-51; appointment to
LegCo, xi, 70-75;
legislative career,
87-88, 112-13; forms
KAU, 79-86; educational
reforms, 30, 88-91,
128f; Emergency legis-

lation, 121-27; Execu-
tive Council, 97, 120,
130; and Kenyatta's re-
turn, 84-85; labor re-
form, 91-94, 100-102,
128; land reform, 94-
96, 112, 128; represen-
tative reform, 96-99,
128, 131-32; social re-
form, 97-98, 102-4, 128;
and Mau Mau, 107-8, 112-
18, 135-36, 176; elec-
toral defeat, 134-50
passim
Mau Mau, 85, 95, 105-8
passim, 111-126 passim,
150-151, 172-73
Mbotela, Tom, 112-17 pas-
sim
Mboya, Chief Paul, 72-73
Mboya, Tom, 57, 143f, 151,
179
Merchant, Colonel, 84
Meru people, the, 134-39
passim
Militants, 113-18
Missions, see individual
missions by name
Mitchell, Sir Phillip
(Gov. 1944-52), 85-87,
100-101
Moi, Daniel Arap, 179
Mombasa General Strike,
101-4 passim, 113
Mombasa Times, 120
Montgomery, H.R., 50, 70
Moore, Sir Henry (Gov.
1940-44), xi, 70-72,
86, 167
Moral Rearmament, 119
Morris Carter Land Com-
mission, 94
Muimi, J.N., 179
Muliro, Masinde, 179
Multiracialism, 81, 89,
111, 132; and Mathu,
75-76, 86, 95, 122,
127; and African elec-
tions, 130, 145
Mungai, John, 114

Murray, John, 53, 58
Murumbi, Joseph, 114

NAACP, xiv, 26
Nairobi District African
Congress, 141
Nationalism in Colonial
Africa, 13
National registration,
see kipande
Native Authority Ordi-
nance of 1937, 103f
Native Registration
Ordinance, 50
Ndegwa, George, 83
New Statesman and Nation,
61
Ngala, Ronald, 143, 179
Ngei, Paul, 113f
Niagara Movement, xiv
Nicolson, Sir Harold, 52
Njonjo, Charles, 135
Njoroge, James, 26
Njoroge, William, 11
Njuri Ncheke, 138
Nkrumah, Kwame, 59
Nyagah, Jeremiah, 135-37
passim, 142
Nyanza Province, 74
Nyeri District, 74

Odede, Fanuel, 114f
Odinga, Oginga, 178f
Ofafa, Ambrose, 112-17
passim
Ogot, B.A., 110
Oguda, L.G., 179
Ohanga, B.A., xii, 13,
87, 97, 119, 131
Ojal, J.M., 65
Okwirry, M., 112-13
Oriyo, Alliance Master,
65
Ormsby-Gore, W.G.A., 71
Otiende, Joseph, 64f
Oxford, see Balliol
College, Oxford

Padmore, George, 59-62
  passim
Pan-African Congress, 84
Pan-Africanism, 59f, 84,
  116
Parliament, see under
  Britain
Patel, A.B., 130
Perham, Dame Margery, 52-
  54, 59, 66-69 passim,
  78, 112, 150, 164
Phelps-Stokes Commission,
  15-18 passim
Political parties, see
  individual parties by
  name
Poll tax, 3
Presbyterian Church, 49
Pyrethrum Board, 132-35
  passim

Race consciousness, 2,
  110f
Registration of Persons
  Ordinance of 1947, 92-
  93
Rhodesia, see Southern
  Rhodesia
Rhodes Trust, 54, 58
Riley, Ben, 71
Riruta, see Kiambu Dis-
  trict
Robeson, Paul, 59
Roman Catholic Mission, 6

Sauti ya Mwafrika, 80
Scotland, 55-57
Scott, H.S., 36, 43
Self-government, 87, 119,
  144, 150f
Self-help, 2, 48, 69, 77-
  78
Smith, James Stephen, 20,
  32-34 passim, 57, 64,
  134
Social reform, 102-4, 128,
  132-35 passim, 145
Society for Civil Liber-

ties, 92
South African Native
  College, see Fort Hare
Southern Rhodesia, 75
Specially Elected Mem-
  ber's Seats, 143-47
  passim
Stanley, Oliver, 71
Stock, Dinah, 60
Suk people, the, 132

Tameno, J. Ole, 118, 178
Tanganyika, General, 126
Taxation, 3ff, 22
Thika District, 144
Thuku, Harry, 14, 23-27
  passim, 79-83 passim,
  112
Towett, Arap, 178
Tribalism, 48-49, 137-42
Tribes, see individual
  tribes by name
Tuskegee Institute, 39,
  68f, 77

Uganda Railway, 3
United Front, The, 139-
  41, 178
United Kenya Club, 119
United Nations Economic
  Commission to Africa,
  149
Universal Negro Improve-
  ment Association, see
  Garvey, Marcus
University College of
  the South West, see
  Exeter University
University of South
  Africa, 37
Up From Slavery, 21, 41

Wade, F.D., 35
Wallace-Johnson, I.T.A.,
  59
Wambui, Eliud Mathu's
  mother, 7

Waruhiu, David, 137, 142
Washington, Booker T., 21,
   26-28 passim, 51; and
   Jabavu, D.D.T., 39-42
   passim; and Mathu, xiii-
   xv, 18-19, 29-31 passim,
   48, 77-78, 88-89, 152
Waweru, Wanyutu, 113, 118
Welbourne, F.B., 108
Williams, Eric, 59
Wilson, Sir Samuel, 26

Wisdom, R.H., 52
World Conference of
   Christian Youth, 57

Young Baganda Associa-
   tion, 24
Young Kikuyu Associa-
   tion, 23ff
Youth Hostel Association
   of Great Britain, 59